The *"How-To-Win"* Trial Manual

WINNING TRIAL-ADVOCACY IN A NUTSHELL
INCLUDING: A "TEST YOURSELF" PRACTICE SESSION
(WITH THE ANSWERS)

by

Ralph Adam Fine
JUDGE, WISCONSIN COURT OF APPEALS

 Juris Publishing

Library of Congress Cataloging-in -Publication Data

Fine, Ralph Adam, 1941-
   The "how-to-win" trial manual : winning trial-advocacy in a nutshell : including a "test yourself" practice session (with the answers) / by Ralph Adam Fine.
     p. cm.
   Includes index.
   ISBN 1-57823-052-7
   1. Trial practice --United States.   I. Title
KF8915.F54   1998
347.73' 75--dc21   98-17563
                                                                       CIP

Copyright ©1998 by Ralph Adam Fine

All rights reserved. No part of this publication may be reproduced in any form or by any electronic or mechanical means including information storage and retrieval systems without permission in writing from the publisher.

Manufactured in the United States of America.

For Kay and Matt

*Winning does not depend on our clients,
our witnesses, our juries, or our judges;
it depends on us!*

ABOUT THE AUTHOR

Ralph Adam Fine has been a judge on the Wisconsin Court of Appeals since 1988. He served as a judge on the Wisconsin circuit court from 1979 to 1988, and presided over in excess of 350 jury trials. He was the presiding judge in the PBS *Frontline* production *Inside the Jury Room*, which was the first time jury deliberations in a criminal trial were filmed and broadcast.

Judge Fine has taught trial-advocacy, evidence, and appellate-advocacy at more than seventy continuing-legal-education programs around the country, at in-house trial-advocacy programs to law-firm litigation departments, and as Professorial Lecturer in Law at the George Washington University National Law Center in Washington, D.C. In January of 1995, the University of Virginia School of Law honored Judge Fine with the Honorable William J. Brennan, Jr., Award for his contributions to the teaching of trial advocacy.

Ralph Adam Fine is the author of the annually supplemented *Fine's Wisconsin Evidence* (Lexis), which Judge Jack B. Weinstein, original co-author of *Weinstein's Federal Evidence*, called "probably the best single-volume state treatise on the subject that I have seen." Judge Fine is also a senior contributing editor and reporter for the four-volume treatise *Evidence in America* (Michie); a contributor to the ABA publications *Emerging Problems Under The Federal Rules of Evidence* (West 2d ed. 1991) and *Emerging Problems Under The Federal Rules of Evidence* (Lexis 3d ed. 1998). He has also written more than thirty professional-journal articles.

In addition to *Fine's Wisconsin Evidence*, Judge Fine has written three books: *Escape of the Guilty* (Dodd, Mead & Co. 1986), which was called "must reading" by the *Wall Street Journal*; *The Great Drug Deception* (Stein & Day 1972); and *Mary Jane versus Pennsylvania* (McCall 1970). He also has two chapters in *Criminal Justice?*, edited by Robert James Bidinotto and published in 1994–1995 by the Foundation for Economic Education, and a chapter on the Eighth Amendment in *A Time for Choices* published in 1991 by the First Amendment Congress. Judge Fine has analyzed legal issues on CBS' **60 Minutes**, ABC's **Nightline** and **Reader's Digest: On Television**, PBS' **MacNeil/Lehrer NewsHour**, CNN's **Both Sides with Jesse Jackson**, as well as a periodic guest on CNN's **Crossfire** and **Larry King Live**.

A 1962 graduate of Tufts University, and a 1965 graduate of the Columbia Law School, Judge Fine is an elected member of the American Law Institute.

INTRODUCTION AND DEDICATION

This book owes it's existence to three people: Herbert J. Stern, Stephen A. Saltzburg, and Peter J. Kenny.

I first met Herb when, as a sitting United States district judge, he came to Wisconsin to teach trial-advocacy to those lawyers who were wise enough to attend his course. That was in the mid-1980s. I was then a state trial judge in Milwaukee, and was long-frustrated with the poor quality of many of the lawyers trying cases in my court. It's not that the lawyers were not smart; most of them were. It's also not that the lawyers did not care; most of them did. The simple fact was that although they were smart and they cared, they were less than effective because they did not know how to use the tools of persuasion.

Herb was similarly frustrated with the low level of trial-advocacy that he saw every day in his Newark, N.J., federal courtroom. As a young prosecutor, Herb had successfully taken on a bribery nest involving major oil companies, mob figures, and many of his state's most powerful politicians. He won against some of this country's most famous and successful criminal-defense lawyers—including the legendary Edward Bennett Williams and Simon H. Rifkind—because he knew how to put together and try a winning case. Those victories were the fruit of Herb's meticulous study and analysis of not only the techniques of skilled trial lawyers—including Williams—but also of Aristotle and the other great rhetoricians of the past. Herb distilled these techniques into easily understood and applied trial-advocacy tools.

Herb took time away from his busy schedule as a federal trial judge to share his trial-advocacy techniques with lawyers around the country, and was in Wisconsin on one such trip when we met at a friend's house for dinner. As we talked, I realized that the persuasion techniques that he articulated with such clarity were those that I had amorphously and instinctively felt—both as a lawyer and as a trial judge. In short, Herb was, I perceived, one of those geniuses whom Alexander Pope had in mind when he wrote: "True wit is nature to advantage dressed; what oft was thought, but ne're so well expressed."

Herb's "true wit" about winning trial advocacy is "expressed" brilliantly in his four-volume treatise TRYING CASES TO WIN. It is also expressed every year at the nine-day Trial Advocacy Institute that he, Steve Saltzburg, and Peter Kenny run at the University of Virginia the first week of every January. At the Institute, Herb enthralls lawyers from all over the country and University of Virginia law students with his cogent and funny exegeses on how to try cases successfully. After each lecture and faculty demonstration, the lawyers and students break up into small groups of eight where they practice the newly learned techniques under the tutelage of experienced trial lawyers and judges who volunteer their time as faculty.

The Trial Advocacy Institute got its start in 1981 when Herb, then one of the nation's youngest federal judges, and Steve Saltzburg, then a professor at the University of Virginia Law School, recognized the need for a place where lawyers could learn trial-advocacy techniques that made sense and worked. Steve, now a law professor at the George Washington University National Law Center, and co-author of the highly acclaimed FEDERAL RULES OF EVIDENCE MANUAL among other books and treatises, was able to get the University of Virginia involved, and the Institute is taught at the law school.

Steve, one of the leading experts in the United States on evidence and civil and criminal trial procedure, is blessed with an almost instinctive ability to cut through the dross surrounding most legal problems to get to the very core. I've been fortunate to share many a platform with him over the years at American Bar Association-American Law Institute programs on evidence and trial practice, and I was honored when he and Herb asked me to join the Institute faculty in the late 1980s. It was at the Institute that I met Peter Kenny, who has served as its Executive Director since the beginning.

After a sterling career as an Army lawyer, Peter joined Virginia CLE—the group that organizes continuing legal education programs for lawyers in Virginia. Lawyers are busy people, and one of Peter's jobs is to make sure that lawyers get a good return on the time and money they spend in attending those programs. Peter's annual task at the Institute, however, is even more complex. He has to coordinate the one-hundred and fifty or so registrants, three waves of faculty and judges, and the final moot courts, where the registrants practice in front of jurors chosen from one of the most preeminent Virginia high schools. Peter is the Institute's "General Domo."

At Herb's suggestion, I have, since 1993, been sharing winning trial-advocacy techniques with lawyers around the country. This book is an outgrowth of my one-day WIN YOUR TRIAL program. The program and this book would not have been possible without the trail-blazing efforts by Herb, Steve, and Peter—who, each in his own special way, have helped thousands of lawyers better represent the people who depend on effective legal representation for their fortunes, futures, liberty, and, in some cases, lives. I stand on their shoulders, and it is to them that I dedicate this book.

Acknowledgments

I would like to thank the following persons who were able to take the time to review the manuscript of this book and give me their very helpful suggestions: Robert G. Harley, Gregory P. Joseph, Peter J. Kenny, Beth J. Kushner, Ronald C. LeMay, and Lowell A. Stanley.

THE CONTENTS OF The *"How-To-Win"* Trial Manual

I. The Royal Road

Most law-school and CLE trial-advocacy courses teach concepts and techniques that hinder rather than help the trial lawyer to effectively represent his or her clients in court. *The "How-To-Win" Trial Manual* teaches powerful and effective techniques that will help every trial lawyer who uses them to win. The techniques go against the "conventional wisdom," but they *work*. Once grasped, the techniques are easy to implement. Once learned, they will never be forgotten.

II. Truth in the Courtroom

Jurors believe that the lawyers know the truth about the case, and that the rules prevent the jury from learning much of what is critical to its decision. *The "How-To-Win" Trial Manual* shows how to use this fact to win your case.

III. The Importance of Belief

In order to persuade others, you must believe, and that belief must be apparent. Everything that you do in the courtroom must, within the ethical and legal rules, convey to the jury that you believe that your client's cause is just.

IV. You Must Be the Truth-Giver

If you are to win your case, the jury must see *you* as the trial's truth-giver.

V. Persistence of Belief

You must persuade the jury from the beginning that your cause is just. Once jurors decide, even tentatively, they will use the tools of rationalization and denial to validate their decisions. Most cases are won or lost in the opening statements.

VI. The Winning Theme

The winning theme must do all of the following: show that your client deserves to win; show that a victory for your client is good for society; be consistent with all of the facts that the jury will believe at the end of the case (including the facts that are adverse to your position); be consistent with what the jury knows from life (that is, the theme must "ring true"); give the jury a simple solution to the dispute; and be consistent with your credibility as the truth-giver.

VII. Constructing a Winning Theme
Learn how to construct a winning theme.

VIII. The Three Main Tools of Persuasion in the Courtroom
The three main tools of persuasion in the courtroom are: primacy, recency, and repetition. In this chapter we see how you can use these tools to win.

IX. Opening Statements
Most cases are won or lost in the opening statements. Learn how to give a powerful and persuasive opening statement—one that argues without being "argumentative."

X. Evidence Is Used to Validate the Lawyer's Promises of Proof
The lawyer as truth-giver takes center-stage. The winning trial lawyer uses evidence to validate his or her arguments.

XI. Use the "Bad Facts" to Win
Don't just "remove the sting," make the facts that are adverse to your position *work for you*. Ralph Adam Fine shows you how to do it every time.

XII. The Burden of Proof
In the opening statement, the burden of proof should be used as a sword, not a shield. Never hide behind your adversary's burden of proof.

XIII. Limit Note Taking
Note-taking distracts the advocate, and encourages the trial lawyer to be responsive rather than pro-active.

XIV. Don't Sound Like a Lawyer
Law schools take common sense away from entering students, and do not give it back when the students graduate. The worst thing you can do in the courtroom is to sound like a lawyer.

XV. The Importance of Empathy
Learn how to make the jury like and empathize with your clients and witnesses. This will make the jury like and want to help them.

XVI. The Opening Statement—An Annotated Demonstration
Analyze a live demonstration of an opening statement that Ralph Adam Fine gave for both sides of the same case at the nine-day, annual Trial Advocacy Institute at the University of Virginia. See the winning techniques in action, and learn how you, too, can use them to win your trials.

XVII. Use the Direct-Examination to Argue Your Case
Contrary to the conventional wisdom, direct-examination should not be used to elicit facts that will later be tied-up in summation. Rather, the direct-examination is your argument to the jury through the witness. Ralph Adam Fine shows you how to use direct-examination to win your trial.

XVIII. Never Ask "What Happened Next?"
Most lawyers' favorite question on direct-examination is also the worst. Read this chapter and you will never again ask: "What happened next?"

XIX. Using Diagrams to Repeat Testimony
Learn how you can use diagrams to win.

XX. The Direct-Examination Maxim
Follow this maxim and the jury will answer your way before the witness even responds. This puts the jury on your side from the get-go.

XXI. How to Protect Your witnesses From Cross-Examination
Make your witnesses invulnerable to cross-examination.

XXII. Two More Winning Tips for Direct-Examination
How you should deal with any baggage that your witnesses may have, and why you should *never* use written questions.

XXIII. Direct-Examination: An Annotated Demonstration
Analyze a live demonstration of direct-examination given by one of the lawyers who took an in-house trial-advocacy course taught by Judge Fine. See how the lawyer uses the winning techniques, and learn how you, too, can use them to win.

XXIV. A Trial is Not an Evidence Test
Why smart lawyers rarely, if ever, object in front of the jury.

XXV. The Three Faces of Cross-Examination

Learn how to use cross-examination to limit the scope of the witness's testimony, to get favorable testimony from the witness, and when and how to discredit the witness.

XXVI. Cross-Examining Problem Witnesses

How to keep the problem witness from pushing you around, *without asking the judge for help*. Also, how to expose biased witnesses and make their biases *work for* **you**!

XXVII. The Cross-Examination Maxim

Follow this maxim and the jury will answer your way before the witness even responds. This keeps the jury committed to your version of the case.

XXVIII. Why Irving Younger Was Wrong

After you read this chapter you too will agree that the central focus of Younger's famous "Ten Commandments of Cross-examination" is self-destructive.

XXIX. Cross-Examination: An Annotated Demonstration

Analyze a live demonstration of cross-examination given by one of the faculty members at the nine-day, annual Trial Advocacy Institute at the University of Virginia. See the winning techniques in action, and learn how you, too, can use them to prevail in your trials. See how the lawyer controls the witness without leading, and how the lawyer argues his case to the jury through the witness.

XXX. Summation

Learn why the conventional wisdom about closing arguments is wrong.

XXXI. The Function of Closing Argument

Learn the real function of the closing argument, and how to use it to nail down your win.

XXXII. A "Test Yourself" Practice Session (including the answers)

See if you can do a direct-examination better than Johnnie Cochran! Read his direct-examination of a witness in the O.J. Simpson criminal trial, apply the techniques you've learned, and then fashion a powerful direct-examination that argues your point to the jury through window of what the witness can give you. Then compare what you have done with the way Ralph Adam Fine would do it.

XXXIII. How To Know the Rules of Evidence Cold

Learn how to easily master the rules of evidence.

XXXIV. *Voir Dire*

What *voir dire* can and cannot do for you.

XXXV. Win Victories, Not Praise

This should be the ultimate goal of every trial lawyer.

Appendix A

A complete copy of the Federal Rules of Evidence, for your easy reference.

Appendix B

An analysis of the Federal Rules of Evidence by their purpose and function, to help you see how the rules relate with one another.

Appendix C

A handy summary on how to use the Federal Rules of Evidence to help you win.

I.
THE ROYAL ROAD

I've been a judge since 1979. For the first nine years, I was a trial judge and presided over more than 350 jury trials, both civil and criminal. During that time, I rarely saw a trial lawyer who tried his or her case effectively. Scary stuff? You bet.

Since 1988, I've been an appellate-court judge. I read briefs and trial transcripts. The transcripts mimic what I saw during my nine years on the trial bench. Most of the appellate briefs I read are little better, although I've seen several gems.

The legal system is a search for the truth. At the trial level, the search is in the trenches—hand-to-hand combat in the muck, with bullets flying all around. On the appellate level, we are limited to making sure that the process before the trial court was fair and complied with the law. At both levels, your job is the same: to persuade a tribunal (a jury or a judge at the trial level, a group of judges at the appellate level) that truth—that justice—is on your side.

Persuasion is one of the most difficult arts. For a few, it is second nature. History is shaped by persons who have risen from dismal, even wretched circumstances to lead great armies and great nations. There are similar giants in the history of trial-lawyering. Most of us who want to be superb, persuasive trial lawyers, however, have to work at it.

It is difficult to develop any skill. I am told that during the height of his powers and fame, Isaac Stern, the great American violinist, practiced eight hours a day—he knew how to get to Carnegie Hall. Similarly, champion chess players not only fill their lives playing chess but also re-play great matches of the past.

Developing great skills as a trial lawyer is especially difficult because trial lawyers are busy people—there is little time to "practice." More importantly, most trial lawyers have been taught—both in law school and in most continuing-legal-education programs—to do it the *wrong way*, and it is difficult to discard bad habits.

In the late 1930s, Arthur Koestler, the Austrian/British writer, teamed up with Langston Hughes, the American poet, to survey education in the

Caucasus region of the then Soviet Union for some Moscow ministry. One day, the local major domo proudly took them to a one-room school. Inside, he beamed, spies who were to be dropped behind Nazi lines were being taught German. Unfortunately for those future (and short-lived) James Bonds, the instructor was teaching them *Yiddish*! Most law schools and continuing-legal-education trial-advocacy programs similarly ill-equip lawyers for their in-court combats.

Trial lawyers who do not know how to try cases persuasively will not, of course, get tortured and shot. They may even win cases. Even in a race between snails, someone will always win. Trial lawyers who do not use the techniques that I show and demonstrate in this book will not, however, win as many cases as they should and could!

In this book, I will teach you the techniques, and show you how to practice those techniques, that will help you win—period. What's more, you will never lose your skills as an effective and persuasive trial lawyer once you learn these techniques. Learning how to win in court is like learning how to ride a bicycle; the skills will stay with you forever.

One last story before we begin. Alexander, the warrior-emperor who had conquered much of the known world by the time he was twenty-six, obviously had mastered the skills of persuasion. He yearned, however, to master the concepts of mathematics that were beginning to exert their influence on both commerce and warfare. He commanded his teacher Aristotle show him an easy way. Aristotle replied that there was "no royal road" to any branch of knowledge, much less mathematics.

There *is* a "royal road" to the mastery of trial skills. Follow me as we walk down that path together.

II.
TRUTH IN THE COURTROOM

In the next several chapters we will learn and practice the techniques of effective and persuasive trial lawyering. Before we do so, we must look at the underlying verity that makes these techniques so powerful.

From our first days in law school we have been taught that a trial is a search for the truth. Indeed, the United States Supreme Court has described it as a "sober search for the truth."[1] But what is "truth" in any trial?

On one level, "truth" is what the jurors say it is. For us, of course, that is the only level that counts. More important, that is the only level that counts for your clients. As a character in *Bleak House* by Charles Dickens cogently observes when his friend protests that he is innocent and that that is the truth: "But the mere truth won't do . . . You must have a lawyer."

Significantly, for any case that goes to trial there is no verifiable "truth." If there were verifiable "truth," the case would not go to trial. It would either not be brought, it would be dismissed on the pleadings or on summary judgment, or it would be settled. Indeed, Rule 11 of the Federal Rules of Civil Procedure recognizes that lawyers can argue facts that are contrary to the facts argued by an adversary and not violate the mandate of honesty imposed by that rule.

Under Rule 11, a lawyer advocating a position in federal court "is certifying that to the best of the person's knowledge, information, and belief" the "allegations and other factual contentions" either do or "likely" will "have evidentiary support."[2] Similarly, a lawyer denying an opponent's contentions also certifies that the denials are "warranted."[3] This would be impossible if the "truth" of the case were verifiable. Simply put, Rule 11 recognizes that lawyer Susan Smith can say that "X" happened, and that lawyer Peter Jones can say that "X" did not happen, and that both of them can be honest and ethical, and in compliance with the rule.

The dynamics in criminal cases are not much different. If the "truth" of innocence were verifiable, the defendant would either not be charged or the case would be dismissed. If the "truth" of guilt were verifiable, the defendant would most likely either plead guilty outright or under a plea bargain. Thus, for the great bulk of criminal cases that do go to trial there is no verifiable "truth" of either guilt or innocence.

Although there is no verifiable "truth" for any case that goes to trial, the jurors do not know that. Indeed, jurors believe that underneath all of the pomp

---

[1] Estes v. Texas, 381 U.S. 532, 551 (1965).
[2] FRCP RULE 11(b)(3).
[3] FRCP RULE 11(b)(4).

and circumstance of the courtroom, and underneath all the posturing by the lawyers, is *the truth*. Jurors want to discover this "truth" and thus to reach a just and fair result. Indeed, jurors are even told that their decision is called a "verdict"—Old French for "true saying."

Jurors not only believe that there is a "truth" in the case, but they also believe that the *lawyers* know that truth. Jurors also recognize that the jury will never learn much of what is critical to their decision. This belief is confirmed every time the trial judge sustains an objection, holds a sidebar conference, or marches the jurors out of the courtroom "so the lawyers and I can discuss a few things." Commenting on the O.J. Simpson criminal trial during her appearance on the February 10, 1995, edition of the television program *American Journal*, Candace Garvey, Nicole Brown's friend and a witness at the trial, reflected: "What you're seeing is a quarter of the information there is. There are so many rules that keep the truth out."

What Jurors Believe the Lawyers Know

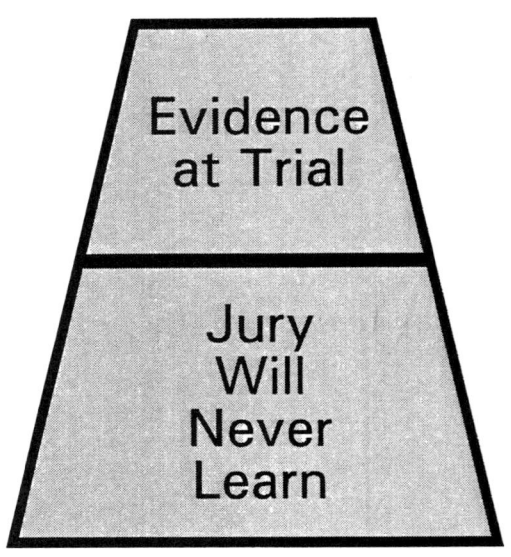

If the jury believes that each of the opposing lawyers knows the truth and lawyer Smith argues "X" and lawyer Jones argues "not X," one of them must be lying. This leads us to the essence of effective, powerful advocacy. As former federal prosecutor and United States district court judge Herbert J. Stern points out in his ground-breaking, magnificent four-volume series, *Trying Cases to Win* (Wiley), the most important factor in any trial is not the facts of the case, it is not the governing law, it is not the jury, it is not the judge, it is the lawyer's personal credibility with the jury. As Judge Stern explains: If "your case is triable (that is, possible for either side to 'win'), would you rather have an edge on the law, an edge on the facts, or Abraham Lincoln as your lawyer?"[4] The answer to this question will guide us as we explore the techniques that will help you win your trial.

III.
THE IMPORTANCE OF BELIEF

There's an old saying that laughter like sorrow is infectious. Belief is infectious too. In his interesting novel on aviation litigation, *Impact*, Stephen Greenleaf describes the trial lawyer on whom the book focuses:

> "Alec Hawthorne was the best . . . not because he was smarter or better prepared or even luckier . . . but because in the bedrock of his soul Alec Hawthorne believed his cause was just and the incandescence of that conviction made twelve men and women believe it as well."

Winston Spencer Churchill, one of the great men of history who mastered the elements of persuasion, also recognized, when he was but twenty-three years old, that the key to persuading others was sincerity: "To convince you must believe."

Everything that you do in your trial must convey to the jury—in an ethical and lawful way—your personal belief in the righteousness of your cause. Early on in his career, Edward Bennett Williams was described by colleagues has having an "affidavit face"—people, especially jurors, believed what he said. To paraphrase Greenleaf, the "incandescence" of that belief must shine forth with such brightness and fervor that the jury will "believe it as well." **You must be the Abraham Lincoln in your courtroom.**

---

[4] 1 Herbert J. Stern, *Trying Cases to Win* 13 (Wiley 1991).

IV.
YOU MUST BE THE TRUTH-GIVER

Trials have five or six components: the theme; the *voir dire* (to the extent permitted); the opening statements; the direct-examination of your witnesses; the cross-examination of your opponent's witnesses; the closing arguments. The pole star that guides you through each of these must be your need to make the jury see you as **the truth-giver in the courtroom—the Abraham Lincoln of your trial**. This book will show you how to reach that goal.

V.
PERSISTENCE OF BELIEF

Devising a theme for your case is the most important task that you have. The theme of a case is critical. Jurors take their jobs very seriously; they want to do what's right. Once they decide who should win, they will struggle to return a verdict that validates that decision.

> "Jurors inescapably bring their own moral sense—of what is right, fair, and reasonable in the circumstances—in deciding the facts of a case. This may be true even if personal morality dictates a result different from the court's instructions. It is understandable when a case requires a jury to apply notions like 'reasonable' conduct; reasonableness is inherently a normal concept. But, from interviewing jurors and observing mock juror deliberations, it appears that almost *every* lawsuit becomes a morality play. It is about someone (allegedly) having done wrong and someone else who is (allegedly) a victim. Jurors routinely include their own views of who should win the lawsuit in their 'factual' determinations."[5]

Jurors not only want to do the right thing, but they also want to decide early. As with us all, indecision is uncomfortable. Once jurors decide, even tentatively, they will struggle to validate that early decision. The mind-sciences call this mechanism **the persistence of belief**.

---

[5] Terry Lunsford, *How Jurors Respond to Complex Commercial Cases*, 19 LITIGATION No.4 50, 53 (Summer 1993) (italics in original).

The skillful trial lawyer recognizes that jurors tend to want to stay with their initial impressions of where justice in the case lies. One of America's most effective trial lawyers, Louis Nizer, explained the mechanism:

> "We believe with heart and soul what we want to believe. Fundamentally, this is the essence of persuasion. If one can be made to wish emotionally that a certain result should obtain, he will find any argument appealing which achieves that goal."[6]

Simply put, we rationalize away facts that conflict with what we want to believe, and we deny those facts that cannot be rationalized.

For years, cigarette smokers accepted tobacco-company assertions that cigarettes were not harmful, even though each pack of cigarettes and every cigarette advertisement proclaimed that smoking caused either cancer or some other disease. Even now, when tobacco companies admit that cigarettes are dangerous, smokers use the tools of rationalization and denial to validate their decision to smoke. They tell themselves that *they* won't get sick—either because they refuse to believe that the risk is all that serious (denial) or because they only smoke "occasionally" (rationalization).

Another example. There are some nine million American youngsters in day care. Yet, according to *The Wall Street Journal*, "high-quality care is so scarce in many places—half to three-quarters of parents who use day care feel they have no choices and must settle for what they can find, studies show—that parents lapse into denial about their kids' experience." The article described this denial:

> "In one center, researchers saw that none of the infants was fed on time, held or even diapered until just before the parents came. But though most suspected problems, 'almost all said they thought their child was the lucky one who got most of the attention.'"

We all use the tools of rationalization and denial to validate our views, whether faith in a particular politician, or ardor for a college or professional sports team. Oliver Wendell Holmes, Jr., put it so well: "One thinks that error exposed is dead, but exposure amounts to nothing when people want to believe." Jurors use the same persistence-of-belief mechanisms.

---

[6] Louis Nizer, *My Life in Court* 443-444.

Your task as a trial lawyer is to make the jury want to believe that right, justice, and truth is on your side. And, you need to hook them from the start. You cannot do either of these things without a powerful and effective theme.

VI.
THE WINNING THEME

A winning theme must do two main things:

1. The theme must persuade the jury that a win for your side is not only "justice" between the parties (the "morality play" about which jury-analyst Terry Lunsford wrote) but also "right" for society.

2. Most important, the theme must be consistent with your credibility as the truth-giver in the courtroom. Thus, your theme:

    A. Must be consistent with what the jury knows from life—it must "ring true."

    B. Must be consistent with the facts that the jury will believe at the end of the case—all of the facts, including those that seem adverse to your position.

    C. Must give the jury a simple solution to the dispute.

    Jury studies reveal that jurors find the simplest story that makes sense of the dispute, even if the lawyers do not.[7] Thus, even though lawyers may attempt to lead the jury the long way—down each leg of the right-triangle, so to speak—jurors will find the hypotenuse. Make it easy for the jury to go down your path. Make it the shortest distance that is logically consistent with the facts.

    D. Must not give the jury theories that are inconsistent with one another, such as "I did not shoot the victim, but if I did, it was self-defense."

---

[7] The Brookings Institution, *Charting a Future for the Civil Jury System* 10 (1992).

E. Must not give the jury theories that *appear* to be inconsistent with one another, such as "The defendant was not negligent, *but, even if* she was, the plaintiff has exaggerated his damages."

The key here is to present theories that are consistent with one another in a way that they do not appear to be inconsistent. Certainly, the defendant in a negligence action could be both free from negligence, and the plaintiff could be overstating his damages.

Never use the phrase "but, even if" to connect two consistent theories. Rather, show the jury that you are making both points, and that both points are consistent: "The defendant was not negligent. *(Moreover) (What's more) (And)*, the plaintiff has exaggerated his damages." As Herb Stern was one of the first to point out, using "moreover" (or "what's more" or "and" or something similar) tells the jury that your argument is consistent and that the two subpoints help, rather than contradict, each other.

F. Must not add weak arguments to strong arguments.

Piling on every conceivable argument tells the jury that you are willing to say anything and make any argument in order to win. This destroys your truth-giver role, and eviscerates strong arguments that, if presented by themselves, would carry the day.

Lawyers throw in everything including the kitchen sink because they do not want to be criticized, by both their client and colleagues, should they lose. The feared refrain is common: "Why didn't you argue . . . ?" In a very real sense, lawyers who succumb to this fear and load their case with every conceivable argument are committing malpractice in an attempt to avoid malpractice.

What writing guru Lajos Egri says about the novel is equally applicable to trials and the need to put together a compelling theme:

> "The author using a badly worded, false, or badly constructed premise finds himself filling space and time with pointless dialogue—even action—and not getting anywhere near the proof of his premise. Why? Because he has no direction."

I have sat through countless trials where the lawyers filled the case with "pointless" evidence without getting anywhere near the heart of a winnable theme. So have most of you. Everything you do in the courtroom, every argument you make—whether in your opening statement, your direct-examination, your cross-examination, or your summation—must do one thing: advance your theme.

An additional word on credibility. Before they caved in, the tobacco companies pulled together a team of scientific experts to present the companies' defense. Their theme: "Nicotine Is Not Addictive."* Everyone laughed, because, even if scientifically accurate from a technical standpoint, the concept was ludicrous as everyone who had ever tried to quit smoking knew. The nicotine-is-not-addictive theme was suicidal. Don't make the same mistake in your trials.

VII.
CONSTRUCTING A WINNING THEME

Let's fashion the skeleton of a theme using a simple example. We represent the plaintiff in a products-liability action. She was styling her hair in front of the bathroom mirror with a hair dryer when she accidently dropped the dryer into the sink below the mirror. Unfortunately, the sink was full of water, and she was injured severely by the resulting electric shock.

We contend that the dryer was unreasonably dangerous and defective—that it is the company's fault that our client got hurt. The hair dryer, however, was beflagged with warnings, alerting consumers that hair dryers and water do not mix. Indeed, the warnings aside, we know this from life, and so do the jurors. Our theme must recognize this and still make the jurors see that justice and right are on our side.

---

* Suein L. Hwang & Yumiko Ono, Tobacco Dream Team: Experts Who Insist Nicotine Isn't Addictive, *The Wall Street Journal*, March 23, 1995.

The theme: Electrical appliances can be dangerous if used near water. Hair dryers are generally used in the bathroom. Bathrooms have sinks and tubs that hold water. People in a hurry are inclined to cut corners and make mistakes. Hair dryers are often used by people in a hurry. We all know all of this, and so do the companies that make electrical appliances. Appliances should be designed so that a simple mistake by the consumer will not result in electrocution—either fatal or non-fatal.

We must then marshall our facts so they support our theme in a logical, common-sense way. As with the formulation of the theme, **the facts that we present to the jury must be *believable*, they must "ring true," they must be consistent with what the jurors know from life**.

- Women routinely wash their hair in the bathroom sink; what our client did was not unusual.

- The bathroom mirror is, typically, located above the sink, as it is in our client's home.

- Women style their hair with dryers while their hair is wet, as did our client.

- All of the above was either known in the industry or should have been known in the industry.

- Our client attempted to drain the water out of the sink before styling her hair, but the sink's drain was clogged, as drains in which hair is washed tend to become.

- The company that made the hair dryer either knew that sinks near which their dryers are used can clog, or it should have known that.

- Our client was late for a very important job interview, and was rushed as well as stressed.

- The company that made the hair dryer either knew that hair dryers are routinely used by people who are in a hurry, or it should have known that.

- Our client was careful to keep the dryer away from the water, by stepping back away from the mirror as far as the short cord would permit.

- The company either knew or should have known that a longer cord would give the user a chance to stand further away from potential danger.

- The dryer slipped from her hand accidentally as she attempted to manipulate the dryer, a hair brush, and a spray bottle of styling lotion.

These facts will prove that the confluence of circumstances causing our client's injuries was foreseeable by the company, and that our client's responses were reasonable. The product was defective because it should and could have been sufficiently shielded to fall into water without becoming a lethal weapon. After all, you will point out, automobile manufacturers design electric gasoline pumps that operate in the gas tank, submerged under gallons of highly flammable gasoline. Additionally, a longer cord would have permitted the client to stand further away from the sink. This, too, would have prevented her injuries.

Now let us assume that we represent the company that made the hair dryer. We will argue that the plaintiff's injuries were her fault, not the company's.

The theme: Companies cannot make products that are absolutely fool-proof without both increasing their cost substantially and decreasing their utility. Moreover, persons in society have a responsibility to exercise a modicum of due care for their own safety. The plaintiff did not.

- The dryer is plastered with labels that warn people not to use the dryer near water.

- There were other outlets in the plaintiff's home that were near mirrors but not water, and she could have used the dryer, brush, and styling lotion at one of those mirrors.

- Making a dryer that could be submerged in water would increase its cost substantially; this would put the hair dryer out of the financial reach of many.

- Making a dryer that could be submerged in water would also make it significantly heavier; surveys show that those who use dryers want them to be light and easily maneuverable.

We will argue that in view of all the warnings on the hair dryer, the company acted reasonably and responsibly in trusting the consumer's good judgment and common sense, and that the plaintiff's injuries were her own fault for which she should take responsibility.

VIII.
THE THREE MAIN TOOLS OF PERSUASION IN THE COURTROOM

Devising a powerful and effective theme is only part of our task, of course. The most robust theme will be ineffective unless we present it to the jury forcefully and with clarity. This is the job of the opening statement. Before we turn to the opening statement, however, we must look at the three main tools of persuasion.

There are three main tools of persuasion: primacy, recency, and repetition. The skilled trial lawyer understands not only the role that each plays but also how to most effectively use each in arguing his or her case to the jury.

1. *Primacy.* The rule of primacy tells us that what we learn first colors the way we look at what follows. This is the tool that sets the jury's gyroscope; once set in favor of a particular result, it is more likely than not that the jury will arrive at that destination.

Let me give you an example of the power of primacy. Assume that the issue is whether rubber checks, those marked "NSF" and returned to the payee, is a serious problem. You are the decision-maker. This is the first thing that you learn:

1,500,000 checks bounce every day;

533,000,000 checks are returned without payment every year

What is your initial view of the problem—serious or not serious? Now look at footnote 8.[8]

2. *Recency.* The rule of recency tells us that we will remember with the most clarity what we learn last. By that time, however, we have been subjected to the rule of primacy, and our analysis has already been affected by what we know. Therefore, even though we may remember with greater clarity what we learn later, our acceptance of the argument supported by this later information is distorted by rationalization and denial. To return to the cigarettes-and-health example, many cigarette smokers still deny to themselves that cigarettes are dangerous even though the scientific evidence is now clear (as the tobacco companies themselves have finally admitted).

3. *Repetition.* Repetition is known as "the mother of learning." And so it is. Ask any actor struggling to learn his or her lines, or any student struggling with complex mathematical formulae.

Repetition has two functions in the courtroom. First, it pounds home the same message over and over again so that even the most obtuse juror will get the point. Second, not all jurors are listening at any given moment. Indeed, science tells us that people generally have an aural attention span of but twenty

---

[8] Less than one percent of checks bounce. This, too, is true. How do you handle this information? You already know about 533 million checks that go unpaid every year. Thus, it is easy to rationalize this new figure by saying to yourself that "the absolute percentage is so low because there are so many checks that are presented for payment." On the other hand, if you first learned that less than one-percent of all checks bounce, you can accept the yearly 533-million figure with greater equanimity—after all, with so many checks out there, a lot of them are going to bounce. Indeed, in 1992, sixty-two billion checks were processed.

"According to the American Collectors Association, a trade group of debt collectors, 'of the more than 62 billion processed by U.S. banks in 1992, 533 million bounced. The association figures that 1.5 million checks are dishonored each day because of insufficient funds, closed accounts or stop-payment requests.'" *The Wall Street Journal*, June 13, 1994, p. B1.

or so seconds. Thus, out of a jury of twelve, but a handful of jurors are listening at any particular moment. Your argument and evidence will thus fall on many "deaf ears" unless you repeat your points over and over again. Luckily, as we will see later on, and contrary to the conventional wisdom, there are perfectly legal and ethical ways to repeat your argument and evidence as many times as you want.

One thought about how to present your evidence to maximize its clarity and impact. You should **"show" as well as "tell."** People remember approximately twenty percent of what they hear, seventy percent of what they see, but *ninety* percent of what they both see and hear. So, blow up exhibits, use projectors, use diagrams.

IX.
OPENING STATEMENTS

The opening statement is the most important part of the trial. Jury studies show that most jurors make up their minds, at least tentatively, during the openings. As we have seen, once jurors decide who should win they will use the tools of denial and rationalization to validate their decision.

During my nine years as a trial judge, I sat in quiet amazement as lawyer after lawyer wasted the precious opportunities presented by the opening statement. They would typically say something like this:

> "May it please the court, ladies and gentlemen of the jury. I represent (the State) (the defendant) (the plaintiff) (the defendant), and this is my chance to tell you what the evidence in this case will show. Of course, what I am about to tell you is not evidence. Evidence comes from the mouths of the witnesses, who will come into court, sit over on that witness chair, and will tell you what they know about this case. My job now is to give you a road map (to show you the cover of a puzzle box), so you can have some idea of where the testimony of each witness will fit.

This is silly. It is also counterproductive. This type of opening statement, which is all too-typical, not only wastes the precious first moments, but it also tells the jury not to credit anything the lawyer says ("what I am about to tell you is not evidence"). Why in heaven's name would a lawyer want to do that? Most lawyers do it this way because they have either been taught that or they are copying what other lawyers do.

A lawyer has but one job in the courtroom and that is to argue his or her case as persuasively as the rules permit. The opening statement is *the* time to set the filters through which the jury will look at the entire case; it is the time to set the jurors' gyroscope to *your destination*.

Step back for a moment to gauge the dynamics at this stage of the trial. The jury has not seen or heard any of the evidence—neither the witnesses nor any of the exhibits. The only thing they know about the case is either what the judge has already told them, or what the lawyers were able to get across during *voir dire*.

As we have seen, the jury believes that each of the lawyers knows the truth about the case, and that only one is telling the truth. This means that the more personal commitment you show, the stronger the jury will perceive your case to be.

When you stand before the jury to deliver your opening statement, you must convey your personal commitment that your cause is righteous and just. There are three rules you must follow if you are to be effective.

1. **Do not read your opening statement.** Truth-givers do not read; they don't have to read because the verity of what they are saying wells up within them. Politicians know this, which is why they all use teleprompters—to give everyone the impression that they are *not* reading.

Lawyers tell me that they read their opening statements because they are afraid that they will forget important points if they do not read, and because they want to say everything just right. These are not reasons, they are excuses by lawyers who are either reluctant or afraid to make the effort to do their job properly. After all, if it were your future or fortune at stake and you had retained Abraham Lincoln to represent you, would you want him to stand in front of the jury box and speak to the jurors one-on-one, or would you want him to stand behind a podium reading a prepared opening statement? Do no less for *your* clients.

Let's look at the excuses lawyers use to read their opening statements. Once we do, we'll see how easy it is *not to read*.

The first excuse that lawyers use to justify reading their opening statements is that they are afraid that they will forget some of the points they want to make. This problem is solved by having, either on the podium or on three-by-five index cards (which you can keep in one of those nifty leather holders), the points you wish to cover in tidy bulleted paragraphs, as in the following example.

- Important job interview
- Running late
    - had to take son to practice
    - heavy traffic
    - cat ran out door
- Washed hair
- Sink wouldn't drain
- Juggling dryer, brush & bottle
- Lost grip
- Jolt
- Fell, hit head
- Amnesia
- Lost job

Stand to one side of the podium, look the jurors in their eyes, and tell them why a verdict in your favor is just and correct—glancing at the notes to make sure you cover all of the points. If the judge lets you stray from the podium, all the better. Do not be afraid to let the jury see you think. You are the truth-giver, not an actor either reading or remembering a prepared script. Mary Wisewell has noted: "There is no music in a rest, but there is music's making." For the lawyer in the courtroom, a pause is not only the prelude to meaning, it can be meaning in and of itself.

The second excuse lawyers use to justify why they read their opening statements is that they want to use precisely the right words. Would these same lawyers read a prepared statement while they were having a critical discussion with a significant other, even though each word *could* be crucial and a wrong word would destroy the relationship? Of course not. Reading an opening statement to a jury affects them in the same way as reading a prepared statement to a significant other affects that person—it casts doubt on your sincerity.

2. **You must argue your case.** All too many law schools and CLE trial-advocacy courses warn that the opening statement is not the time for argument. They teach that argument comes at the end of the case, after the jury has heard all of the evidence, not at the beginning. This is nonsense.

Everything you do in the courtroom has but one goal: To argue your case—by which I mean persuasively advance your client's cause. This requires that you structure your opening statement so it is the most persuasive it can be.

There are essentially three ways lawyers structure their opening statements: 1) chronological, 2) witness-by-witness, and, 3) the "story." The "story" approach is gaining in popularity, but none is as effective as making the opening statement an **argument**.

The chronology is easy to do. The lawyer using this structure for his or her opening statement starts with the first day and takes the jury through the various events until he or she reaches the morning of trial. Interesting? Not very. Persuasive? No. By lashing the lawyer to the mast of the events as they happened, the chronology prevents the lawyer from organizing the facts in their most persuasive order.

The witness-by-witness approach is even easier to do than the chronology. Here, the lawyer need only go through each folder of his or her trial notebook and regurgitate for the jury what each witness is expected to say. We've all heard this type of opening statement. It, too, is not very interesting and is hardly persuasive.

The "story" is better than both the chronology and the witness-by-witness approach, but not much. The story may hold the jury's interest better than a straight chronology or a witness-by-witness account, but it is not persuasive; it does not put the lawyer's personal commitment on the line, it does not advocate. Let me show you what I mean.

One of the most prominent lecturers on the techniques of trial advocacy is James W. McElhaney, a professor at Case Western Reserve University School of Law, and a columnist for both *Litigation*, a publication of the American Bar Association Section of Litigation, and the *ABA Journal*. In the January 1995 issue of the *ABA Journal*, Professor McElhaney urges the "story" approach to the opening statement. This is his example of a suggested opening statement that tells a story:

> "Ladies and gentlemen, if you had been in the corporate headquarters of the Midwest Lawn Mower Co. on the third of March, 1993, you would have seen five corporate officers have the opportunity to avoid a tragedy.
>
> "The lawn mower company had just received a report that one of the new, model Z100 riding mowers actually threw a spinning lawn mower blade 150 feet when a little boy in Kalamazoo, Mich., pushed the emergency stop button on his father's new mower. Fortunately no one was hurt.
>
> "If you had come back one week later—March 10, 1993—you would have seen those five men and women decide that the flying lawn mower blade was just a freak accident that would never happen again, and was not even worth investigating.
>
> "Then, if you had been at Mark Stein's house on August 23, 1993, when Mark was mowing the front lawn, you would have seen the result of that corporate decision."[9]

Interesting? Mildly, although it is larded with too many facts that are not consequential at this point: the dates and the model number. Persuasive? Again, mildly.

In my trial-advocacy lectures to lawyers around the country, I demonstrate the difference between a "story," as exemplified by Jim McElhaney's example, and an "argument" by using the facts of the McElhaney example to craft the start of an opening statement the way I would do it. Although the precise words are different each time I do the demonstration, the substance of the example is the same:

---

[9] James W. McElhaney, *Opening Statements*, 81 ABA JOURNAL 73–74 (January 1995).

"Ladies and gentlemen. Mark Stein sits here without any legs. He sits here without any legs because they were cut off at the knees when a lawn mower blade made by these people over here flew out when Mark pushed the 'stop' button on their lawn mower.

"You see, Mark was mowing his family's lawn on a sunny Sunday morning, just before he was going to go to his Little League game, when his mother called him. So Mark pushed that 'stop' button. Mark thought that that was the safe thing to do—to stop the lawn mower. Well, pushing that 'stop' button caused the spinning blade to fly off and cut Mark's legs off at the knees. He never made it back into the house that day. And, of course, he has never played Little League again—ever.

"Ladies and Gentlemen, I will prove to you that Mark Stein lost his legs that day because these people ignored a similar accident, just months before the blade cut off Mark's legs. You see, Ladies and Gentlemen, there was another little boy who tried to stop this very same model lawn mower by pushing the 'stop' button. And what happened when he did? The lawn mower blade flew 150 feet in the air, barely missing his legs.

"Did the lawn mower company, the defendant in this case, know about that near tragedy? You bet they did. I will prove to you that within days, this company got a report about that near miss. And I will prove to you that the company's president met with her engineering staff and the members of their safety-compliance committee, and they all discussed the problem of the flying lawn mower blade.

"And what did they do? I will prove to you that they did nothing. They sat around a large mahogany table and did absolutely nothing. In fact, I will prove that they decided that the flying lawn mower blade was just a freak accident that wasn't worth bothering about, and I will bring into this courtroom the minutes of that meeting where they actually said that.

"Unfortunately for Mark Stein, their powers of prediction were no greater than their ability to make a lawn mower that was safe. And, as a result, Mark Stein has no legs, and until he is old enough to get fitted with artificial limbs, he will have to roll around in a wheelchair while his friends and classmates frolic and play."

This is an opening statement that is persuasive, and, as we will see, it is an argument without being argumentative. Indeed, I will demonstrate for you later, as I do in a live demonstration for lawyers attending my trial-advocacy seminars, what happens if the opposing lawyer should be foolhardy enough to object.

3. **You must demonstrate commitment.** As we have seen, the jurors believe that each of the lawyers knows the "truth" of the case. Accordingly, the more personal commitment you show, the more likely it is that the jurors will believe your contentions. President Theodore Roosevelt understood this dynamic well. Historians recently discovered one of his typewritten speeches. Next to one paragraph, he wrote the following handwritten comment: "Argument weak; speak loudly!" This is but a variant of the young Churchill's recognition that "To convince you must believe." Again, to paraphrase Stephen Greenleaf's *Impact*, the incandescence of your belief in the justness of your client's cause must shine out.

Allowing your personal commitment to shine out so that it lights up the courtroom is powerful stuff. Indeed, the law recognizes how powerfully persuasive a lawyer's expression of personal opinion is to a jury, and, thus, in every court in the nation it is absolutely *verboten* for a lawyer to say to a jury "I know." Yet, you can come close and be on the safe side of the ethical and legal restraints. In the next few pages, I will show you how.

Although the lawyer's personal commitment is a critical component of successful trial advocacy, many lawyers seem almost apologetic in presenting their client's case. Thus, in the criminal prosecution of O.J. Simpson, Marcia Clark actually sounded ashamed for prosecuting a man she presumably believed had brutally slain two defenseless people: "You may not like me for bringing this case," she told the jury. "I'm not winning any popularity contests for doing so." Why not, if Simpson was guilty?

Christopher Darden's apologia was even worse than Clark's. He actually said this to the jury:

"Nobody wants to do anything to this man. We don't. There is nothing personal about this, but the law is the law."

Huh? Nobody wants to do anything to this brutal killer? Why not? No wonder the jury was ready to believe that the prosecutors really didn't believe that Simpson was guilty.

The apologies by Clark and Darden aside, and I concede that these are extreme examples of incompetence, most lawyers are afraid to show commitment to the jury, even when permitted by ethical and legal restraints. Even lawyers with great reputations hurt their cases by not using as a tool of advocacy the jury's belief that the lawyer knows the truth. In the Oklahoma City bombing trial of Terry Nichols, Mike Tigar, Nichols' chief lawyer, made this mistake during the following *voir dire* of one of the potential jurors. First, Tigar, who was arguing that Nichols was innocent, explored the potential juror's views on punishment. This, in my view, is a major blunder. If you have an innocent client, and you have faith in the system, the jurors will never reach the punishment phase. Discussing punishment when you will also argue innocence is making an "even if" argument that weakens both alternatives. Second, Tigar must have recognized that he was weakening his "innocence" contention, because this is how he tried to explain to the potential juror why he was asking about the juror's views on capital punishment:

> "You notice I'm talking hypothetically? And that's because none of us here can say what the evidence will be. We think we know."[10]

How's that again? "We think we know"? This translates as: "Gee, I'm going to argue that Nichols is innocent, but I really don't know that. We're all going to have to see how the evidence unfolds." In my view, this is a suicidal way to argue a case. But, unfortunately, it is the way most lawyers do it. They routinely hide behind the "witnesses," the "evidence," and what the jury "will be able to conclude at the end of the case." This is the way they usually phrase their promises of proof:

> "Ladies and Gentlemen, witnesses will tell you that the defendant was driving too fast. The evidence will show that he went through a red light, and smashed into the plaintiff's car. At the end of the case you will be able to conclude that he failed to exercise ordinary care and was thus negligent."

If you hired Abraham Lincoln, would you want him to hide behind what the witnesses will say, to hide behind what the evidence will show, to hide

---

[10] *United States v. Terry Lynn Nichols*, 96-CR-68 (U.S.D.C. Colo.) Transcript of proceedings, October 10, 1997. Tigar made a similar mistake during the trial, when he introduced himself to witnesses that he was about to cross-examine: "My name is Michael Tigar. I'm one of the lawyers appointed to help out Terry Nichols." *Id.*, Transcript of November 7, 1997 (Cross-examination of Thomas Brown); "I'm Michael Tigar. I'm one of the lawyers appointed to help Terry Nichols in this case, sir." *Ibid.* (Cross-examination of Brett Mills).

behind what the jury will be able to conclude at the end of the case? I think not. If you were the plaintiff in the above example, you would want Abraham Lincoln to stand in front of the jury and put *his* credibility on the line for you:

> "Ladies and Gentlemen, I will prove to you that the defendant was driving too fast. I will prove that he went through a red light, and smashed into the plaintiff's car. And I will prove to you that he failed to exercise ordinary care and was thus negligent."

As Herb Stern has shown in his pioneering trial-advocacy seminars and books, "I will prove" is the way to let the incandescence of your belief glow without crossing the line by saying "I know." "I will prove" can be used any place where you would be able to say "the evidence will show." In fact, what separates an improper "argumentative" opening statement from an opening statement that is forceful and persuasive is whether you can put "the evidence will show" in front of an assertion. If you can, the assertion is not "argumentative," and you should use the more powerful "I will prove." Consider these two examples:

> A lawyer's declaration in an opening statement, "I ask you to use your verdict to send a message to this company and companies every where that they cannot make and sell dangerous products" is "argumentative" and improper; it is impossible to insert "the evidence will show" (or "I will prove," for that matter) in front of the offending phrase.

> A lawyer's declaration in an opening statement that "the defendant was driving too fast" is not "argumentative"; "the evidence will show" (or "I will prove") fits easily in front of the phrase. Why settle for "the evidence will show" when you can use the more forceful and committed "I will prove"?

Before we move on, I promised to show what happens to an opponent who objects to a forceful, persuasive opening statement, and the judge sustains the objections. Let's look at the start of my Mark Stein open again, this time with some objections. I have put into italics what I've added as a result of the sustained objections. My editorial comments are in small capital letters.

> "Ladies and gentlemen. Mark Stein sits here without any legs. He sits here without any legs, because they were cut off at the knees when a lawn mower blade made by these people over here flew out when Mark pushed the 'stop' button on their lawn mower.

[THIS IS A POWERFUL BEGINNING. ALTHOUGH BEING HURT, THE DEFENSE LAWYER HAS NO BASIS UPON WHICH TO OBJECT.]

"You see, Mark was mowing his family's lawn on a sunny Sunday morning, just before he was going to go to his Little League game, when his mother called him.

[IS THE DEFENSE LAWYER GOING TO OBJECT TO "SUNNY"? I THINK NOT. BUT, LET'S ASSUME THAT HE DOES. LAWYERS OBJECT FOR A VARIETY OF REASONS, AND THE DEFENSE LAWYER MAY WANT TO OBJECT MERELY TO THROW THE PLAINTIFF'S LAWYER OFF BALANCE. LET'S ALSO ASSUME THAT WE HAVE A BAD JUDGE, A BULLY. THE RESPONSE BY THE PLAINTIFF'S LAWYER IS SIMPLE, HOWEVER. NOTICE HOW HE DEALS WITH THE INTERRUPTION AND THE JUDGE'S UNREASONABLE COMMENTS AND DIRECTION. THE IMPORTANT THING TO REMEMBER IS: COMPLY WITH THE JUDGE'S DIRECTIONS, BUT DO NOT BACK DOWN FROM YOUR POINT.]

Defense Counsel: I object to the word "sunny." It is argumentative.

The Court: Sustained.

Plaintiff's Counsel: Well, it was sunny that morning, and I'll bring in the official weather charts to prove it.

The Court: The objection was sustained. I don't see the relevance of whether it was sunny or not. Move on.

Plaintiff's Counsel: Yes, Your Honor. I will prove, Your Honor, that the grass was dry that morning, and was precisely in the condition for which lawn-mower makers design the blade mechanisms for their mowers. The grass was not wet and heavy; it was dry because that morning and for three days before that it was sunny.

[SEE HOW THE LAWYER IS ABLE TO BACK UP, SHOW A LEGITIMATE REASON WHY "SUNNY" IS RELEVANT, AND COME BACK TO THE VERY POINT TO WHICH A SUSTAINED OBJECTION WAS MADE. THIS IS THE ESSENCE OF EFFECTIVE TRIAL-LAWYERING, AND REQUIRES TOTAL AND THROUGH PREPARATION.]

"*Now, when his mother called him,* Mark pushed that 'stop' button. Mark thought that that was the safe thing to do—to stop the lawn mower.

Defense Counsel: I object to what was in Mark's mind.

The Court: Sustained.

Plaintiff's Counsel: Ladies and gentlemen, I will prove to you that when Mark Stein's mother called him, he had three choices. Mark could have ignored his mother. But Mark will tell you why he did not. First, I'll prove to you that Mark is not in the habit of ignoring his mother. And Mark will tell you that himself. Second, I'll prove to you that Mark was waiting for his mother to give him a ride to his Little League game. And Mark will tell you that too. In fact, I'll prove that when Mark was mowing the lawn that sunny morning he was in his Little League uniform, and I will bring into this courtroom the photographs from the hospital showing him in that uniform, or what was left of it, when he was taken there after the lawn mower blade cut off his legs.

When responding to his mother's call, Mark could have either left the mower running or tried to stop it. I will prove to you that Mark did not think that leaving the mower running was a good idea, and he'll tell you why. You see, there were little children playing nearby and Mark was afraid that they might get hurt if he left the mower running. So, ladies and gentlemen, Mark felt that stopping the mower was the safest thing to do, and he naturally assumed that the 'stop' button would do that. Well, pushing that 'stop' button caused the spinning blade to fly off and cut Mark's legs off at the knees. He never made it back into the house that day. And, of course, he has never played Little League again—ever.

> [A LAWYER WHO HAS THOUGHT HIS OR HER CASE THROUGH, IS PREPARED FOR ANYTHING—INCLUDING AN OPPONENT WHO OBJECTS AT EVERY TURN AND A JUDGE WHO SUSTAINS THE OBJECTIONS. OBJECTIONS, ESPECIALLY WHEN THEY ARE SUSTAINED, CAN BE TURNED INTO LADDERS WITH WHICH TO REACH GREATER HEIGHTS OF ADVOCACY AND PERSUASION. THE IMPORTANT POINT TO REMEMBER IS NOT TO BACK DOWN. A JURY WILL LOSE RESPECT FOR YOU AS THE TRUTH-GIVER IF THEY SEE YOU COWERING FOLLOWING AN ONSLAUGHT OF SUSTAINED OBJECTIONS.]

The above illustration was, of course, based on Professor McElhaney's example. Let me give you one from an actual trial that demonstrates how to not back down in the face of a sustained objection when you are right.

The example comes from the transcript of a serious medical malpractice case that went to trial. The plaintiff claimed that her physician, a family practitioner, failed to diagnose a rare ailment. One of the plaintiff's expert witnesses was a gastroenterologist who had never worked as a general practitioner. In her opening statement, the defense lawyer bore down on this:

> "He testified, when I asked him questions at his deposition, that he would defer to the board certified family practice physician as to whether [the defendant physician] exercised reasonable care. In other words, he was acknowledging that he doesn't know what the family practice practitioner is."

At this point, the plaintiff's lawyer interrupted: "I'll object, Your Honor. That's argumentative." The trial judge sustained the objection, adding: "That is argumentative." The defense lawyer continued on this part of her argument for several more sentences, and pointed out that the gastroenterologist "testified that he never did a residency in family practice," that he "couldn't take the board certification exam for family practice because he doesn't have the credentials," and submitted that she believed "it would be appropriate to take that into consideration when listening to [the gastroenterologist]'s testimony." She then left the point.

The defense lawyer's recovery after the sustained objection was better than most—she did not leave the issue entirely. Yet, it could have been better. Consider the following hypothetical response, picked up right after the judge sustained the plaintiff's objection to "In other words, he was acknowledging that he doesn't know what the family practice practitioner is" as argumentative. For the sake of this example, we'll call the gastroenterologist "Dr. King."

> "Ladies and gentlemen, as you know, lawyers get to talk with the witnesses that the other side may call to testify. These are not ordinary conversations, however. They are under oath, and are taken down word-for-word, just as the testimony in the trial is taken down word-for-word by the court reporter here.
>
> "Now, I asked Dr. King some questions, and he responded under oath. I will prove to you that he is not a family practitioner and has never been one. Indeed, he's admitted that under oath. Your Honor, I am reading from page 15 of Dr. King's deposition:
>
> > 'Q   You are not a family practitioner?

        A   No, I am not.

        Q   And, in fact, you have never been a family
            practitioner?

        A   That's right.'

"And I will prove that Dr. King is not even qualified to take the board certification exam for family practice, and he's admitted this as well, Your Honor, I'm quoting from Dr. King's deposition, page 16:

        'Q   Are you qualified to take board certification
             exam for family practice?

        A   No?'

"In fact, I will prove that Dr. King said right here in this deposition that he would defer to a board certified family practice physician as to whether [the defendant physician] exercised reasonable care. Again, Your Honor, page 16 of Dr. King's deposition:

        'Q   In fact, you would defer to a board certified family
             practice physician as to whether [the defendant physician]
             exercised reasonable care?

        A   Yes.'

"Ladies and gentlemen, based on all of this, I submit, and I will prove to you, that Dr. King does not know what a family practice practitioner is, and that the evidence, including Dr. King's own statements under oath, will confirm that."

Notice, by coming back to the sentence to which the objection was sustained, how the lawyer is sending a message to the jury:

"I am the truth-giver in this courtroom. The judge may have sustained my opponent's objection, but I did nothing wrong. As proof of that, I am repeating what I asked, and the judge is letting me do it."

And the judge will let her do it, because she was perfectly within her rights to say what she said, and, after the foundation, the judge will see it. None of the defense lawyer's "arguments" in this example was "argumentative"—the phrase "the evidence will show" can be placed before every one.

X.
EVIDENCE IS USED TO VALIDATE THE LAWYER'S PROMISES OF PROOF

As we have seen, in giving their opening statements, most lawyers hide behind the witnesses and the evidence. That is, the lawyers see the function of the opening statement to either lay out a "road map" of the evidence or to show to the jury the cover of the puzzle box. This has it all backwards.

The witnesses and the evidence exist to *validate* the lawyer's arguments. This is a principle that underlies not only an effective opening statement, but also direct- and cross-examination, as well as the closing argument. Let me repeat:

The witnesses and the evidence exist to *validate* the lawyer's arguments.

Contrary to the conventional wisdom, the witnesses and the evidence must take a back seat to the lawyer's personal credibility and commitment. Again, all this is founded on the fact that the jurors believe that the lawyers know the truth, *and that the technical rules of trial will keep the jurors from learning much of what is critical to their decision.* Thus, to be an effective advocate, a lawyer giving an opening statement must put his or her own credibility on the line and, in effect, say to the jury *I know that this is a fact **without using those words**.* Thus an effective opening statement uses the TWO STEP:

1. "I will prove . . ."

2. ". . . and I will bring into this courtroom (Mrs. Jones, who will tell you so) (a document that says so) ([opposing party]'s prior testimony that admits it)."

You've seen this technique used in the examples. You will see it again.

What makes the technique so effective is that it works synergistically to both bolster your promise of proof and enhance your own believability and credibility as the truth-giver. Thus, when you come to a point that can only be proved by circumstantial evidence the jury will have before it a track-record of validated promises of proof.

The synergism of the two-step is lost if the lawyer jumps first to the evidentiary basis for his or her point. For example, in the Mark Stein/lawn-mower blade example, a plaintiff's lawyer with a copy of the safety committee's minutes might be tempted to go directly to those minutes in the opening statement—as in illustration number one—rather than use the two-step—as in illustration number two:

1. Ladies and gentlemen, when the near-miss accident was reported to the company, they held a meeting, and the minutes of that meeting show that they looked at the accident as just a freak accident that wasn't worth bothering with.

2. Ladies and gentlemen, when the near-miss accident was reported to the company, they held a meeting. I will prove to you that they concluded that the flying lawn mower blade was just a freak accident that wasn't worth bothering with, and I will bring into this courtroom the minutes of that meeting where they actually said that.

XI.
USE THE "BAD FACTS" TO WIN

Every trial has facts that both support and weaken a party's position; if not, the case would not go to trial. How a lawyer handles the bad facts of his or her case can make the difference between winning and losing.

Some lawyers will actually try to either deny or ignore the bad facts, presumably with the hope that the adversary will not find about them. Thus, the O.J. Simpson prosecution team's presentation of Mark Fuhrman to the jury as a boy scout. The typical result of this head-in-the-sand Ostrich-like position is to get kicked where the Ostrich is most vulnerable. More usually, however, lawyers try to "remove the sting," as they are taught to do.

The following is a typical example of "removing the sting." In a criminal prosecution for bank-robbery, the government's main witness is the defendant's accomplice. The prosecutor brings out the witness's bad background, as is permitted by Rule 607 of the Federal Rules of Evidence ("The credibility of a witness may be attacked by any party, including the party calling the witness."). This is an example of removing the sting during the prosecutor's opening statement:

> "Ladies and gentlemen, you will hear from Sam Smith how he helped the defendant rob the bank. I wish I could tell you that Mr. Smith has led a perfect life.[11] He hasn't. Indeed, he'll tell you that this is the third armed robbery in which he's been involved, and that he's also been convicted of perjury."

This is much better, of course, than ignoring the witness's baggage, hoping that the defense lawyer might be asleep at the switch. It is also much better for the prosecutor to foreshadow the accomplice's testimony in the opening statement than to wait until the accomplice's direct-examination. As we will see in a few pages, it is much better for the lawyer to **use** the bad stuff as part of his or her proof.

There is a story, most likely apocryphal, about a lawyer representing a man claiming serious and disabling injuries as the result of an automobile accident. The lawyer is ready to begin her opening statement. As she heads for the jury box, the defense lawyer calls her over to his table and whispers in her ear: "Sally, I just wanted to warn you, the nice guy that I am, that we have a video tape of your client shoveling snow."

The plaintiff's lawyer walks over to the jury box and begins her opening statement without missing a beat. During that portion of her presentation discussing the plaintiff's injuries, she says:

> "Now let me tell you something about what kind of man Bob Rogers is. Most people, I will prove to you, when faced with this type of injury would be bedridden for weeks, if not for months. In fact, I'm going to bring into this courtroom Bob Rogers' physician, and she will tell you that. It's not that staying in bed that long is necessary to the healing process; it is not, and Mr. Rogers' doctor will also tell you that. It's just that most people can't stand the pain, and prefer to be pampered during the healing period, and the doctor will tell you that too.

---

[11] By the way, this sentence is technically "argumentative" because the words "the evidence will show" (or, "I will prove") cannot be placed before it. Nevertheless, this type of comment in an opening statement is common, and judges generally permit it as a form of transition.

"Now, Bob Rogers is, I will prove to you, made of sterner stuff than that. In fact, during the first several weeks of his recuperation period, we had that heavy snow storm. Remember? It snowed some five to eight inches around town, and I'll show you the official weather reports that say that.

"In any event, Mr. Rogers' wife had to get to work that day, but their driveway was snowed in. So what did Mr. Rogers do, despite the awful pain? Ladies and gentlemen, I will prove to you that Bob Rogers pulled himself out of his sick-bed, walked into his garage, got his snow-shovel, and shoveled the entire driveway. And, as I'll prove to you, although this did not affect his healing period, and his doctor will tell you that, that it was hard and painful work. But, ladies and gentlemen, Bob Rogers wanted his wife to be able to get to work that day."

Let's analyze this example. Assume that everything that the plaintiff's lawyer said was true. There are three ways to present those facts.

1. Ignore the defense lawyer's warning and not mention the tape at all, either in the opening statement or on direct-examination of the plaintiff. After the defense lawyer shows the tape on his cross-examination of the plaintiff, explain it away on re-direct.

2. Deal with the tape in the opening statement, but do it this way:

    "Ladies and gentlemen, you may have seen that defense counsel whispered something to me before I started my opening statement. He told me that they had a surveillance tape of my client showing him shoveling snow. Let me explain that."

3. Do it the way she did it.

The first approach is suicidal, The jury will believe that the plaintiff's testimony is a made-up story to explain away the tape, which shows him not as disabled as he claims. The second way of dealing with the tape is little better. Again, however, the jury will discount the explanation because it is presented *as an explanation.*

What makes the way the lawyer actually did it so powerful? By presenting the facts as she did, the plaintiff's lawyer *makes them work for her* as part of her case. Then, when the defense lawyer shows the jury the tape (if he does), that tape bolsters rather than weakens the plaintiff's claim.

As the snow-shoveling example shows, there are two inter-related rules that govern the effective presentation to the jury of the bad facts in your case:

1. **The explanation must come before the accusation.**

2. **The explanation must be presented as a positive aspect of your proof.**

Let me give another example. The only way that the government was able to convict mafia boss John Gotti was through the testimony of his long-time associate and underboss, Sammy "The Bull" Gravano. Yet, Gravano was hardly Mother Teresa. According to his recent biography, Peter Maas's *Underboss*, Gravano was a burglar, bank robber, car thief, extortionist, loan shark, and a killer who, according to Maas, admitted to his involvement in "18 or 19 murders."

I do not know how the prosecutors presented Gravano to the jury; I will assume that they followed the conventional wisdom and "removed the sting" by bringing out Gravano's sordid past themselves. If they did it this way, the journeyman's way, OK, but they could have done better.

The following is a brief excerpt from a hypothetical opening argument by the government in Gotti's prosecution. It makes Gravano's past work as a positive aspect of the government's case:

> "Ladies and gentlemen, this is a trial about greed, violence, corruption, and murder. It is about John Gotti, who, I will prove, led one of the biggest criminal enterprises in this nation's history. In fact, I will prove to you that John Gotti's criminal enterprise was so big and so far-flung, that he could not oversee it all by himself. He needed helpers, he needed henchmen. And to control these helpers, these henchmen, who, I will prove, were thugs, thieves, and killers, he needed a man who was even more ruthless, more heartless, more brutal, and more cruel than any of them were. Such a man is not easy to find, I'll prove to you. But John Gotti found such a man, and that man was Sammy, known as 'The Bull,' Gravano.

"Sammy 'The Bull' Gravano" started life as a common thug. He then progressed up the ladder of crime to burglary, robbery, extortion, and murder. Just the kind of résumé John Gotti was looking for in an underboss. Indeed, Sammy 'The Bull' Gravano, selected by John Gotti to be his chief henchman, to be his underboss, will tell you how, during his fairly short life, he's been involved in eighteen or nineteen murders—so brutal was his life that he can't even remember how many.

"But, ladies and gentlemen, even Sammy Gravano had his limits. The turning point, I will prove to you, came when he and John Gotti were watching the news about the Desert Storm operation against Sadaam Hussein. Gotti rooted for Iraq, and told Gravano that he hoped that American servicemen and women would die in the desert. Gravano may be a killer, but he is an American, and Gotti's disloyalty started the chain of events that led to Gravano being willing to testify against his former crime boss."

XII.
THE BURDEN OF PROOF

One of the legal rules that come into play in any trial, civil or criminal, is the burden of proof. Most lawyers, whether they are trying civil or criminal cases, argue the burden of proof if their opponent bears that burden.

The typical criminal defense lawyer stands behind his or her client, and solemnly proclaims that the defendant is cloaked with the presumption of innocence and that this presumption of innocence prevails at the end of the trial unless the prosecutor proves guilt beyond a reasonable doubt. There is only one thing that the average juror thinks during this demonstration: "Guilty. The guy is guilty."

Truth-givers do not rely on burdens of proof. What would you think if your daughter came home from school with a sealed note that accused her of stealing several candy bars from the cafeteria, and, in response to your questions, remarked: "I don't have to say anything. I don't have to prove my innocence. The school has to prove me guilty."?

Some jurors may be linear, and follow the beyond-a-reasonable-doubt instruction and acquit persons whom they believe to be factually, but not provably, guilty. I don't believe that it happens very often, however. Certainly, the odds of an acquittal are greater if you can persuade the jury that the defendant is factually innocent, rather than relying on the burden of proof.

I am not saying that the burden of proof in a criminal case is not important. It is very important. As we'll see later, the beyond-a-reasonable-doubt argument can be critical during closing argument, at the end of the trial. But in the opening statement it should be used as a sword and not as a shield:

> "Ladies and gentlemen, Her Honor has told you that we don't have to prove anything in this courtroom, and that you cannot return a verdict of guilty unless the prosecutor here proves guilt beyond a reasonable doubt. But we're not going to rely on that. Ladies and gentlemen, Sam Smith sits here an innocent man, and I am going to prove it to you."

You can, and should, say this even if Smith will not testify (although my preference is that the defendant should, if at all possible, testify—jurors want to hear what the defendant has to say, and they know that if any of them were falsely accused of a crime they would shout their denials from every rooftop in town).[12] Innocence can be proved by the government's evidence or lack of evidence.

The burden of proof in a civil case, a preponderance of the evidence, is meaningless. A preponderance of anything can be so small that it cannot be measured. Several years ago, General Electric announced that their engineers had developed a light that could go from "off" to "on" to "off" in five femtoseconds. There are as many femtoseconds in a second as there are seconds in thirty million years. Take the proof equivalent of a femtosecond, divide it by a trillion, and add the result to one side of an equally balanced case, and, under the law, that side has prevailed by a preponderance of the

---

[12] Edward Bennett Williams, the great criminal defense trial lawyer, used to say: "If a defendant doesn't take the stand, he might as well take his toothbrush to court on the last day and say 'goodbye.' " Evan Thomas, *The Man To See* 111 (1991).

Williams was an absolute master at winning in court. In the 1950s, he was asked to represent Bernard Goldfine, who was then in jail on a contempt-of-Congress charge for refusing to testify before a congressional committee investigating the scandal involving Sherman Adams, President Dwight Eisenhower's right-hand man in the White House. Goldfine was a rough-and-tumble wheeler-dealer and fixer, and had a coterie of lawyers who did his bidding. One of those lawyers was a man by the name of Ralph Slobodkin, whom Goldfine used mainly as a bill-collector and gofer. Williams met with Goldfine and told him that Goldfine didn't have a defense. Goldfine, who hired Williams, complained to one of his hangers-on: "Who does that young momzer [Yiddish for "bastard"] from Washington think he is, telling me I have no defense? Defense? If I had a defense, I'd still have Slobodkin!" Evan Thomas, *The Man To See* 135–136 (1991).

evidence. The problem is, of course, that the burden of proof in a civil case comes into play only when the decision-maker is in total balance. That *never* happens.

As with the burden of proof in a criminal case, the burden of proof in a civil case does have a defensive use in the closing-argument portion of the trial. In the opening, however, it, like the burden of proof in a criminal trial, should be used as a sword, not a shield. Consider the following two examples, the first by the plaintiff's lawyer, and the second by the defense lawyer:

1. "Ladies and gentlemen, as Her Honor has told you, we have the burden of proof in this case. We gladly accept that burden, and I will prove to you that on March 15, Sam Jones, the man sitting at this table, sped through a red light and rammed his 1989 Dodge van into the side of Sarah Smith's little Miata."

2. "Ladies and gentlemen, Her Honor has told you that we don't have to prove anything in this courtroom, but I will prove to you that Mr. Jones did not run a red light, and I will bring into this courtroom two eye witnesses who will tell you that. What's more, I will prove that he was driving well within the speed limit and that the plaintiff caused the accident."

XIII.
LIMIT NOTE TAKING

Note pads are the bane of every trial lawyer. They force the lawyer to write rather than to listen. This is true during all stages of the trial, and excessive note-taking is especially harmful during the opening statements. Note-taking lures the lawyer who represents the defendant, either in a civil or criminal case, into responding to the arguments of the plaintiff or of the prosecutor, rather than formulating a persuasive opening statement that can stand on its own.

An opening statement must be positive, not responsive. This does not mean, however, that the defense lawyer should not deal with points made by his or her adversary. It means that those points should be dealt with at the place in the defense's opening statement where they make logical and persuasive sense. During my years as a trial judge, I saw too many defense lawyers, in both civil and criminal cases, do an opening statement that repeated and attempted to answer the opening statement given by the plaintiff or prosecutor—either in direct order or reverse order.

XIV.
Don't Sound Like a Lawyer

An Oklahoma City lawyer attending one of my trial-advocacy lectures once told me that the problem with law schools was that, in a parody of the old western town of Dodge City's gun ordinance, they made you check your common sense when you entered but did not give it back when you left. One of the ways law schools rob their students of common sense is by teaching them to sound and write like lawyers.

Every profession and occupation has its jargon. Most professions, however, confine the jargon to discussions among members. Lawyers, however, make the mistake of using the jargon and stilted language in the courtroom when they are attempting to persuade lay people to reach a certain decision. The following are actual questions asked by lawyers in trials over which I presided:

"After you terminated the conversation, what course of action did you take?"

"Did you have occasion to notice the roadway where you observed the vehicle?"

"In what manner of speed was the vehicle moving?"

"Does that photograph fully and accurately portray the scene at the time you had occasion to take the photograph?" The witness scratched his head and murmured "what?" Then the lawyer, shaken from his efforts to sound like a lawyer, got to the nub: "Did it look like that?"

Why do lawyers use stilted language in the courtroom? For the same reason cops and some doctors do—they want to sound "professional," whatever that means, or "smart."[13] Herman Melville once wrote:

---

[13] Cops, of course, are notorious for never getting out of cars; they exit vehicles. They never watch anybody; they "surveil." My favorite snippet of testimony from a doctor in a trial over which I presided is: "He continued to progress in a negative fashion."

"A man of true science uses but few hard words, and only when none other will answer his purpose; whereas the smatterer in science thinks that by mouthing hard words he proves that he understands hard things."

Don't try to "sound" like a professional "by mouthing hard words." You should try to sound *right*. Use simple language, and avoid the pet jargon that most lawyers use. Juries will resent you if you try to lord it over them with "hard words."

The words on the left side of the chart are "lawyer" words and you should avoid them.

No		**Yes**
State	⇒	Tell me
Occasion	⇒	-------
Observe	⇒	See, hear, taste, smell, feel
Vehicle	⇒	Car, truck, van, bus,
Proceed	⇒	Go, walk, run, drive
Exit (verb)	⇒	Leave, get out of
Transpire	⇒	Happen
Explain to Jury	⇒	Tell me

An important part of oral advocacy is the painting of pictures for the listener. The words "observe," "vehicle," and "proceed" tell us very little. "Where did you first see the rusty Volkswagen bus?" is far more effective than "when did you first see the vehicle?" "Explain for the jury" is condescending and presumptuous; it says, in effect, "Doctor, you and I know all this technical stuff, why don't you please explain it to those twelve dummies sitting over there." Use the word "transpire," and half the jury will believe that someone died. The word "occasion" is but a mere static word, unless used to refer to an event or a party. If you mean to ask: "Did you see Sam Smith that day?" don't phrase it: "Did you have occasion to see Sam Smith that day?" In one of the trials over which I presided, a witness responded to: "Did you have occasion to see Sam Smith that day?" with "Yes, but I missed him."

There is another phrase that you must never utter in the courtroom. Never, ever, say "for the record"—either in front of the jury or before the judge.

When you ask a witness to "state" something "for the record," you are telling the jury that the question and answer are mere formalities, perfunctory stuff that doesn't mean anything.

This same psychology applies to arguments that you make to the judge. A sentence, objection, or argument that starts with the phrase: "Your Honor, for the record, let me . . . " Will be rejected. I used to think that I was idiosyncratic when the word "denied" echoed in my brain when lawyers made motions "for the record." The moment I heard that apologetic phrase, I knew that they had little or no faith in their arguments. If the advocate has no faith, why should the tribunal? Later on, I learned from discussions with judges all over the country that my knee-jerk reaction was shared by every judge I asked.

XV.
THE IMPORTANCE OF EMPATHY

One of the most important tools of persuasion is empathy. A person whom a jury likes, for whom it has compassion, affection, respect, sympathy, and understanding, is a person whom the jury will want to believe and help. Thus, one of the skillful trial lawyer's most important jobs is to try to make his or her client and witnesses sympathetic. Luckily, the ground has already been plowed for us.

Hollywood has recognized from the American film-industry's inception that the audience needs to relate to the main character: get the hero on the screen in the first two minutes or so and make the audience care about that person. There are, essentially, five ways to do this: make the character skilled at what he or she does (a great auto mechanic, for example, who is able to fix the car the boys in the shop have struggled with for years); make the character a victim of undeserved tragedy; put the character in jeopardy (Pauline was always in "peril"); give the character a sense of humor (both Sally and Harry in the movie where they meet); make the character a "good person" (we will empathize with a man whom we first see rescuing a little girl from a raging fire even though in the middle of the movie he blows up a school—we may not like what he has done, but we will be more likely to find underlying causes for that criminal act than we would if we first see him blowing up the school.)

You can use these Hollywood techniques to get the jury rooting for and believing in your clients and witnesses. Additionally, juries, like the rest of us, want to know about the person with whom they are dealing. Is the person stable (long-time employee in a position of sensitivity and trust) or flighty? Is the person caring and concerned (Little League coach, PTA member, community volunteer)? You must make your client and witnesses live for the jury; they must be made into real-life, three-dimensional human beings. Shakespeare said it best, when he had Shylock describe his own feelings:

> "Hath not a Jew eyes? Hath not a Jew hands, organs, dimensions, senses, affections, passions? . . . If you prick us, do we not bleed? If you tickle us, do we not laugh? If you poison us, do we not die?"

The jury must see your clients and witnesses as persons who bleed when pricked, laugh when tickled, and die when poisoned.

If you represent an institutional client, personalize it by making the "client" an employee. If possible, this employee should be the person whose decision is the subject of the lawsuit The person should sit at counsel table throughout the entire trial, just as if he or she were the *real* client with a stake in the outcome. Rule 615 of the Federal Rules of Evidence permits you to exempt this person from sequestration.

XVI.
THE OPENING STATEMENT—AN ANNOTATED DEMONSTRATION

So far we have discussed the theme of the case and the opening statement. We've explored some brief examples to help illustrate the points. There is an old saying that one demonstration is worth a thousand explanations. One of the great trial-advocacy programs for lawyers is the nine-day Trial Advocacy Institute at the University of Virginia run by former federal judge Herbert J. Stern and George Washington University law professor Stephen A. Saltzburg with Executive Director Peter J. Kenny. Every January, lawyers from all over the country come to Charlottesville to learn the techniques of effective trial advocacy. I have been honored to be on the Institute's faculty. Like many of the other faculty members, I have put on demonstrations.

One year, Herb and Steve asked me to do back-to-back opening statements for both sides in one of the Institute's case files. The purpose of the demonstration was to show that a lawyer could argue both sides of an issue, and let the incandescence of his or her belief shine out for both.

The case file is *Rock v. United States Postal Service*. Norman Rock, a black postal employee sued his employer because he was denied a promotion, and claims that he was the victim of race and sex discrimination, and that the decision-maker, a postal supervisor by the name of Al Haig, engaged in illegal reprisal by passing over Rock to get back at Rock for filing an earlier discrimination complaint. This is the nub of the case. It is generally all the jurors will know before opening statements.

The following is a transcription of my arguments that Friday evening—less than two hours after being given the assignment. An annotated version follows, to show what I was attempting to accomplish. Let me emphasize that I did not write out these openings and, obviously, did not read them to the group. I did, of course, have a few jotted points that I wanted to cover. The following is the opening as I gave it, together with obvious misstatements, which I have marked with [sic].

FOR THE PLAINTIFF:

"Ladies and gentlemen, as Her Honor has told you, the name of this case is Norman Rock versus the United States Postal Service. Now we all know what the Postal Service is. It's the post office. And in the next few minutes that I have, I'm going to tell you a little bit about who Norman Rock is, and why he would come into this courtroom, with the word "truth" emblazoned over the portal, to sue his employer, the United States Postal Service, the postal service of the United States of America, represented by these fine lawyers from the United States Department of Justice in Washington, D.C., and from the United States Attorney's office here in Cincinnati.

"Norman Rock has worked for the postal service since 1973. He started out, as most people start out in the postal service, as a mail clerk. About nine months later, he was promoted to be distribution clerk. Less than a year after that, he was foreman of mails. After four years as foreman of mails, he was promoted again to be foreman of platform operations. Two years later, 1981 we're at now, he was promoted to be supervisor of mails. And since 1985, for the last eight years, he has been general supervisor of mails.

"Norman Rock, through his progressive experience at increasing higher levels, has, I will prove to you ladies and gentlemen, devoted his life to the United States post office. And he's not one of these nine-to-fivers, either. Because from 1975 until 1985, after putting in a full-day's work, and even more, I will prove to you, at the post office, in these various increasing levels of responsibility, that his supervisors entrusted him with over the years, Norman Rock went home for a quick bite, I will prove to you, and then went to school.

"For nine years, Norman Rock went to night school to get a Bachelor of Science degree in Business Administration. He also, during that time, took a number of internal post-office courses to better his opportunities within the service and to make his performance and the fulfillment of his responsibilities, I will prove to you, even more knowledgeable, even more efficient.

"Just as Norman Rock was reaching the level, which I will prove to you is reached by similarly situated persons—persons who have similarly come up through the ranks—and just as he was getting ready to enter into the upper levels of management in the post office, he ran into this man sitting right here, Al Haig, Field Director for Mail Processing. And it was Norman Rock's bad luck to run into a man who has, we will prove to you ladies and gentlemen of the jury, a perverse hatred and fear of black men.

"Al Haig has proven over the last several years to be a stone wall in the road, we will prove to you, of Norman Rock's career. Ladies and gentlemen, we will prove to you throughout the next several days that it's the racist attitude, forgive me, it's the racist, sexist attitude, because we will be bringing into this courtroom an expert in these areas who will tell you that it is not uncommon for certain white men to have a special fear and hatred of black men. Al Haig's perverse hatred and fear of black men has stopped Norman Rock's career in its tracks, and that's why we're here today, I will prove to you.

"Now, in 1990 Norman Rock ran into that wall for the first time. Because the next level of his progressive experience of promotions came up. And the position was Tour Superintendent. And the Tour Superintendent is responsible for all the activities on his or her tour at the particular postal station at which he or she is working. And Norman Rock, with this progressive, continuous higher levels of experience, applied for the position. The position of Tour Superintendent, like everything else in government, like all positions in government, has certain designated criteria that the appointing people have to follow. And the reason for this is clear, and we'll prove that to you, folks. That during the dark ages when cronyism was rampant in government, enlightened folks realized that you can't trust promotion in government to the unfettered whim or discretion of an appointing person. So they established specific and detailed criteria that the appointed person has to meet in order (A) to be considered for the job, and (B) to be given the job.

"And the most important criteria for the position of Tour Superintendent is set out in this official document. And this is what it requires: 'Associate level understanding of management principles.' That's number one: 'Associate level understanding of management principles.' Number two: 'Extensive, progressive experience in supervisory positions in the area of mail processing.' That's number two. Number three is 'Well-developed human relations and communications skills.' And number four is: 'Physically able to work in a standing position for an extended period.'

"In 1990, Norman Rock had this incredible progressive experience in mail processing. He applied. Al Haig gave the job to a black woman, with, we will prove, ladies and gentlemen, far inferior qualifications. Norman Rock was disappointed at the time, and, we will prove to you, had this sixth sense, I guess, that it wasn't a level playing field. That there was something funny going on. And we will prove to you that as a result of those feelings, feelings, which we will prove to you, that only people who have been the victims of discrimination can really feel, he filed a discrimination complaint. Well, this was the first time he hit the brick wall, and the complaint was dismissed, and Norman Rock chalked it up to experience.

"Two years later, however, another Tour Superintendency opened up. And Norman Rock applied again. And again, as luck would have it, this man, Al Haig, was the man with the responsibility of making the appointment. Ladies and gentlemen, we'll prove to you that Norman Rock considered very carefully as to whether he should apply again, the deck being stacked, in his view.

"He applied. In a sense, and he'll tell you this, he swallowed his pride and applied again despite what happened with Al Haig back in 1990, and despite all these vibes he was getting. And again, Al Haig picked someone with far, far, we will prove, inferior qualifications: Rose Climber.

"Let me tell you a little bit about Rose Climber. You know, in addition to his progressive experience and work for the postal service since 1973, in addition to his nine years of going to night school to get a Bachelor of Science degree in Business Administration, in addition to his taking internal post-office courses, Al [*sic*] Rock is also a sergeant in the Army Reserves, and it was his tough luck, back in 1990 and 1991, when operation Desert Storm took place, that he had to go to Saudi Arabia. And they filled his position temporarily with Rose Climber.

"Now, we'll show you, ladies and gentlemen, that the person who filled that position temporarily with Rose Climber is a man no longer with the postal service by the name of William Donovan, a black man. Rose Climber came in at that point in her career, and we're just talking a couple of years ago now, at that point in her career she had a total of seven years with the United States

Postal Service. For four years, she stood at a mail-sorting machine her seven to eight hours a day. Then she was given a supervisory position. And then when Norman Rock went to Saudi Arabia to slosh around in the sand, protecting the interests of his government, Rose Climber was designated to fill in temporarily. And she came up with what everybody thought was a wonderful idea. It's this idea upon which they're hanging their hats, folks. She decided that if she moved the tour of duty back one-half hour, she'd save a lot of money in overtime expense. Except, we will prove, ladies and gentlemen, that although money was saved in overtime expense, the manner in which that was implemented by Rose Climber cost the United States government far more in terms of lost productivity, in terms of litigation expenses, than the savings during that period of time. Because you know what happened? Like a lot of people who don't have experience, we will show, ladies and gentlemen, she figured she is now a supervisor, she now can do what she wants, and she can deliver edicts from on high. Rather than working with the employees to explain the shift, to work with the union and explain the shift, she sprung it on them folks, and we'll prove that. And, as a result, there was all hell to pay for a while. People's lives were disrupted, we'll show. They complained, they filed grievances. The union filed grievances. Lawyers were tied up in litigation. The morale dropped.

"Rose Climber, the man [*sic*] Al Haig selected for a position that requires 'associate level understanding of management principles' and an 'extensive progression experience in supervisory positions,' had experience limited to four years working as a mail clerk by a sorting machine, two years as Supervisor of Mails, a position that Norman Rock held from 1981 to 1985. In addition, she took a one-month course inside the post office on managerial training, and she's currently going to night school in communications at the Lucius Quintus Community College.

"Ladies and gentlemen, by any fair analysis, by any unbiased, unprejudiced analysis, by any level-playing-field analysis, we will prove to you there is no dispute, no doubt, that the only one of those two candidates who had the required extensive, progressive experience in supervisory positions in the area of mail processing was Norman Rock. But there was that brick wall. The brick wall erected by race-based sexism. Hard thing to prove, folks, but we're going to prove it. And we're going to prove it right out of the mouth of Al Haig. Because no matter how good these racists are, they slip. They slip. And Al Haig, under oath, testified that during his entire nine years as a supervisor he could not remember ever, ever, ever having promoted an Afro-American man. And listen to his excuse. Because it is an excuse, we will prove to you, ladies and gentlemen, that has echoed through the centuries by people who try to hide their motives and make decisions that are based on racial hatred, ethnic hatred, or sexism.

"He was asked . . ."

Member of Group: "Objection, Your Honor."

The Court: "Overruled"

"We will prove to you, ladies and gentlemen, that he was asked 'Have you ever promoted an African-American male?' And what was his answer? Ladies and gentlemen, we'll prove to you, and he said this under oath: 'I don't believe so. But I would have if he was qualified.' Ladies and gentlemen, we will prove to you, and I submit that your own common knowledge and experience will tell you independent of our proof, that that is the refuge of a racist.

"Norman Rock has been deprived of an opportunity to advance up the career ladder to which he has devoted his entire life, because of Al Haig. But there's more. Because there's complicity, complicity with the United States Postal Service, who has let this go on. Because all these facts, and Her Honor will tell you, that this isn't the first time that this matter was heard. An independent agency of the United States government, called the Equal Employment Opportunity Commission, heard the facts that you're going to hearing during the course of this trial, totally independent of the postal service, totally independent agency, they heard the facts that you're going to hear. And what was their conclusion? The conclusion was that Al Haig discriminated against Norman Rock. Unfortunately, as we will show, ladies and gentlemen, that wasn't the end of it. Otherwise we wouldn't be here. Because under the rules, it all comes back to, guess where, the United States Postal Service. And the United States Postal Service rejected the determination of the independent agency, Equal Employment Opportunity Commission, that Al Haig discriminated against Norman Rock and, as a result, Norman Rock is entitled to his promotion.

"Ladies and gentlemen, it will be your opportunity to remove that brick wall. It'll be your opportunity to set things right, and re-write what should have been written correctly originally. Thank you Your Honor."

I took a two-minute break, and, before I started the argument on behalf of Norman Rock, I shared this with the group:

"I'm reminded of the story that they used to tell about Abraham Lincoln. He walked into a courthouse in Illinois one afternoon, and in those days legal matters didn't take forever because you didn't have all these fancy gizmos that produce reams of paper. And so, he'd been in that courtroom that morning in a different matter, and he was making an argument to the judge, and the judge looked down at Abraham Lincoln and said: 'Mr. Lincoln, you were here this morning. You argued exact opposite theory for your client this morning and I found in your favor.' And Abe Lincoln said: 'Judge, I may have been wrong this morning, but I'm right now.'"

FOR THE DEFENDANT:

"If it please the court, counsel. Norman Rock didn't get a job that he wanted. And he's crying racism and he's crying sexism, he's crying reprisal—at least that's in his complaint, he alleges Al Haig is trying to get even with him for something. Norman Rock has come into this courtroom and has accused Al Haig of being a racist. He has accused Al Haig of being a sexist. And he's accused Al Haig of promoting Rose Climber to get even with him. As Her Honor has told you, we don't have to prove a thing in this courtroom, but we will prove to you that each and every one of those charges against this good man is false.

"Al Haig is not a racist, we will prove to you. Al Haig is not a sexist, we will prove to you. He's not a racist-sexist, whatever that is, and we will prove that to you too. And the only reason he promoted Rose Climber was because, in his honest view, Rose Climber was the best qualified applicant for that position, period. And we will prove that to you as well.

"Now let me tell you a little bit about Al Haig. We've heard a lot of things, quite frankly, that are somewhat disturbing. Al Haig has worked with the mails for more than twenty-five years, since 1967. For the last nine years, he's been Field Director of Mail Processing here in Cincinnati. And that means it's his responsibility to make sure the mail gets delivered. And when you think of the enormous quantity of mail that flows through all the postal stations under his supervision, day after day. The millions of letters of all shapes, sizes and in all condition. The thousands of boxes, again of all shapes and sizes and condition. You'll wonder how Al Haig is able to sleep at night.

"Ladies and gentlemen, we're going to prove to you why the United States mail is the envy of the world, and we'll prove to you why the Cincinnati service is the envy of the nation. And I will show you how Al Haig has been a part of that service for the last quarter century.

"Now, it's not only the responsibility of making sure the mail gets out on time that sometimes, I'll show you, keeps Al Haig up at night, but Al Haig has another responsibility that is perhaps, we'll show you, even more significant to the efficient processing of the mail service here in Cincinnati than his general supervisory position. Because Al Haig knows, and we'll prove to you, that a supervisor's most important job is to select good employees. Because no matter how good the supervisor is, even if you had Superman, the man of steel, working, the supervisor can't do everything alone. So the most important responsibility is to get good employees. And Al Haig knows that what you need in this modern day and age is an aggressive self-starter, who doesn't have to be led around by the hand. And it's not only important to the postal service, to which Al Haig has devoted twenty-five years of his life, but it's also important to him, personally, because, and your common sense will tell you, but we'll prove it anyway, that there's nothing more debilitating to a supervisor than to have an employee who can't get the job done right. So it was in Al Haig's interest, not only for the postal service, to get the good employee, but, I'll prove to you, in his own personal interest to pick good employees, the responsibility for which he ultimately bears.

"Now, Al Haig, as you've heard, has had a chance to make two promotions to the position of tour superintendent. The tour superintendent is the person who's responsible for the working conditions and general processing of the mail during his or her tour. And, in 1990, selected a woman whom he felt, and we will prove to you, ladies and gentlemen, was better qualified than any other applicant for that position. The woman's name was Shirley Walker. Ms. Walker is black. A black woman. Now Al Haig [sic] was also an applicant, and when Al Haig [sic] discovered that he was passed over -- I'm sorry, when Norman Rock discovered that he was passed over in favor of a black woman, he became jealous, and we'll prove that to you, ladies and gentlemen, he became bitter, and we'll prove that to you, ladies and gentlemen, and he filed a complaint, a discrimination complaint.

"Now, Norman Rock couldn't claim racial discrimination back then because Ms. Walker was black. So he claimed sex-discrimination. Ladies and gentlemen, we will prove to you that that charge was absurd, and we will bring into this courtroom the official documents dismissing that charge.

"Then, in 1991, another position opened up for Tour Superintendent, and Al Haig, understanding the need for the postal service to become more efficient, understanding the need for the postal service to do things a little differently than had been done in the past, selected an aggressive self-starter, somebody who wasn't bogged down with the 'that's the way it's always been done' mentality that a lot of people have, and selected Rose Climber.

"Now let me tell you a little bit about Rose Climber. Rose Climber started out as a mail clerk, that's right. And for four years, she worked on the front lines. And during those four years she developed a keen insight as to what was needed to improve the efficiency of the service—something you can't tell by walking the parapets. During those four years, though, she developed an understanding of what was needed. And after those four years, she was promoted to supervisor. And then, Desert Storm comes about and Norman Rock goes to Saudi Arabia. And who chooses her to fill in for Norman Rock? William Donovan, a supervisor at the time, a black man, picked Rose Climber, a white woman, to fill in for Norman Rock because he was convinced in his own mind, and he will come into this courtroom and tell you so, that Rose Climber was an up-and-coming young postal employee from whom great things were expected.

"And ladies and gentlemen, it wasn't only William Donovan who saw the promise in Rose Climber, it was Norman Rock! Norman Rock, who sits here today and calls Al Haig a racist, we'll show you, ladies and gentlemen, seven months before they both applied for the position Tour Supervisor [*sic*] had this to say about Rose Climber, whom he rated as doing an excellent job, and to whom he gave the highest possible rating. And this is what he wrote in September of 1990. If it please the court, this has already been admitted pursuant to our pre-trial stipulation. September of 1990, Norman Rock speaking: 'Ms. Climber is doing an excellent job. Her communication skills are excellent and she is an aggressive self-starter. Her knowledge of departmental operations are improving at a good rate.' And, indeed, they were. Because she was on the job for a very short period of time in Norman Rock's position, a position he had held for years, and immediately put into operation an idea that saved and will save the postal service, we'll prove to you, ladies and gentlemen, hundreds of thousands of dollars. The idea to move back the starting time, to save on this incredible overtime. Move it back one-half hour.

"Now, ladies and gentlemen, we'll show you that what she did when she had this idea was to go to her immediate supervisor, William Donovan, and William Donovan will come into this courtroom and will tell you that he thought it was a fantastic idea. And that when he took it to Al Haig, Haig agreed and they implemented it and they saved the United States Postal Service lots of overtime expense. Now, it didn't sit right with some people.

Postal service employees, we will prove to you, sometimes don't like changes. And there was a rise in complaints. And even though the shift applied to everybody equally, we'll prove to you, ladies and gentlemen, there were discrimination complaints, based on this half-hour shift that applied to everybody equally. And we'll prove to you, ladies and gentlemen, that discrimination complaints are common in the post office, almost irrespective of what the change is.

"When Al Haig had to make a decision to pick a Tour Superintendent, and he wanted an aggressive self-starter who wasn't bogged down in the ways of the past, he appointed Rose Climber not, and this is important, ladies and gentlemen, we'll prove to you, not despite her relative newcomer status but precisely because of it. Because she proved she could bring a fresh look to the postal service, increase efficiency, and save money. And in light of all of this, and in light of Norman Rock's words seven months before they both applied for the position, calling her work excellent, commending her for being an 'aggressive self-starter,' his claim of race-discrimination, sex-discrimination, race/sex-discrimination, race/sex reprisal, rings hollow indeed, And, in fact, ladies and gentlemen, we will prove to you, that that's the reason that the final agency action immediately before we were brought into this courtroom totally exonerated Al Haig and upheld his decision. Ladies and gentlemen, I thank you for your attention, and I thank Your Honor for her patience."

THE ANNOTATION

I am reprinting in small type the transcription of my two opening statements in the *Rock* file so that you can have easy reference to the text in connection with my comments.

FOR THE PLAINTIFF:

"Ladies and gentlemen, as Her Honor has told you, the name of this case is Norman Rock versus the United States Postal Service. Now we all know what the Postal Service is. It's the post office. And in the next few minutes that I have, I'm going to tell you a little bit about who Norman Rock is, and why he would come into this courtroom, with the word "truth" emblazoned over the portal, to sue his employer, the United States Postal Service, the postal service of the United States of America, represented by these fine lawyers from the United States Department of Justice in Washington, D.C., and from the United States Attorney's office here in Cincinnati.

[I AM PLAYING THE DAVID-VERSUS-GOLIATH CARD.]

"Norman Rock has worked for the postal service since 1973. He started out, as most people start out in the postal service, as a mail clerk. About nine months later, he was promoted to be distribution clerk. Less than a year after that, he was foreman of mails. After four years as foreman of mails, he was promoted again to be foreman of platform operations. Two years later, 1981 we're at now, he was promoted to be supervisor of mails. And since 1985, for the last eight years, he has been general supervisor of mails.

[GET NORMAN ROCK ON THE SCREEN EARLY AND SHOW THAT HE IS SKILLED AT WHAT HE DOES. AS YOU WILL SEE, THIS SETS THE "PRIMACY" STAGE FOR THE ARGUMENT THAT ROCK MET THE JOB-CRITERION OF "PROGRESSIVE EXPERIENCE" IN POSTAL SERVICE SUPERVISORY POSITIONS.]

"Norman Rock, through his progressive experience at increasing higher levels, has, I will prove to you ladies and gentlemen, devoted his life to the United States post office. And he's not one of these nine-to-fivers, either. Because from 1975 until 1985, after putting in a full-day's work, and even more, I will prove to you, at the post office, in these various increasing levels of responsibility, that his supervisors entrusted him with over the years, Norman Rock went home for a quick bite, I will prove to you, and then went to school.

[NORMAN ROCK IS DEDICATED. NOTE THE USE OF THE PHRASE "PROGRESSIVE EXPERIENCE." THE JURY DOES NOT YET KNOW THAT THIS IS ONE OF THE FORMAL CRITERIA FOR THE JOB. I WANT THE JURY TO ASSOCIATE THE PHRASE "PROGRESSIVE EXPERIENCE" WITH NORMAN ROCK.]

"For nine years, Norman Rock went to night school to get a Bachelor of Science degree in Business Administration. He also, during that time, took a number of internal post-office courses to better his opportunities within the service and to make his performance and the fulfillment of his responsibilities, I will prove to you, even more knowledgeable, even more efficient.

[ROCK CARES.]

"Just as Norman Rock was reaching the level, which I will prove to you is reached by similarly situated persons—persons who have similarly come up through the ranks—and just as he was getting ready to enter into the upper levels of management in the post office, he ran into this man sitting right here, Al Haig, Field Director for Mail Processing. And it was Norman Rock's bad luck to run into a man who has, we will prove to you ladies and gentlemen of the jury, a perverse hatred and fear of black men.

[NORMAN ROCK IS THE VICTIM OF UNDESERVED MISFORTUNE.]

"Al Haig has proven over the last several years to be a stone wall in the road, we will prove to you, of Norman Rock's career. Ladies and gentlemen, we will prove to you throughout the next several days that it's the racist attitude, forgive me, it's the racist, sexist attitude, because we will be bringing into this courtroom an expert in these areas who will tell you that it is not uncommon for certain white men to have a special fear and hatred of black men. Al Haig's perverse hatred and fear of black men has stopped Norman Rock's career in its tracks, and that's why we're here today, I will prove to you.

> [NORMAN ROCK IS THE VICTIM OF UNDESERVED MISFORTUNE. HAIG IS A BAD MAN. THIS LATTER POINT IS ONE THAT HAS TO BE PROCLAIMED. THE JURY WILL NOT FIND FOR ROCK UNLESS IT IS CONVINCED THAT HAIG IS A RACIST. NO JURY WILL HAVE THE COURAGE TO MAKE THAT ASSESSMENT UNLESS THE LAWYER DOES IT FIRST.]

"Now, in 1990 Norman Rock ran into that wall for the first time. Because the next level of his progressive experience of promotions came up. And the position was Tour Superintendent. And the Tour Superintendent is responsible for all the activities on his or her tour at the particular postal station at which he or she is working. And Norman Rock, with this progressive, continuous higher levels of experience, applied for the position. The position of Tour Superintendent, like everything else in government, like all positions in government, has certain designated criteria that the appointing people have to follow. And the reason for this is clear, and we'll prove that to you, folks. That during the dark ages when cronyism was rampant in government, enlightened folks realized that you can't trust promotion in government to the unfettered whim or discretion of an appointing person. So they established specific and detailed criteria that the appointed person has to meet in order (A) to be considered for the job, and (B) to be given the job.

> [THIS IS THE "WHAT'S GOOD FOR SOCIETY" THEME. THE CIVIL SERVICE AND ITS PROTECTIONS WERE DESIGNED TO NOT ONLY ADVANCE FAIRNESS FOR THE AFFECTED EMPLOYEES, BUT ALSO TO INCREASE EFFICIENCY. NOTE THAT I'VE AGAIN ASSOCIATED NORMAN ROCK WITH THE PHRASE "PROGRESSIVE, CONTINUOUS HIGHER LEVELS OF EXPERIENCE." THE JURY STILL DOES NOT KNOW THAT THIS IS A FORMAL CRITERION FOR THE JOB.]

"And the most important criteria for the position of Tour Superintendent is set out in this official document. And this is what it requires: 'Associate level understanding of management principles.' That's number one: 'Associate level understanding of management principles.' Number two: 'Extensive, progressive experience in supervisory positions in the area of mail processing.' That's number two. Number three is 'Well-developed human relations and communications skills.' And number four is: 'Physically able to work in a standing position for an extended period.'

> [THESE ARE THE CRITERIA AND NORMAN ROCK FITS THEM TO A "T." THE JURY ALREADY KNOWS FROM MY EARLIER STATEMENTS THAT NORMAN ROCK HAS HAD "EXTENSIVE, PROGRESSIVE EXPERIENCE IN SUPERVISORY POSITIONS IN THE AREA OF MAIL PROCESSING."]

"In 1990, Norman Rock had this incredible progressive experience in mail processing. He applied. Al Haig gave the job to a black woman, with, we will prove, ladies and gentlemen, far inferior qualifications. Norman Rock was disappointed at the time, and, we will prove to you, had this sixth sense, I guess, that it wasn't a level playing field. That there was something funny going on. And we will prove to you that as a result of those feelings, feelings, which we will prove to you, that only people who have been the victims of discrimination can really feel, he filed a discrimination complaint. Well, this was the first time he hit the brick wall, and the complaint was dismissed, and Norman Rock chalked it up to experience.

[THE JURY CAN ACCEPT MY REPRESENTATION THAT ROCK "HAD THIS INCREDIBLE PROGRESSIVE EXPERIENCE IN MAIL PROCESSING" BECAUSE THEY HAVE HEARD IT SO OFTEN AND THE POINT WAS VALIDATED RIGHT UP FRONT WHEN I WENT THROUGH THE LIST OF HIS POSITIONS WITHIN THE POSTAL SERVICE. I AM ALSO REPEATING THE POINT THAT NORMAN ROCK IS THE VICTIM OF UNDESERVED MISFORTUNE.]

"Two years later, however, another Tour Superintendency opened up. And Norman Rock applied again. And again, as luck would have it, this man, Al Haig, was the man with the responsibility of making the appointment. Ladies and gentlemen, we'll prove to you that Norman Rock considered very carefully as to whether he should apply again, the deck being stacked, in his view.

[A LOW-KEY USE OF THE "JEOPARDY" THEME; NORMAN ROCK'S HAS TO DECIDE WHETHER TO PUT HIS SELF-ESTEEM, PRIDE, AND FAITH AT RISK.]

"He applied. In a sense, and he'll tell you this, he swallowed his pride and applied again despite what happened with Al Haig back in 1990, and despite all these vibes he was getting. And again, Al Haig picked someone with far, far, we will prove, inferior qualifications: Rose Climber.

[AGAIN, AND DESPITE HIS FAITH, NORMAN ROCK IS THE VICTIM OF UNDESERVED MISFORTUNE.]

"Let me tell you a little bit about Rose Climber. You know, in addition to his progressive experience and work for the postal service since 1973. In addition to his nine years of going to night school to get a Bachelor of Science degree in Business Administration. In addition to his taking internal post-office courses, Al [sic] Rock is also a sergeant in the Army Reserves, and it was his tough luck, back in 1990 and 1991, when operation Desert Storm took place, that he had to go to Saudi Arabia. And they filled his position temporarily with Rose Climber.

[BEFORE I WILL TALK ABOUT ROSE CLIMBER, HOWEVER, I REPEAT ROCK'S ATTRIBUTES SO THE COMPARISON WILL BE STARK. UNLIKE NORMAN ROCK, ROSE CLIMBER IS THE BENEFICIARY OF UNDESERVED FORTUNE (LUCK).]

"Now, we'll show you, ladies and gentlemen, that the person who filled that position temporarily with Rose Climber is a man no longer with the postal service by the name of William Donovan, a black man. Rose Climber came in at that point in her career, and we're just talking a couple of years ago now, at that point in her career she had a total of seven years with the United States Postal Service. For four years, she stood at a mail-sorting machine her seven to eight hours a day. Then she was given a supervisory position. And then when Norman Rock went to Saudi Arabia to slosh around in the sand, protecting the interests of his government, Rose Climber was designated to fill in temporarily.

[AGAIN, UNLIKE NORMAN ROCK, ROSE CLIMBER IS THE BENEFICIARY OF UNDESERVED FORTUNE (LUCK), ALL THE WHILE NORMAN ROCK, WHO IS MORE QUALIFIED, IS IN THE DESERT.]

"And she came up with what everybody thought was a wonderful idea. It's this idea upon which they're hanging their hats, folks. She decided that if she moved the tour of duty back one-half hour, she'd save a lot of money in overtime expense. Except, we will prove, ladies and gentlemen, that although money was saved in overtime expense, the manner in which that was implemented by Rose Climber cost the United States government far more in terms of lost productivity, in terms of litigation expenses, than the savings during that period of time. Because you know what happened? Like a lot of people who don't have experience, we will show, ladies and gentlemen, she figured she is now a supervisor, she now can do what she wants, and she can deliver edicts from on high. Rather than working with the employees to explain the shift, to work with the union and explain the shift, she sprung it on them folks, and we'll prove that. And, as a result, there was all hell to pay for a while. People's lives were disrupted, we'll show. They complained, they filed grievances. The union filed grievances. Lawyers were tied up in litigation. The morale dropped.

[INEXPERIENCE HAS ITS COSTS. AND HAIG PICKED CLIMBER BECAUSE OF THIS?]

"Rose Climber, the man [sic] Al Haig selected for a position that requires 'associate level understanding of management principles' and an 'extensive progression experience in supervisory positions,' had experience limited to four years working as a mail clerk by a sorting machine, two years as Supervisor of Mails, a position that Norman Rock held from 1981 to 1985. In addition, she took a one-month course inside the post office on managerial training, and she's currently going to night school in communications at the Lucius Quintus Community College.

[HER QUALIFICATIONS ARE BUT AN IRONIC SHADOW OF NORMAN ROCK'S]

"Ladies and gentlemen, by any fair analysis, by any unbiased, unprejudiced analysis, by any level-playing-field analysis, we will prove to you there is no dispute, no doubt, that the only one of those two candidates who had the required extensive, progressive experience in supervisory positions in the area of mail processing was Norman Rock. But there was that brick wall. The brick wall erected by race-based sexism. Hard thing to prove, folks, but we're going to prove it. And we're going to prove it right out of the mouth of Al Haig. Because no matter how good these racists are, they slip. They slip. And Al Haig, under oath, testified that during his entire nine years as a supervisor he could not remember ever, ever, ever having promoted an Afro-American man. And listen to his excuse. Because it is an excuse, we will prove to you, ladies and gentlemen, that has echoed through the centuries by people who try to hide their motives and make decisions that are based on racial hatred, ethnic hatred, or sexism.

> [HAIG IS A RACIST, AND, AGAIN NORMAN ROCK IS THE VICTIM OF UNDESERVED MISFORTUNE. THIS IS THE FIRST STEP OF THE TWO-STEP—THE PROMISE TO PROVE.]

"He was asked . . ."

Member of Group: "Objection, Your Honor."

The Court: "Overruled"

> [THE JUDGE, PLAYED BY PROMINENT LAWYER AND COURT-TV HOST RIKKI KLIEMAN, CORRECTLY OVERRULES THE OBJECTION. HAIG'S DEPOSITION TESTIMONY IS OBVIOUSLY ADMISSIBLE AND CAN BE USED DURING THE OPENING STATEMENT.]

"We will prove to you, ladies and gentlemen, that he was asked: 'Have you ever promoted an African-American male?' And what was his answer? Ladies and gentlemen, we'll prove to you, and he said this under oath: 'I don't believe so. But I would have if he was qualified.' Ladies and gentlemen, we will prove to you, and I submit that your own common knowledge and experience will tell you independent of our proof, that that is the refuge of a racist.

> [NOTICE THE USE OF THE TWO-STEP: I PROMISE TO PROVE IN THE PARAGRAPH BEFORE THE OBJECTION AND THEN QUOTE HAIG IN THIS PARAGRAPH TO VALIDATE MY PROMISE. AS DISCUSSED, THIS IS MORE EFFECTIVE THAN IF THE FIRST STEP, THE PROMISE, WERE OMITTED.]

"Norman Rock has been deprived of an opportunity to advance up the career ladder to which he has devoted his entire life, because of Al Haig. But there's more. Because there's complicity, complicity with the United States Postal Service, who has let this go on. Because all these facts, and Her Honor will tell you, that this isn't the first time that this matter was heard. An independent agency of the United States government, called the Equal Employment Opportunity Commission, heard the facts that you're going to hearing during the course of this trial, totally independent of the postal service, totally independent agency, they heard the facts that you're going to hear. And what was their conclusion? The conclusion was that Al Haig discriminated against Norman Rock. Unfortunately, as we will show, ladies and gentlemen, that wasn't the end of it. Otherwise we wouldn't be here. Because under the rules, it all comes back to, guess where, the United States Postal Service. And the United States Postal Service rejected the determination of the independent agency, Equal Employment Opportunity Commission, that Al Haig discriminated against Norman Rock and, as a result, Norman Rock is entitled to his promotion.

> [THE EXPLANATION (WHY THE FINAL AGENCY ACTION VINDICATED HAIG) BEFORE THE ACCUSATION (HAIG MUST HAVE BEEN RIGHT, THE FINAL AGENCY ACTION VINDICATED HIM) WITHOUT EVEN ACKNOWLEDGING THAT THERE CAN BE THE ACCUSATION. STATED ANOTHER WAY, I AM USING THE FINAL-AGENCY-ACTION VINDICATION AS A POSITIVE ASPECT OF MY PROOF—TO SHOW "COMPLICITY" (BY LOGICAL INFERENCE IF I HAVE NO DIRECT PROOF OF COLLUSION). IT IS A FAIR AND EFFECTIVE ARGUMENT.]

"Ladies and gentlemen, it will be your opportunity to remove that brick wall. It'll be your opportunity to set things right, and re-write what should have been written correctly originally. Thank you Your Honor."

> [THE FINAL "DO JUSTICE" PLEA. TECHNICALLY, THIS IS "ARGUMENTATIVE," BUT ALL JUDGES PERMIT THIS KIND OF FINAL WORD, AS LONG AS IT IS NOT TOO LONG.]

FOR THE DEFENDANT:

"If it please the court, counsel. Norman Rock didn't get a job that he wanted. And he's crying racism and he's crying sexism, he's crying reprisal—at least that's in his complaint, he alleges Al Haig is trying to get even with him for something. Norman Rock has come into this courtroom and has accused Al Haig of being a racist. He has accused Al Haig of being a sexist. And he's accused Al Haig of promoting Rose Climber to get even with him. As Her Honor has told you, we don't have to prove a thing in this courtroom, but we will prove to you that each and every one of those charges against this good man is false.

> [I CANNOT IGNORE THE HORRIBLE CHARGES. I MUST GRASP THE NETTLE AND PUT THE FULL WEIGHT OF MY PERSONAL ADVOCACY BEHIND MY CLIENT'S DECISION-MAKER, AL HAIG. THE SUBTHEME HERE IS ALSO THAT HAIG IS AN UNDESERVED VICTIM OF THE CHARGE OF RACISM AND SEXISM.]

"Al Haig is not a racist, we will prove to you. Al Haig is not a sexist, we will prove to you. He's not a racist-sexist, whatever that is, and we will prove that to you too. And the only reason he promoted Rose Climber was because, in his honest view, Rose Climber was the best qualified applicant for that position, period. And we will prove that to you as well.

[I MUST PUT MY PERSONAL ADVOCACY ON THE LINE.]

"Now let me tell you a little bit about Al Haig. We've heard a lot of things, quite frankly, that are somewhat disturbing. Al Haig has worked with the mails for more than twenty-five years, since 1967. For the last nine years, he's been Field Director of Mail Processing here in Cincinnati. And that means it's his responsibility to make sure the mail gets delivered. And when you think of the enormous quantity of mail that flows through all the postal stations under his supervision, day after day. The millions of letters of all shapes, sizes and in all condition. The thousands of boxes, again of all shapes and sizes and condition. You'll wonder how Al Haig is able to sleep at night.

[FIRST, TO PRESERVE MY OWN CREDIBILITY, I HAVE TO ACKNOWLEDGE THAT THE CHARGES, IF THEY WERE TRUE, ARE HORRIBLE. SECOND, THIS SHOWS THAT AL HAIG IS SKILLED AT WHAT HE DOES AND IS DEDICATED.]

"Ladies and gentlemen, we're going to prove to you why the United States mail is the envy of the world, and we'll prove to you why the Cincinnati service is the envy of the nation. And I will show you how Al Haig has been a part of that service for the last quarter century.

[AL HAIG IS SKILLED AT WHAT HE DOES.]

"Now, it's not only the responsibility of making sure the mail gets out on time that sometimes, I'll show you, keeps Al Haig up at night, but Al Haig has another responsibility that is perhaps, we'll show you, even more significant to the efficient processing of the mail service here in Cincinnati than his general supervisory position. Because Al Haig knows, and we'll prove to you, that a supervisor's most important job is to select good employees. Because no matter how good the supervisor is, even if you had Superman, the man of steel, working, the supervisor can't do everything alone. So the most important responsibility is to get good employees. And Al Haig knows that what you need in this modern day and age is an aggressive self-starter, who doesn't have to be led around by the hand. And it's not only important to the postal service, to which Al Haig has devoted twenty-five years of his life, but it's also important to him, personally, because, and your common sense will tell you, but we'll prove it anyway, that there's nothing more debilitating to a supervisor than to have an employee who can't get the job done right. So it was in Al Haig's interest, not only for the postal service, to get the good employee, but, I'll prove to you, in his own personal interest to pick good employees, the responsibility for which he ultimately bears.

[AL HAIG HAS A SELFISH REASON TO PICK THE BEST EMPLOYEE: IT MAKES HIS JOB EASIER. NOTE HOW I'VE BEGUN TO USE THE PHRASE "AGGRESSIVE SELF-STARTER," MAKING IT A *DE FACTO* QUALIFICATION FOR THE JOB, SO THAT WHEN THE JURY LEARNS THAT THE PHRASE COMES FROM NORMAN ROCK'S EVALUATION OF ROSE CLIMBER IT WILL HAVE EVEN

> MORE IMPACT. IT'S HIS ADMISSION AND RECOGNITION THAT SHE IS QUALIFIED FOR THE JOB.]

"Now, Al Haig, as you've heard, has had a chance to make two promotions to the position of tour superintendent. The tour superintendent is the person who's responsible for the working conditions and general processing of the mail during his or her tour. And, in 1990, selected a woman whom he felt, and we will prove to you, ladies and gentlemen, was better qualified than any other applicant for that position. The woman's name was Shirley Walker. Ms. Walker is black. A black woman. Now Al Haig [sic] was also an applicant, and when Al Haig [sic] discovered that he was passed over – I'm sorry, when Norman Rock discovered that he was passed over in favor of a black woman, he became jealous, and we'll prove that to you, ladies and gentlemen, he became bitter, and we'll prove that to you, ladies and gentlemen, and he filed a complaint, a discrimination complaint.

> [CONTRARY TO BEING A VICTIM OF UNDESERVED MISFORTUNE, NORMAN ROCK IS A WHINER, SOMEONE WHO CAN'T ACCEPT THE UPS AND DOWNS OF LIFE.]

"Now, Norman Rock couldn't claim racial discrimination back then because Ms. Walker was black. So he claimed sex-discrimination. Ladies and gentlemen, we will prove to you that that charge was absurd, and we will bring into this courtroom the official documents dismissing that charge.

> [AGAIN, CONTRARY TO BEING A VICTIM OF UNDESERVED MISFORTUNE, NORMAN ROCK IS A WHINER, SOMEONE WHO CAN'T ACCEPT THE UPS AND DOWNS OF LIFE. EVEN THE EEOC FELT HIS COMPLAINT LACKED MERIT.]

"Then, in 1991, another position opened up for Tour Superintendent, and Al Haig, understanding the need for the postal service to become more efficient, understanding the need for the postal service to do things a little differently than had been done in the past, selected an aggressive self-starter, somebody who wasn't bogged down with the 'that's the way it's always been done' mentality that a lot of people have, and selected Rose Climber.

> [MAKING THE "BAD STUFF" (CLIMBER'S INEXPERIENCE) WORK FOR ME AS A POSITIVE PART OF MY CASE. I'M NOT EXPLAINING, OR "REMOVING THE STING," I'M MAKING HER INEXPERIENCE A VALUABLE JOB-QUALIFICATION. AGAIN, I HAVE THROWN IN THE PHRASE "AGGRESSIVE SELF-STARTER."]

"Now let me tell you a little bit about Rose Climber. Rose Climber started out as a mail clerk, that's right. And for four years, she worked on the front lines. And during those four years she developed a keen insight as to what was needed to improve the efficiency of the service—something you can't tell by walking the parapets. During those four years, though, she developed an understanding of what was needed. And after those four years, she was promoted to supervisor. And then, Desert Storm comes about and Norman Rock goes to Saudi Arabia. And who chooses her to fill in for Norman Rock? William Donovan, a supervisor at the time, a black man, picked Rose Climber, a white woman, to fill in for Norman Rock because he was convinced in his own mind, and he will into this courtroom and tell you so, that Rose Climber was an up-and-coming young postal employee from whom great things were expected.

[ROSE CLIMBER HAS WORKED HARD TO GET TO WHERE SHE IS. SHE KNOWS WHAT IT'S LIKE TO BE ON THE FRONT LINES; SHE'S IN TOUCH WITH THE POSTAL EMPLOYEES WHO MAKE THE SERVICE WORK, UNLIKE ROCK WHO HAS BEEN IN SUPERVISORY POSITIONS FOR TOO LONG. SHE WAS NO MERE LINE-WORKER, HOWEVER. EVERYONE RECOGNIZED HER PROMISE.]

"And ladies and gentlemen, it wasn't only William Donovan who saw the promise in Rose Climber, it was Norman Rock! Norman Rock, who sits here today and calls Al Haig a racist, we'll show you, ladies and gentlemen, seven months before they both applied for the position Tour Supervisor [sic] had this to say about Rose Climber, whom he rated as doing an excellent job, and to whom he gave the highest possible rating. And this is what he wrote in September of 1990. If it please the court, this has already been admitted pursuant to our pre-trial stipulation. September of 1990, Norman Rock speaking: 'Ms. Climber is doing an excellent job. Her communication skills are excellent and she is an aggressive self-starter. Her knowledge of departmental operations are improving at a good rate.' And, indeed, they were. Because she was on the job for a very short period of time in Norman Rock's position, a position he had held for years, and immediately put into operation an idea that saved and will save the postal service, we'll prove to you, ladies and gentlemen, hundreds of thousands of dollars. The idea to move back the starting time, to save on this incredible overtime. Move it back one-half hour.

[EVEN NORMAN ROCK SAW THE PROMISE IN ROSE CLIMBER. ALSO, NOTE HOW, UNTIL WE SEE THAT THE PHRASE COMES FROM NORMAN ROCK, I MADE "AGGRESSIVE SELF-STARTER" A *DE FACTO* QUALIFICATION FOR THE POSITION. ALSO, NOTICE HOW I SEGUE FROM NORMAN ROCK'S PRAISE FOR ROSE CLIMBER TO A VALIDATION OF THAT PRAISE BY WHAT SHE DID WHEN GIVEN THE OPPORTUNITY. THIS IS NOT A CHRONOLOGY. IT IS NOT A "STORY." IT IS AN ARGUMENT.]

"Now, ladies and gentlemen, we'll show you that what she did when she had this idea was to go to her immediate supervisor, William Donovan, and William Donovan will come into this courtroom and will tell you that he thought it was a fantastic idea. And that when he took it to Al Haig, Haig agreed and they implemented it and they saved the United States Postal Service lots of overtime expense. Now, it didn't sit right with some people. Postal service employees, we will prove to you, sometimes don't like changes. And there was a rise in complaints. And even though the shift applied to everybody equally, we'll prove to you, ladies and gentlemen, there were discrimination complaints, based on this half-hour shift that applied to everybody equally. And we'll prove to you, ladies and gentlemen, that discrimination complaints are common in the post office, almost irrespective of what the change is.

> [ROSE CLIMBER DID NOT IMPOSE THE RULE CHANGE, SHE WENT THROUGH CHANNELS. THIS IS AN ANSWER OF THE CHARGE MADE IN THE POSTAL SERVICE'S OPENING STATEMENT. BUT I ANSWER IT IN MY OWN WAY, AND, BY NOT REFERRING TO THE CHARGE, MAKE IT A POSITIVE ASPECT OF MY PROOF. MOREOVER, THE RISE IN COMPLAINTS ARE BECAUSE POSTAL WORKERS ARE LIKE THAT (THE RISE IN DISCRIMINATION COMPLAINTS, DESPITE THE FACT THAT THE SHIFT CHANGE APPLIED TO ALL EMPLOYEES EQUALLY, UNDERSCORES THIS).]

"When Al Haig had to make a decision to pick a Tour Superintendent, and he wanted an aggressive self-starter who wasn't bogged down in the ways of the past, he appointed Rose Climber not, and this is important, ladies and gentlemen, we'll prove to you, not despite her relative newcomer status but precisely because of it. Because she proved she could bring a fresh look to the postal service, increase efficiency, and save money. And in light of all of this, and in light of Norman Rock's words seven months before they both applied for the position, calling her work excellent, commending her for being an 'aggressive self-starter,' his claim of race-discrimination, sex-discrimination, race/sex-discrimination, race/sex reprisal, rings hollow indeed, And, in fact, ladies and gentlemen, we will prove to you, that that's the reason that the final agency action immediately before we were brought into this courtroom totally exonerated Al Haig and upheld his decision. Ladies and gentlemen, I thank you for your attention, and I thank Your Honor for her patience."

> [THE "NOT DESPITE HER RELATIVE NEWCOMER STATUS BUT PRECISELY BECAUSE OF IT" TAKES WHAT IS, ARGUABLY, ONE OF THE WEAKEST ASPECTS OF MY CASE, AND MAKES IT THE KEY STRENGTH. THIS IS MAKING THE "BAD STUFF" TO WORK FOR YOU.]

XVII.
USE THE DIRECT-EXAMINATION TO ARGUE YOUR CASE

Most lawyers look upon the direct-examination as a chance to let their witnesses tell their stories. Thus, they sit back, or lean back, or slouch over the podium, content to pepper the witnesses' narrative with a series of "what happened next" questions. Contrary to the conventional wisdom, this is all wrong.

Letting the witnesses tell the story, letting them pull the oars of your case, puts the burden and the focus on the wrong person in the courtroom. First, it makes the witness, who is not allowed any notes, *remember and relate* the incident in its most persuasive way. No wonder most witnesses are nervous wrecks.

Second, as we have discussed already at length, jurors believe that you (and your opponent) know the truth of what really happened. This is why your direct-examination must be *your argument to the jury*, albeit confirmed by the witnesses' responses. Stated another way, the direct-examination of any witness is that part of your summation that can be validated by that witness. It is your summation through the window of what the witness can give you.

If you follow the techniques discussed in these chapters on direct-examination, your direct-examination of every witness will be clear, memorable, persuasive, and invulnerable to cross-examination. Most important, you will have advanced your theme, and by having your witnesses validate and confirm your argument, you will have enhanced your own personal credibility and standing with the jury. This synergism will increase your odds of winning.

XVIII.
NEVER ASK "WHAT HAPPENED NEXT?"

The "what happened next" question makes religious any lawyer who asks it, because he or she is praying that the witness remembers the script. Of course, very few witnesses *do* remember the script. And, if the witness *does* remember what to say, more often than not it will sound as canned as it is. In the next several pages, we will discuss and demonstrate what's wrong with the "what happened next" question. We will also explain and demonstrate how to make your argument to the jury through the witness clear, memorable, and persuasive.

- "What happened next?" often elicits a muddled, confused, wandering, narrative from the witness.

This prevents the jury from grasping the point that you are trying to make—the point is buried under tons of straw. Consider this example from the O.J. Simpson criminal trial.

Marcia Clark is examining the limousine driver, Allen Park, the fellow who testified that O.J. Simpson initially did not answer the door when Park arrived to take him to the airport that fateful night. We pick up the examination where Clark has established that Park arrived at Simpson's house early.

> Q What happened next?
>
> A I had a little bit of time, so I just stepped out of the car and had a cigarette, and listened to the radio for a little bit.
>
> Q When you stepped out of the car, where did you go?
>
> A I just went to the back of it, the limousine, and sat on the curb.
>
> Q And after you finished the cigarette, what did you do?
>
> A Got back in the car and proceeded to wait for maybe five minutes or so and about 10:40 was when I pulled up to the front gate after I pulled around first. I came around Ashford onto Rockingham, looked in the driveway, and it just didn't look accessible as the other driveway. So I backed up and came back over to Ashford.
>
> Q All right. So you got back into your car at what time, after having a cigarette?
>
> A Just before 10:40.
>
> Q And what did you do then?
>
> A Just what I told you.

Do we really care about the cigarette, and the radio? The point is that Simpson did not answer the door the first time the limousine driver tried it. I suggest that the following line would have been better.

> Q What time did you get to Mr. Simpson's house that night?
>
> A Sometime before 10:40.
>
> Q Were you early or late?
>
> A I was early.

Q Did you try Mr. Simpson's door at that time, or did you wait?

A I waited.

Q **Why did you wait?** [You don't really care what this answer is, but you don't want the jury speculating as to the answer (some might think that Simpson waved to Park).]

A I was told to be there at a certain time, and I didn't want to disturb him if he was not ready.

Q After you waited, did you then try Mr. Simpson's door?

A Yes.

Q When?

A At 10:45.

Q Was that when you were told to be there?

A Yes.

Q Did Mr. Simpson answer the door at 10:45?

A No.

When asking the "what happened next" question, a lawyer will often get an answer he or she did not expect—one that either *undercuts* the argument or derails it. Consider the following example, also from the Simpson criminal trial.

Denise Brown, Nicole Brown's sister, testified about the time when they went to Buffalo and watched a football game with Simpson. Prosecutor Christopher Darden asked these questions on direct-examination:

Q Both he and your two sisters watched the game that day, is that correct?

A Yes, we did.

Q And after the game, did you go to the defendant's house?

A   Yes, we did.

Q   All three of you? You and both your two sisters?

A   Yes.

Q   Did anything unusual happen at the football game?

A   Actually, no. A friend of O.J.'s was there. He came over and said hello to us, and Nicole said hello, kissed him on both cheeks, I said hello, she introduced me to him, and that was it.

During my nine years as a trial judge I have seen this scenario play out time after time when the lawyer asks the equivalent of "what happened next": the deadly "did anything unusual happen?"

The reason most lawyers ask the "what happened next" question, and its variant, the "did anything unusual happen" question, is that they don't want anyone to think that they are leading the witness. Some lawyers even add the phrase "if anything," as in "what happened next, if anything?" I guess law school's teach that asking a leading question on direct-examination is only slightly less sinful than pederasty.

No less an authority than John Henry Wigmore tells us that a "leading question" is one that "suggests the *specific* answer desired," and that a question may "legitimately suggest to the witness the *topic* of the answer," without being leading.[14] (Emphasis added.) Of course! Thus, if Darden wanted to elicit that Simpson hit Nicole Brown that day in Buffalo, he could have done it this way, without all the beating around the bush:

Q   Were you with Nicole and O.J. that day?

A   Yes.

Q   Did you see him hit her that day?

Leading? Not in my view, although I concede that some judges might sustain an objection based on "leading." The skillful lawyer handles it this way, without backing down:

---

[14]   3 WIGMORE, EVIDENCE § 769 at 155 (Chadbourn rev. 1970).

Q   Were you with Nicole and O.J. that day?

A   Yes.

Q   Did you see him hit her that day?

Counsel: Objection. Leading.

The Court: Sustained.

Q   Ms. Brown, were you with O.J. and Nicole that day?

A   Yes.

Q   Did you see them interact?

A   Yes.

Q   Tell me whether or not you saw O.J. hit her that day.

The same type of judge who thinks that "Did you see O.J. hit Nicole that day?" is a leading question, will also think that adding "tell me whether or not" cures the problem. If you still get a sustained objection, you can move on to:

Q   Did you see them interact?

A   Yes.

Q   Did he or did he not hit Nicole that day?

The simple fact is that not only Wigmore but the rules also recognize that a question may legitimately suggest to the witness the topic of the answer. Trials would take forever if the rule were otherwise. Can you imagine the chaos that would result if a lawyer was limited to asking: "I can't give you any clues, but tell me something interesting that you think bears on this case." That is the logical consequence of a judge's sustaining an objection to "Did he hit her that day?"

No lawyer has to rely on a "did anything unusual happen" to elicit that someone was hit, was shot, or was tossed out of a thirteenth-story window. In fact, the rules also let you *lead* when you have to. Consider this example.

Q   What color was the car?

The witness freezes and looks at you with owl-like eyes. What do you do? You do what the rule permits.

Q   Was it red?

Counsel: Objection, leading.

The Court: Sustained.

Q   What color was the car?

A   It was red.

Rule 611(c) of the Federal Rules of Evidence, and its state counterparts, expressly permit this. The rule provides:

> "Leading questions should not be used on the direct examination of a witness *except as may be necessary to develop the witness' testimony.*"

(Emphasis added.)

Keep Questions and Answers Short.

In *Dialogue for Writers*, best-selling author, editor, and publisher Sol Stein advises novelists to give the reader but "one thought at a time." He warns: "Anything over three sentences per speech runs into danger." This maxim applies to direct- and cross-examination as well.

As we've seen earlier, any person's attention span for information received aurally is quite limited, fifteen to thirty seconds at the most. Letting a witness ramble on in response to a "what happened next" question guarantees that most of the jury will miss *the point* that you are trying to make. This is true even where the witness is the "good" witness that every trial lawyer prays for, or is an "expert." Let's look at the following excerpt from John Grisham's *The Runaway Jury*.

We pick up the story where the plaintiff's lawyer is having the witness, a former high-level tobacco-company employee, describe a long-missing document that purportedly showed that the tobacco companies in the book knew that nicotine was addictive.[15]

"Q And the next paragraph?

"A The writer suggested [to the president] that the company take a serious look at increasing the nicotine levels in its cigarettes. More nicotine meant more smokers, which meant more sales, and more profits."

Powerful stuff to be sure, and Grisham meant it to be that way. But look how much more powerful it would be if the lawyer did not ask a "what happened next?"-type question, but broke down the components himself rather than let the witness given them to the jury in one large package. Remember, not all jurors are paying attention all of the time.

Q Did you read the next paragraph as well?

A Yes.

Q What was the subject of that paragraph?

A Nicotine.

Q Did the writer of that memorandum suggest that the company do something about the nicotine levels in the cigarettes it was making?

A Yes.

Q Did the writer suggest that the nicotine levels in the cigarettes be increased or decreased?

A Increased.

Q Did the writer tell the company's president how increased nicotine levels would affect the number of people who smoked?

A Yes.

---

[15] Grisham acknowledges that the "best evidence rule" would most likely have prevented this testimony, but has the presiding judge receive it nevertheless.

Q   Would increasing the nicotine levels in cigarettes mean more or fewer smokers?

A   More smokers.

Q   More smokers than if the nicotine levels were not increased?

A   Yes.

Q   Would this mean more or fewer sales?

A   More sales.

Q   Would this mean more or less profit for the company?

A   More.

Q   Would the profits be substantial?

A   Yes.

Doing it this way accomplishes three main things:

> First, the jury knows the critical answers before the witness responds. This cements in their minds these building blocks of the lawyer's argument.

> Second, the logical connection between increased nicotine levels and higher company profits is made in small, incremental steps. The jurors are not forced to digest the entire package in one question and answer.

> Third, doing it this way, rather than as Grisham has it, permits the lawyer to repeat the good stuff. No juror will be inattentive through the whole series, and thus no juror will miss this phase of the lawyer's argument. If the three points (increased nicotine levels leads to more smokers, which leads to more sales, which leads to higher profits) are presented by the witness in one fleeting answer some of the jurors may not be paying attention for the twelve or so seconds it takes the witness to give that answer in response to Grisham's "And the next paragraph?"

Finally, notice how each of the steps logically builds on what has come before—how each successive step rings true.

There are other problems with the "what happened next" question.

- "What happened next?" puts the burden on the witness to tell the story in its most clear and persuasive way—all without notes.

I'm often amused when lawyers, who insist on reading their opening statements and closing arguments, and in writing out their examinations question-by-question, trust their witnesses to get the "story" just right, all without a note. It just can't be done, as the Darden direct-examination of Denise Brown quoted earlier illustrates. You can put your witnesses at ease if you reassure them that you will do the rowing—all they have to do is sit back and answer your questions truthfully in short, responsive replies. If you do not ask "what happened next?" questions, they will not have to fret about how to best present their aspect of your case.

- The "what happened next" question prevents orderly development of your argument, in the sequence that *you* want.

This, too, is illustrated by Darden's direct-examination of Denise Brown.

- The "what happened next" question prevents legitimate repetition.

Once the witness has covered a point in his or her narrative, saying "let's go back for a minute" in order to cover some skimmed-over point in greater detail will draw an "asked and answered" objection from an opponent, or, more deadly, a "move on" from an impatient judge. As we have seen, it might also bring a "Just what I told you," as it did in response to Marcia Clark's "And what did you do then?" question to limousine driver Allen Park. Let me give an example of how to can repeat testimony you that want to imprint on the jury as often as you wish.

Assume for a moment that you are prosecuting John Smith for bank robbery. A teller is on the witness stand, and you are trying to establish what those first few moments were like. This is the way it is typically done:

Q Where do you work?

A   In the Statesville Bank.

Q   Calling you attention to July 15th of last year, did anything unusual happen to you that day?

A   Yes.

Q   What?

A   We were robbed.

Q   Do you see anyone in the courtroom today whom you saw in the bank on July 15th?

A   Yes.

Q   Where is he sitting, and what is he wearing?

A   He's sitting over there in the tan suit.

Q   Let the record reflect that the witness has identified the defendant.

The Court: The record will so reflect.

Q   What if anything did you see the defendant do that day?

A   He walked in the bank and held us up.

Q   When you say he held you up, what did he do?

A   He pointed a gun at me and Louise, she's the other teller, and demanded money.

Q   What happened next?

A   We gave him the money and he ran out?

Q   What happened next?

A   We rang the alarm.

The problem with this all-too-typical examination is that it relies on the witness to "tell the story," rather than letting the lawyer make his or her argument to the jury *through the witness*. Consider the following better way:

Q Let's talk about July 15th of last year, the day your bank was robbed. Did you see the defendant that day?

A Yes.

Q Do you see him today?

A Yes.

Q Can you point him out, please.

A He's sitting over there in the tan suit.

Prosecutor: I ask that Mr. Smith's lawyer agree that she has pointed to Mr. Smith.

Defense Lawyer: She has.

Q Where were you when you first saw him on July 15th?

A I was working in the bank.

Q The Statesville Bank?

A Yes.

Q What do you do in the Statesville Bank?

A I'm a teller.

Q Where was the defendant when you first saw him?

A Just inside the front door.

Q In the bank?

A Yes.

Q   What was he wearing?

A   Slacks, a sweater, and a hat.

Q   Could you see his face?

A   Yes.

Q   Did he have anything in his hand?

A   Yes.

Q   What was it?

A   A gun.

Q   Was it a big gun or a small gun?

A   A big gun.

Q   Was the gun dark or light?

A   It was light, shiny.

Q   Was he holding the gun in his left hand or his right hand?

A   In his left hand.

Q   Was it pointing at you or away from you.

A   It was pointing directly at me.

Q   Could you tell whether it was a revolver, with a round cylinder in the middle, or an automatic, a flatter gun.

A   Oh it was a revolver all right, just like the ones in the westerns.

Q   Could you see any bullets in the cylinder?

A   Yes, it looked full.

Q   You said he was pointing the gun directly at you, could you see down the barrel?

A   Yes.

Q   How did that make you feel?

A   I was scared.

Using short questions and answers this way makes the robbery more real for the jury than the generally unfocused answers usually given in response to the "what happened next?"-type question. Notice how both the questions and answers have substantive information—no juror is going to miss what's going on.

An Examination Must be Linear.

An examination, whether a direct-examination or a cross-examination, must be a linear chain of points that you want to make to the jury through the witness. The first point is preceded by an **Introduction Question** and are connected by **Transition Questions**, as in the following diagram:

Examination Train

Figure 1   **The Examination Train**

The first point the lawyer makes is that the defendant came into the bank with a revolver and pointed it at the teller. It is preceded by an **Introduction Question**: "Let's talk about what happened to you on July 15th, the day your bank was robbed." The lawyer then uses the following tools to focus—to orchestrate—the arguments she makes through the witness:

- **Looping**—tying a question in with a previous answer so as to imprint in the juror's minds the repeated fact ("Was the *gun* dark or light?").

- **Broad to Narrow**—moving in to get a more and more detailed description of what's happening ("Could you see any bullets in the cylinder?").

- **Choice**—avoiding "leading" by giving the witness a choice of two or three possibilities ("Was he holding the gun in his left hand or his right hand?")

Together with the old standby "**Tell me whether or not**," these tools of orchestration help to focus the witness's testimony so when the lawyer reaches the point when he or she wants to close the point with something that is best expressed by the witness directly (generally because the witness's words have independent significance or carry an emotional overlay), the witness does not have to guess or wonder what the answer should be. More important, neither does the jury. I call the use of these tools the **Examination Funnel**, which can be expressed in the following diagram (the **W** in the diagram stands for the key point that you want to come from the witness):

Figure 2 The Examination Funnel

Examination Funnel

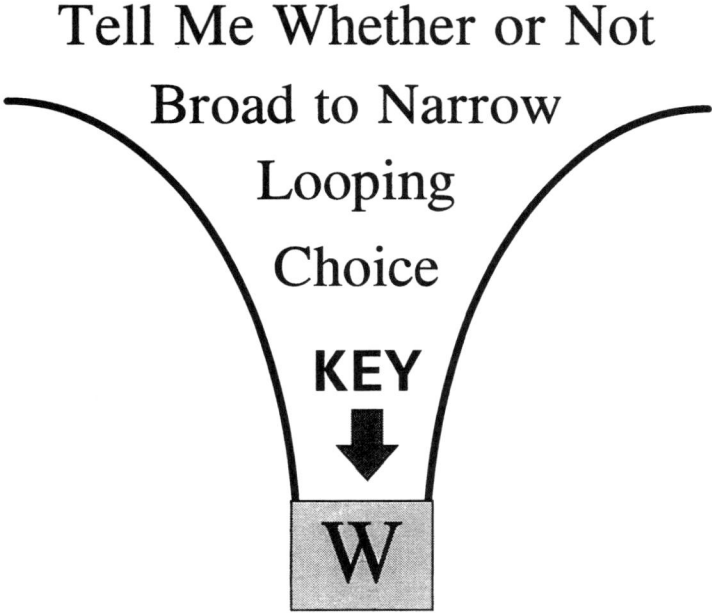

Let's continue with the examination:

> Q Ms. Jones, let's turn our attention to anything the **defendant** might have said that day. Did you hear him say anything?
>
> A Yes.
>
> Q What was the first thing you heard him say?
>
> A "Nobody move. This is a robbery."
>
> Q Where was he standing when he said "Nobody move. This is a robbery"?
>
> A He was still by the door.
>
> Q Was he still holding the gun?
>
> A Yes.
>
> Q Where was the gun pointed when he said "Nobody move. This is a robbery"?
>
> A At me.

The lawyer makes the transition to her second point (the defendant announcing the holdup) with a **Transition Question**, and then uses the orchestration tools to make her examination of the teller clear, memorable, and persuasive. The lawyer will not use written questions, but, rather uses notes that list the points—the arguments—she wants to make to the jury through the witness. They might look something like this, and help to keep the lawyer on track:

- First time teller sees defendant
- "Nobody move. This is a robbery."
- Defendant jumps counter.
- (And so on)

Again, note how the questions and answers in our examples are all short—per Sol Stein's maxim. This keeps the jurors' attention, as they engage in what Herb Stern calls the "Wimbledon Effect"—their heads going back and forth between the lawyer asking the questions and the witness answering those questions. Asking questions this way permits you to repeat the good stuff as often as you want, by moving in for as close a look (at the gun, the clothes, or anything else) as you want—it is all a legitimate area of inquiry because the details that the witness can remember goes to the credibility of her testimony. This is not leading the witness, it is orchestrating his or her testimony to make your argument to the jury—to advance your theme.

Keeping the questions and answers short, and moving in for a closer look, makes the testimony (the witness's validation of your argument to the jury) memorable and permits you to repeat and emphasize the facts that are important to your argument. Consider this example of Marcia Clark's direct-examination of one of the police officers who first arrived at the murder scene. This is one of the few times Clark was effective, as she argues to defuse a defense theory about ice cream that was found at the scene:

Q   About that ice cream, did you have any way of knowing how frozen it was when it was purchased?

A   No.

Q   Do you know whether is was yogurt or ice cream?

A   No, I don't.

Q   Could you tell by looking at it?

A   No.

Q   Do you know whether Nicole Brown put it into the freezer when she got home, and took it out just before she went outside with the tap?

Cochran: Objection. Calls for speculation.

Clark: As did counsel's questions.

The Court: Overruled.

Q   Do you know how long it took for that particular brand to melt?

A No, I don't.

Q Do you know whether it was frozen in the middle and maybe melted around the sides?

A It appeared to be a little bit of mass in the middle with the fluids surrounding it, but I don't know. As I said, I didn't touch it.

Q So you don't know whether the core was still frozen?

A No, I don't.

Q You know of any way to tell the difference between ice cream that's been melted for two versus two and a half hours?

A No.

Q Or two and a half hours and two hours and fifteen minutes?

A No, I don't.

Q Do you know the way anybody could tell the difference between that?

A No.

Johnnie Cochran objected to this question and answer on the ground that it called "for speculation," thereby validating and reinforcing Clark's point. Judge Lance Ito sustained the objection.

Clark is clearly arguing her case to the jury through the witness. She is, in essence, giving her summation to the jury *via* her questions, through the window of what the witness has to offer. What makes her direct-examination about the ice cream so powerful, is that the jury knows the answers before the witness responds. Arguments that are based on answers that the jury already knows makes those arguments invulnerable.

As the Clark ice-cream example shows, you cannot make this kind of effective argument with "what happened next" questions; it simply cannot be done. And this leads us to the final and most important problem with the "what happened next" question:

- It prevents *you*-the truth-giver—from arguing your case to the jury.

The following is a road map you should follow with every point you wish to make:

1. Know the point—where you want to go; that is, know the conclusion that you want the jury to reach.

2. Figure out how you can get there:

- by starting with a point that no one can dispute, and

- so that each step along the way logically and ineluctably follows.

For some of you, this may require a change in the way you think—in the way that you analyze. Many persons are spatial thinkers—they process and present information without significant regard to logical, incremental order. Successful trial advocacy, however, requires linear thinking—going from points A to H by, as Herb Stern is fond of saying, "making all the stops along the way"—A to B to C to D to E to F to G to H. The first chart illustrates how many lawyers present their arguments in court: their opening statements, their direct- and cross-examinations, and their summations. They go from A to G to E to B to C to H to F to D, with the occasional diversion to non-relevant areas.

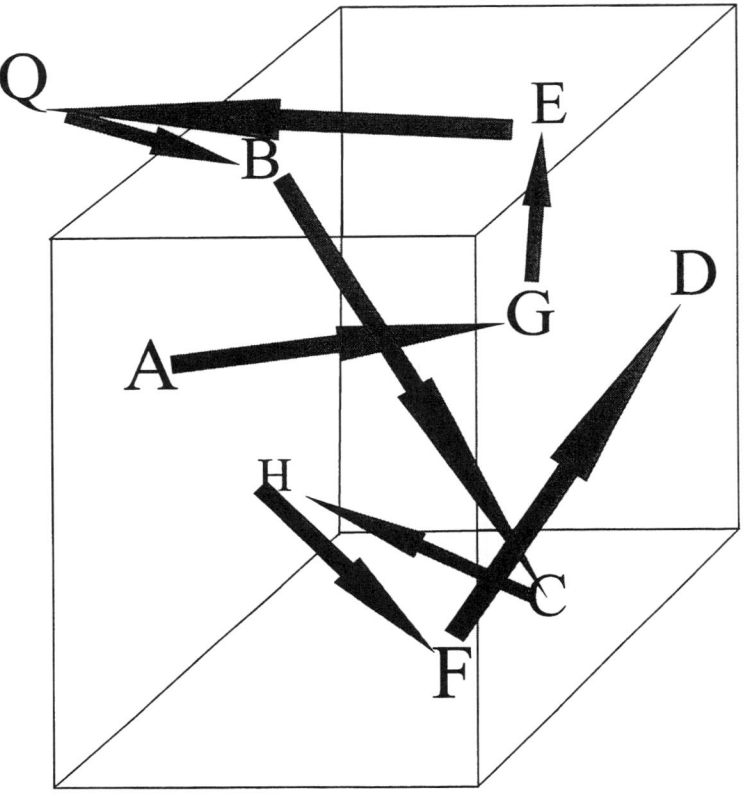

Figure 3   The Spatial Way of Examination

Johnnie Cochran's direct-examination of O.J. Simpson criminal-trial witness Denise Pilnak in the "test yourself" chapter, Chapter XXXII, is an example of a non-linear, non-focused approach to direct-examination, complete with diversions into inconsequentia.

Figure 4   The Linear Way of Examination

If you follow the direct-examination road map and make all the stops along the way with short questions that orchestrate and focus the examination, your points will ring true and your argument will be iron-clad and conclusive.

XIX.
Using Diagrams to Repeat Testimony

Diagrams give you a perfect opportunity to get all the good stuff repeated. As an illustration, let's look at the bank-robbery example, which we will pick up three questions and answers before the end of the first point (in an actual trial, the witness will draw the diagram at the end of his or her direct-examination testimony):

Q   Could you tell whether it was a revolver, with a round cylinder in the middle, or an automatic, a flatter gun.

A   Oh it was a revolver all right, just like the ones in the westerns.

Q   Could you see any bullets in the cylinder?

A   Yes, it looked full.

Q   You said he was pointing the gun directly at you, could you see down the barrel?

A   Yes.

Counsel: At this time, I would like Ms. Jones to step down from the witness stand and go over to the easel.

The Court: All right.

Q   Ms. Jones, could you please draw a diagram of what the inside of the bank looks like.

A   OK (draws).

Q   Where were you standing when you first saw the defendant?

A   Here, behind the teller cage.

Q   And where was the defendant when you first saw him?

A   Here, next to the front door.

You can see where this is going—you get to do a mini-repeat of the direct-examination, this time with the witness drawing in the various landmarks. There are two important points to remember when using this technique:

    1. The diagramming comes *after* the witness's testimony.

    2. Do not present the witness or the jury with a pre-made diagram. You want the jury to follow the witness as he or she adds each element to the picture. If you present to the jury an already-made-up diagram, the jury will be swamped with too much information at once and will not be able to concentrate on the arguments that you are making through the witness as he or she adds to the diagram in response to your questions. If you want to use a pre-made up diagram in closing argument or for the jury's use in the jury room, you can have the witness identify it *after* he or she has roughed out the diagram piece-by-piece in response to your questions. Thus, in the following example, the examiner has just completed the diagram aspect of her examination of the witness:

Q   Ms. Jones, are you a skilled draftsman?

A   No, not at all, as you can see.

Q   Did we discuss your testimony before you came into court?

A   Yes.

Q   And did I ask you to rough out what the inside of the bank looks like, and where inside the bank you and the defendant were?

A   Yes.

Q   I show you what's been marked as Government Exhibit 7, and ask you whether this professionally done drawing shows the things that you have drawn for us on the rough diagram, Exhibit 23?

A   Yes, it does.

Q   And is Exhibit 7, this professionally-made diagram, an accurate representation of the inside of the bank on July 15th, and your testimony?

A   Yes.

Counsel: I offer Exhibit 7 into evidence.

That's it. The exhibit passes muster under Rules 901(a) and 901(b)(1) of the Federal Rules of Evidence and their state counterparts.[16]

XX.
THE DIRECT-EXAMINATION MAXIM

As we have seen, a direct-examination is your argument to the jury, your summation through the window of what the witness can give you. You are not seeking facts, you are making an argument. As we have already discussed, the witness's job is to confirm and validate your version of the facts: you are the truth-giver in the courtroom, but you must demonstrate through the witnesses and the evidence that your version of what happened is correct. In order for this to work, you must obey this maxim:

Except for preliminary questions, do not ask a question on direct-examination unless one or more of the following is true:

1. The jury knows the answer before the witness responds, or

2. The witness's answer is either contemporaneously corroborated or has been pre-corroborated, or

---

[16] Rule 901 Requirement of Authentication or Identification.

(a) *General provision.* The requirement of authentication or identification as a condition precedent to admissibility is satisfied by evidence sufficient to support a finding that the matter in question is what its proponent claims.

(b) *Illustrations.* By way of illustration only, and not by way of limitation, the following are examples of authentication or identification conforming with the requirements of this rule:

(1) *Testimony of witness with knowledge.* Testimony that a matter is what it is claimed to be.

3. When one or two is not possible, the questions should start far enough back from the conclusion so that the jury sees that the witness's response rings true, that is, that the answer given by the witness is consistent with what the jurors' life experiences tell them to expect.

Let us examine each of these elements.

We saw how the first element operated in Marcia Clark's ice-cream direct-examination. The jury knew the answers to her questions—indeed, the witness wasn't even really needed. Jurors will accept your argument when it flows logically from facts they accept as true.

The third element is but a more refined variant of the first element. This is how it works. Assume that you represent a person who claims that she was fired from her job because she would not have sex with her boss. You are seeking, among other things, damages for the pain and disability for an ulcer that she claims was caused by the harassment and discharge. Your medical expert is on the witness stand, and you want to argue to the jury through him that the harassment and discharge caused her ulcer. There are two ways to do this.

The first approach is the way most lawyers do it. After establishing the witness's credentials, the lawyer asks the question, trusting the witness's persona and credibility to persuade the jury that his diagnosis and opinion are correct:

Q   Doctor, did you examine Ms. Rogers at my request?

A   Yes.

Q   And what did you find?

A   I found that she had a well-developed ulcer.

Q   Doctor, did you form an opinion to a reasonable degree of medical probability as to what caused Ms. Rogers' ulcer.

A   I did.

Q   Please tell the jury what your opinion is.

A   In my opinion, Ms. Rogers' ulcer was caused by the stress and worry she felt as a result of losing her job, and the related stress caused by pressures to have sexual relations with Mr. Jones when she worked at the company.

This is the journeyman way. It is OK, provided the jury accepts the witness and believes his testimony. But, and this is important, the jury's acceptance or rejection of your argument that your client has an ulcer and that the ulcer was caused by the defendants rests on the jury's assessment of the witness.

There is a better way to do it, however, and that is to start the questioning at a point where the jury will know the answers before the witness responds. As we have seen, if the jury knows the answers and those answers support your argument, the jury will accept your argument.

Start the questioning far enough back and then progress incrementally, so that each additional point that you are arguing to the jury naturally and logically flows from the previous point—that is, so that each answer "rings true" and is consistent with what the jurors know from their life experiences. Let's consider the following example:

Q   Doctor, can stress cause an ulcer?

A   Yes.

Q   Doctor, can tension cause an ulcer?

A   Yes.

Q   Doctor, can worry over the loss of a job cause an ulcer?

A   Yes.

Q   Doctor, can stress caused by the loss of a job cause an ulcer?

A   Yes.

Q   Doctor can stress in the work environment caused by a boss demanding sex cause an ulcer?

A   Yes.

Q Doctor, did you examine Ms. Rogers to see if she has an ulcer?

A Yes, I did.

Q Does she have one.

A Yes.

Q Doctor, please tell us whether or not Ms. Rogers' loss of her job, and the related stress and tension was, in your opinion, a cause of her ulcer.

By the time you get to the last question, the jury is already primed to accept the answer, *based on what they know from life*. This insulates from successful attack the point you are making. Let me give you a real-life example.

A number of years ago, a case came before the appellate court on which I sit that involved a claim that a fellow broke his neck when a Caterpillar frontloader that he was driving tipped over. He was not wearing a seat belt, and he was thrown from the cab to the ground, a distance of ten feet. He claimed that he broke his neck *before* he was thrown from the cab. His theory was that the tipping of the front-loader snapped his head down to his chest with such force that it broke his neck. The defense theory, on the other hand, was that the plaintiff's neck broke when he hit the ground head first.

The judge refused to instruct the jury that in determining whether the plaintiff was contributorily negligent it could consider that the plaintiff was not wearing a seat belt. The jury returned an eleven-million dollar verdict, and Caterpillar appealed.

In Wisconsin, as elsewhere, a defendant is entitled to a seat-belt instruction only if there is expert evidence in the record that failure to wear the belt was a substantial factor in causing the plaintiff's injuries. Unfortunately for Caterpillar, there was no such evidence. Caterpillar did not call an expert witness to give this testimony. The following is the closest Caterpillar's highly paid lawyers came to establishing that falling from a height of ten feet and hitting the ground head-first was a substantial factor in causing the plaintiff's neck injuries.

The witness was the plaintiff's doctor, and he is being cross-examined by Caterpillar's lawyer:

Q "What caused, in an anatomical sense, the spinal cord injury?" Was it "striking an object?"

A "I'm told from the records of . . . neurosurgeons . . . that he had a hyperflexion injury. In other words, he flexed his neck acutely, suddenly, very suddenly and very extremely. He extremely flexed his neck so his chin went down in the direction of his chest; that's all I know of that incident. It's all second hand."

My, my. Putting aside the failure of Caterpillar's lawyers to call their own expert to lay the foundation necessary to get the judge to give to the jury the standard seat-belt-defense instruction, they could have easily gotten the requisite expert opinion from plaintiff's physician, if they had only known how to ask the questions:

Q Doctor, how much did the plaintiff weigh on the day of the accident.

A 180 pounds.

Q How far did he fall when he fell from the cab of the front-loader?

A Ten feet.

Q How fast was he going when he hit the ground?

A Twenty-five feet per second.

Q Did he land head first?

A Yes.

Q How much force did he hit the ground with?

A Well, depends on how fast he stopped.

Q Well, he hit the ground head first. Assume that his head stopped in one-tenth of a second. How much force did his head hit the ground with.

A One-thousand, five-hundred pounds.

Q   If we assume that his head stopped in one-hundredth of a second, with how much force would his head have hit the ground then?

A   Fifteen thousand pounds.

Q   Doctor, can a person injure his neck if he falls some ten feet and lands on the ground head first with whatever force it is?

A   Yes.

Q   Doctor, can such a fall, from a height of ten feet, actually break the neck?

Even though this would have been cross-examination of the plaintiff's witness, his physician, the answers are compelled because the witness understands that the jury is answering the questions along with him and that his answers had better conform to what the jury knows to be true. This is why Wigmore called cross-examination the "great engine" for getting at the truth. We'll look at cross-examination and that "great engine" later, but the point here is that if a *direct-examination* is structured along these lines, the jury will not have to rely on the witness's credibility or persona to agree with you. They will agree with you because they already know the answer from their life experiences or, at the very least, the answer "rings true." In a sense, you are asking the jury to board the train when it is stopped at the station or, at the very least, going slowly, rather than jumping on when it is screaming along at ninety miles an hour. Once the jurors are on the train, you can easily lead them, step by step, to your argument's ultimate destination.

The second element of the three-part test, the requirement that the witness's answer be either contemporaneously corroborated or pre-corroborated, applies when you are in an area where the jurors' life experiences have no bearing to the line of questioning—no answer will "ring true," irrespective of how far back in the syllogism you go. Then, you must strive to have the jury already know the answer from what it has accepted either from the undisputed facts in the case or from a neutral, disinterested source of impeccable credentials. Let me explain.

Assume for a moment that your client claims that he met with the defendant on January 9th in San Francisco. Let's further assume that the defendant denies the meeting; indeed she denies even being in San Francisco on that day. You have a disinterested witness who can place the defendant in

San Francisco the evening before the meeting. There are two ways to approach this problem:

> First, you could have your client testify about the meeting, let the defendant deny the meeting during her testimony, and then call the disinterested witness in rebuttal.
>
> Second, you could call the disinterested witness to testify in your case-in-chief before your client testifies. He will testify that he saw the defendant in San Francisco the evening of January 8th. When your client then testifies that he met with the defendant in San Francisco on January 9th, that testimony will be pre-corroborated.

The key, of course, as we have previously discussed in the context of making the "bad facts" in your case work for you, is to present the explanation as a positive aspect of your proof. Thus, when the jury hears that the defendant was in San Francisco on the evening of January 8th, they will not know that the defendant denies being in the city on January 9.

> Note: The jury will most likely know from the defense opening statement that the defendant denies being in San Francisco on January 9. This is why you have to lay the groundwork in *your* opening statement, by presenting the January 8th evidence as a positive aspect of your proof without telling the jury that you are anticipating the denial.
>
> Consider the following:
>
>> Ladies and gentlemen, the critical meeting between Mr. Smith and Ms. Jones took place in San Francisco, right in the middle of winter, on January 9. I will prove that Ms. Jones arrived in San Francisco for the meeting at least the day before, on January 8th, because she was seen in the restaurant in the Ritz Carleton Hotel the evening of the 8th, and I will bring into this courtroom the person who saw her there.
>
> This is much better than:
>
>> Ladies and gentlemen, the critical meeting between Mr. Smith and Ms. Jones took place in San Francisco, right in the middle of winter, on January 9. Now, Ms. Jones claims that

the meeting never happened. In fact, Ms. Jones claims that she wasn't even in San Francisco on that day. But we have a witness who will testify that he saw Ms. Jones on the evening of January 8th, in the restaurant of a San Francisco hotel.

In the first example, the jury does not know about the denial—your point about January 8 comes in before the jury knows that there is a dispute over this, and your point is thus not burdened with the heavy clothes of "explanation." As we mentioned earlier, this is the great benefit of going first!

Another example. In the O.J. Simpson criminal trial, one of the criminalists was beaten up on cross-examination because he did things that did not seem to be very scientific. As I recall, the prosecution later called a national expert in the preservation of evidence who testified that what the criminalist did was OK. That disinterested national expert should have testified first, pre-corroborating the criminalist's technique, and the prosecution's opening statement should have been structured the same way. If that had been done, the explanation would have come in as a positive aspect of the prosecution's case before the jury even knew that there was an accusation of sloppy work. The evidence given by the disinterested national expert would have been accepted by the jury as something they already knew (from the case) by the time the criminalist testified. The criminalist's testimony, and the techniques he described in that testimony, would have thus been protected by the earlier witness.

XXI.
HOW TO PROTECT YOUR WITNESSES FROM CROSS-EXAMINATION

As we've discussed, the witnesses' function is to validate your arguments to the jury by confirming the facts that underlie those arguments. Again, *you are the truth-giver in the courtroom.* If you follow the rules of direct-examination discussed in the last chapter, the jury will accept the facts that underlie your arguments *because those facts will either confirm what they already know or those facts will "ring true."* But, there's more. You want the witnesses to be both liked by the jury and believable. There are two reasons. First, having the jury both like and believe the witness enhances the confirming power of that witness's testimony. Second, if the jury likes and believes a witness you have presented to it, the jury is more apt to like and believe you. This is crucial.

There are several ways to protect witnesses from a jury's natural skepticism and lack of trust. First, as we have already discussed, you want to make the witness likable: skilled at what he or she does; a victim of undeserved tragedy; in jeopardy; have a sense of humor; "good"; and, of course, a person who bleeds when pricked, laughs when tickled, and dies when poisoned.

Second, you should structure the preparation of the witness and his or her testimony so that the jury sees, as far as possible, a disinterested observer coming into court to share what he or she knows (obviously the client and members of the client's family, or the client's employees are not disinterested). There are three rules that govern this structure and preparation.

1. **Don't let the witness sell.**

Juries distrust salespeople. I remember a plaintiff in a products-liability trial over which I presided who claimed to have carpal-tunnel injury. He was the most articulate witness most lawyers could ever want. He described his injury and the resulting pain with an eloquence Shakespeare would have envied. Just as the Eskimos have a thousand words for snow because the phenomenon is so important to them, this fellow had a thousand similes for the pain he suffered: it was like getting hit on the big toe with a hammer; it was like getting root-canal work without an anesthetic; and, to top it off (especially for the women jurors), his pain was worse than childbirth. The jury hated him. They not only found no liability, they inserted "0" in the damages portion of the verdict (which had to be answered irrespective of the answers on liability).

Selling is *your* job, not your client's. He or she must appear to the jury as the stoic—unhappy, but accepting the misfortune of injury. You *can*, however, get across to the jury the severity of the pain and the depth of the disability by using **surrogate witnesses**: family members ("I see John in pain all the time. He tries not to let on, but I can see it. He always has a smile, but beneath the smile I sense tears."); physicians and therapists ("John's pain is incredible. He tells me that he can hardly lift a stick, no less than play golf anymore."); employers and co-workers ("I can see that John really tries to get the job done, but he's not his old self anymore. He tries to lift those boxes, he wants to pull his own weight, but he just can't anymore. He's in pain all the time."); friends ("John used to be such a happy-go-lucky person, it is a shame what happened.") Note: the opinions about how John feels, etc., are admissible under Rule 701 of the Federal Rules of Evidence and its state counterparts.[17] What John has told his physicians and therapists is admissible under Rule 803(4) of the Federal Rules of Evidence and its state counterparts.[18]

2. **Don't let the witness exaggerate.**

Witnesses are often tripped up because they try to appear more knowledgeable than they are. This is a variant of "selling"; they want to be so helpful that they will exaggerate little things (sometime big things) in order to help—either your case or their ego. Sometimes this exaggeration is deliberate, sometimes it is inadvertent. Irrespective of whether it is deliberate or inadvertent, exaggeration can kill you—not only because the witness's power to confirm the facts that you give to the jury will be weakened, but also because the witnesses you call reflect on your own personal credibility and standing with the jury.

An area where the perception of exaggeration is common is the recalling of conversations. A typical question and answer about a conversation that the witness had with another person generally goes something like this:

Q   Did you have a conversation with Susan Jones on Monday, September 13, 1993?

A   Yes.

Q   Tell us what you said to her and what she said to you.

---

[17]   Rule 701 Opinion Testimony by Lay Witnesses

If the witness is not testifying as an expert, the witness' testimony in the form of opinions or inferences is limited to those opinions or inferences which are
  (a) rationally based on the perception of the witness and
  (b) helpful to a clear understanding of the witness' testimony or the determination of a fact in issue.

[18]   Rule 803 Hearsay Exceptions.
Availability of Declarant Immaterial. The following are not excluded by the hearsay rule, even though the declarant is available as a witness:
. . .
(4) *Statements for purposes of medical diagnosis or treatment.* Statements made for purposes of medical diagnosis or treatment and describing medical history, or past or present symptoms, pain, or sensations, or the inception or general character of the cause or external source thereof insofar as reasonably pertinent to diagnosis or treatment.

The witness then proceeds to recite, presumably from memory, a word-for-word account of the conversation, as if it were transcribed. No one, not even an unaided John Dean of *Watergate* fame, can recall conversations verbatim.[19] Jurors know this, either consciously or subconsciously. You must, therefore, be honest with them, as in the following illustration:

> Q Did you talk to Susan Jones on Monday, September 13, 1993?
>
> A Yes.
>
> Q In all fairness, Mr. Jones, do you remember word for word what was said?
>
> A No.
>
> Q Do you remember what was said in substance?
>
> A Yes.
>
> Q Then tell us in substance, please, what you said to her and what she said to you.

XXII.
TWO MORE WINNING TIPS FOR DIRECT-EXAMINATION

Two final points before we leave the subject of direct-examination.

1. Do not use written questions.

Written questions, like too much note-taking and a written opening statement or closing argument, are the bane of trial lawyering. There are three problems with them:

> A. You will be looking at your list of questions during the time the witness is answering the question you just asked. This is a no-no. You must look at the witness and listen to his or her answer

---

[19] John Dean, White House Counsel under President Richard Nixon, brought down Nixon's presidency with his testimony before the special Senate committee chaired by Senator Sam Ervin. Nixon's defenders attacked Dean for having *too good* a memory; he was seemingly able to recall conversations word-for-word.

if you want the jury to believe that the answer is important. Frankly, if you are not paying attention to what the witness is saying, why should the jury?

B. When you listen to the witness's answer and see how the jury is responding, you will come up with questions that you could not have prepared—to get the good stuff repeated, to move in for a closer look, or to emphasize a particular point. You must listen to the witness because often the witness will give you a nice big bowl of caviar—a phrase or nuance upon which you can build, or an expression that calls for further exploration. You cannot do this with written questions.

C. Written questions look like a script. This, by itself, weakens your persona as the truth-giver. Truth-givers know the truth and do not need scripts. And, if you've prepared the witness for his or her testimony with your written questions, your adversary may be able to look at them—and cross-examine your witness on them—under the authority given to the trial judge by Rule 612 of the Federal Rules of Evidence and its state counterparts.[20] This would be deadly.

---

[20] Rule 612 Writing Used to Refresh Memory

Except as otherwise provided in criminal proceedings by section 3500 of title 18, United States Code, if a witness uses a writing to refresh memory for the purpose of testifying, either

(1) while testifying, or

(2) before testifying, if the court in its discretion determines it is necessary in the interests of justice,

an adverse party is entitled to have the writing produced at the hearing, to inspect it, to cross-examine the witness thereon, and to introduce in evidence those portions which relate to the testimony of the witness. If it is claimed that the writing contains matters not related to the subject matter of the testimony the court shall examine the writing in camera, excise any portions not so related, and order delivery of the remainder to the party entitled thereto. Any portion withheld over objections shall be preserved and made available to the appellate court in the event of an appeal. If a writing is not produced or delivered pursuant to order under this rule, the court shall make any order justice requires, except that in criminal cases when the prosecution elects not to comply, the order shall be one striking the testimony or, if the court in its discretion determines that the interests of justice so require, declaring a mistrial.

Note: Some states, unlike FRE 612(2), have made the disclosure mandatory if the writing has been shown to the witness before he or she testifies.

As with preparing to deliver your opening statement without reading it, you can jot down, either on a yellow pad or on three-by-five index cards, the points you want to cover. As Herb Stern teaches, if you see the point, the question will immediately come to you, and there is no need to work out the *wording* of the question. Thus, "San Francisco meeting, January 9," should be sufficient for you to cover with your client the events leading up to and surrounding that meeting. After all, you've lived with the case for a couple of years at least. Something is awfully amiss if you don't know the facts and how they apply to your theme of the case well-enough not to need to have your questions written out.

2. **The "bad stuff" goes towards the end of your direct-examination, but you have to end on a strong, positive note.**

Occasionally, you will have to call as a witness a person who has vital confirming information for your arguments, but will also have substantial personal or professional baggage. You bring this out *towards* the end of the direct-examination, but not *at* the end.

Given the powers of primacy and recency, you want to start and end strong. Thus, get the good stuff out early, before the jury sees the witness's baggage, deal with that baggage, and end on a re-confirmation of the material that you need. If the "bad stuff" makes the witness a bad person, you must keep your distance so as not to destroy your persona as the likable truth-giver. Let me give an example.

Assume that you are prosecuting a high-profile murder. One of the witnesses has sold his story to a supermarket tabloid for $50,000. He is the only person who saw the defendant in your city on the day of the murder. Additionally, he says that he saw the defendant with a knife that looks like the knife used to kill the victim.

The court has denied your motion *in limine* to prevent the jury from learning about the sale of the story to the tabloid. You must both (A) make this fact work for you, and (B) not let it either distract the jury or detract from the confirming value of his testimony. Let me suggest the following stages of the direct-examination of this witness:

1. Get the jury to like and empathize with the witness by using the techniques we've already discussed.

2. Present your argument to the jury through the witness in the ways we've already discussed.

3. Deal with the baggage towards the end of the examination:

   Q   Mr. Jones, you came here because you were subpoenaed, that is we served you with a piece of paper that gave you no option but to come into court and tell us what you saw on October 19th?

   A   That's right.

   Q   You would prefer not to be here?

   A   You got that right.

   Q   Why is that, Mr. Jones?

   A   Because I get paid only when I work, and I need the money.

   Q   Yes, you've told us that you have three children in college and your wife is on disability?

   A   Yes.

   Q   How much did you make last year, Mr. Jones?

   Counsel: How is that relevant, Your Honor?

   The Court: Sustained.

   Q   One of the supermarket tabloids gave you $50,000 for your story about this case.

   Counsel: Objection, leading.

   The Court: Sustained.

   Q   Well, have they given you any money for your story in this case?

A   Yes.

Q   How much?

A $50,000.

Q   Given your family situation, is that money that you need or is it money that you do not need?

A   I need it, you bet I do.

Q   By the way, Mr. Jones, did the tabloid tell you that they wanted you to make up a story of what happened on October 19, that day that you saw the defendant with the knife you described, or did they tell you that they wanted the 100% honest total truth for their newspaper?

A   They wanted the truth.

Q   Did you give them the truth?

A   Yes.

Q   Did you also tell us the truth about what you saw?

A   Yes.

Q   Did you tell us the same thing that you told the tabloid?

A   Yes.

Q   And that was that you saw the defendant on October 19th with the knife that you've described for us—the one with the gold and black dragon on the hilt?

A   Yes.

Q   And was that the truth?

A   Yes.

Q   I have no further questions at this time.

XXIII.
DIRECT-EXAMINATION: AN ANNOTATED DEMONSTRATION

The following is a demonstration of effective direct-examination techniques. Again, we will be using the *Rock v. United States Postal Service* case file. The direct-examiner is Anne Willis Reed, who, with the rest of the litigation department of the Milwaukee law firm of Reinhart, Boerner, Van Deuren, Norris & Rieselbach, took a hands-on trial-advocacy course that Professor Steve Saltzburg and I taught. The following took place at one of the hands-on practice sessions. It is a transcription of her direct-examination of a lawyer playing the role of William Donovan. Notice how she orchestrates without leading, how she argues her case to the jury through the witness, and how she uses the other techniques we've discussed.

Q   What's your name, sir?   [NO "STATE YOUR NAME FOR THE RECORD."]

A   Bill Donovan

Q   Mr. Donovan, are you retired from the United States Postal Service?

A   I am, and very well.

Q   When you retired from the United States Postal Service, what was your job?

A   I was the Tour Superintendent at the Cincinnati post office for Tour Three. I was EAS 20.

Q   And is Tour Superintendent for Tour Three at the Cincinnati Post Office the job that Norman Rock is now suing because he didn't get?   [HE KNOWS WHAT THE JOB IS ALL ABOUT.]

A   That's the way I understand it.

Q   So he was applying to replace you in your job?

A   Yes ma'am.

Q And while you had that job, Tour Superintendent for Tour Three, who supervised Norman Rock?

A Well, I supervised Norman Rock. [HE KNOWS ROCK'S ABILITIES.]

Q And when Norman Rock went to Desert Storm, who was it who made the decision to detail Rose Climber into that position while he was gone?

A I did.

Q Mr. Haig did not make that decision?

A No.

Q Who was it who saw the idea that Rose Climber had to reduce overtime on Tour Three?

A I'm sorry?

Q Who was it who saw, who noticed, the idea that Rose Climber had to reduce overtime on Tour Three?

A Well, I heard about it.

Q And who brought it to Mr. Haig's attention?

A I did.

Q What . . . strike that, when did Tour Three start and finish when Rose Climber started in that position?

A Well, it finished at 3:30 in the afternoon.

Q I'm sorry. Let's start with when it commenced. Did it commence at 3:30 in the afternoon or 4 O'Clock in the afternoon?

A I'm sorry. It commenced at 4 O'Clock in the afternoon.

Q And did it end at 11:30 at night or midnight?

A Midnight.

Q   And what change did Ms. Climber make to those hours?

A   Well, she suggested that we change it to be a half an hour earlier: 3:30 to 11:30.

Q   3:30 to 11:30. What is primary mail, Mr. Donovan?

A   Primary mail is first class, generally speaking, that needs to get out of the post office where you're at and get somewhere else outside of our local delivery area.

Q   What percentage of mail handled by the Cincinnati post office on a given day is primary mail?

A   Better than half.

Q   How important is primary mail to the efficient operation of the Cincinnati post office?

A   Well, it's critical that we take care of it on time.

Q   What's the dispatch window?

A   The dispatch window is where we collect the primary mail. It's the broad geographical description of where that happens.

Q   How close to 4 O'Clock in the afternoon is the peak time for getting primary mail to those dispatch windows and out to other cities?

A   We have a very tight time window then because all trucks and things go out just about that time.

Q   How important is it that Tour Three employees be at their job with their coats off, settled, time cards punched, at 4 O'Clock at that peak time to handle primary mail?
                              [NICE IMAGE TO HELP JURY UNDERSTAND.]

A   It's very important.

Q How much difference did it make to move that starting time forward by half an hour to give those employees a half an hour before 4 O'Clock to get themselves in, settled, coats off?

A It really made all the difference in the world.

Q Well, let's see if we could put that in monetary terms. Did it save you money?

[NICE SEGUE. THIS CANNOT BE DONE WITH WRITTEN QUESTIONS.]

A Well, yes, it did, because we didn't have to pay nearly as much overtime from the Tour Two anymore.

Q How much money did you save?

A Ooodles. (Laughter)

Q Tens of thousands of dollars a month?

A Yes, certainly.

Q Had you held the job of General Superintendent, the job that Rose Climber was detailing at . . . Let me ask you a different question. How long had Norman Rock held that job of General Superintendent before he went to Desert Storm?

A Oh, I think that was four or five years.

Q In four or five years did he ever come up with that idea?

A No, he never suggested it to me.

Q Let me ask you a little bit tougher question. Had you had that job of General Superintendent before you were promoted to Tour Superintendent?

A Yes, that's the normal progression.

Q How long did you hold the job?

A Six years.

Q   Did you ever come up with that idea?

A   No ma'am.

Q   How good an idea was that?

A   Well, I thought it was an excellent idea when Rose Climber gave it to me.

Q   How pleased were you when you heard about it?

A   Well, I went right to Al Haig and told him what a good idea I thought it was because of it.

Q   How impressed were you with Rose Climber when you saw the tens of thousands of dollars a month that were saved by her idea?

A   Well, considering that she had filled into a spot that ordinarily she wouldn't've even have gotten, I was very impressed that she came up with that idea.

[GOOD SERIES OF QUESTIONS TO REPEAT THEME THAT ROSE CLIMBER IS INNOVATIVE AND THINKS OUTSIDE OF THE BOX.]

Q   I'd now like to switch to another subject, and that is your own history in the post office and that of other black males who have worked there. How long did you work in the postal service?

[LESS-THAN-SMOOTH TRANSITION BECAUSE OF THE "I'D NOW LIKE TO SWITCH TO ANOTHER SUBJECT." THIS SHOULD BE OMITTED. GET RIGHT TO IT: "MR. DONOVAN, LET'S TALK ABOUT YOUR OWN EMPLOYMENT HISTORY WITH THE POST OFFICE AND THAT OF OTHER BLACK MALES WHO HAVE WORKED THERE."]

A   Twenty-eight years.

Q   Were you promoted during that time?

A   Oh yes.

Q   How many times?

A   I would think twelve times, altogether.

Q   Were there any of those times when you were promoted over a white male?

A   I was in competition with white males for some of my promotions, yes.

Q   Were there any of those times when you were promoted over a woman?

A   Yes, there were.

Q   What about Mr. Rock, he was in the postal service for eighteen years, wasn't he?

A   Yes ma'am.

Q   Was he promoted five times?

A   That would be about right.

Q   How many of those promotions did you make the decision to give him?

A   Two.

Q   In either of those two promotions were there white males who were competing for the spots?

A   Yes, more than once.

Q   In either of those two promotions were there women who were competing for the spots?

A   In both of them.

Q   Did you review Mr. Rock during the time that he worked under you when he was General Superintendent and you were Tour Superintendent?

A   Yes, I did.

Q   Did you review him in 1989.

A   Yes.

Q   What review did you give him?

A   Very good.   [DONOVAN HAS NO AX TO GRIND; HE LIKES ROCK.]

Q   And did you review him again in 1990?

A   Yes.

Q   And what review did you give him then?

A   Also very good.

Q   In 1990, what recommendation did you make about his salary?

A   I recommended him for a one-step increase in salary.

[GOOD SERIES OF QUESTIONS THAT MAKE HER POINT THAT DONOVAN IS DISINTERESTED AND NEUTRAL. THIS PREPARES THE JURY FOR THE CONCLUDING SALVO. NOTE: IN REAL LIFE, THE EXAMINER SHOULD HAVE CONTEMPORANEOUSLY CORROBORATED EACH OF DONOVAN'S RESPONSES WITH THE ACTUAL DOCUMENTS MEMORIALIZING THE REVIEWS.]

Q   Now, I'd like to turn to yet another subject, and that is the subject of grievances. Are you aware that Mr. Rock is making a claim in this case that he was retaliated against for making a sexual-discrimination grievance?

[SHE SHOULD HAVE GONE RIGHT TO IT: "LET'S TALK ABOUT GRIEVANCES IN THE POSTAL SERVICE." ALSO, THE FINAL SALVO, AS YOU WILL SEE, SHOULD COME AFTER THIS LAST SERIES OF QUESTIONS AND ANSWERS. THE MATERIAL BETWEEN THE PRECEDING SERIES AND THE FINAL SALVO (THAT IS, THE FOLLOWING MATERIAL) SHOULD HAVE BEEN IN THE MIDDLE OF THE EXAMINATION.]

A   Yes.

Q   How common are grievances in the postal service? How commonly do you have to deal with that?

A   Well, we see more and more of them now.

Q   How common is Mr. Haig as Field Processor of the Mails the subject, the target, of a grievance. How common a case is that?

Member of the Group: That's where I'd object. I'd say no foundation.

Ralph Adam Fine: Let's say that the judge sustains it, what do you do?

Q   Have you had an opportunity to see grievances as they come in in your role as Tour Superintendent of Tour Three?

[SHE DOESN'T BACK DOWN.]

A   Yes. I'm informed of them.

Q   Give me an idea of the proportion that concern Mr. Haig.

A   Well, ultimately they all do.

Q   If you are the kind of person who takes grievances personally, how long are you going to remain successfully in Mr. Haig's job?

A   Not very long.

Q   Mr. Haig was your boss, isn't that right?

A   Yes.

Q   You talked together every day?

A   Oh yes.

Q   Do you recall him ever saying anything about being upset, or hurt, or offended that Mr. Rock had mentioned him in his grievance?

A   I knew that there had been a grievance. But no, he never said anything like that to me.

Q   How many promotion decisions do you think you made, Mr. Donovan, in the time you were Tour Superintendent in Tour Three?

[SHE'S LAYING THE FOUNDATION FOR HER FINAL SALVO.]

A   You mean of other employees?

Q   Yes, give me some sort of estimate.

A   Well, all of the promotions underneath me I'd know about and I would be involved in. There were probably dozens.

Q   You came to know Mr. Rock quite well during the many years that he worked under you in the postal service, is that true?

A   Yes.

Q   And you observed Ms. Climber in the time you detailed her to Mr. Rock's position?

A   Yes.

Q   Do you like Mr. Rock?

A   Yes, I do.

Q   As you watched them, though, in the same job, which of them brought more energy to the position?

A   Rose Climber really came on like a ball of fire.

Q   Which one had more new ideas?

A   Rose Climber had a lot of fresh ideas.

Q   Which one really seemed to have more drive?

A   Rose Climber.

Q   Which one saved the post office more money in overtime?

A   Rose Climber.

Q   If you had been the person making the decision about who should replace you as Tour Superintendent of Tour Three, and your choices were Norman Rock or Rose Climber, which one would you have chosen?

Member of the group: I'd object, but if I do, I'm going to get creamed, whether it's sustained or not.

And so he would, and that leads us to our next area: a trial is not an evidence test.

XXIV.
A TRIAL IS NOT AN EVIDENCE TEST

As we know by now, what makes the techniques discussed in this book work is that the jurors believe both that the lawyers know the truth of the case, and that there are many things that are critical to the jury's decision that the jurors will not learn. Thus, jurors believe that at least one of the lawyers is either lying to them or trying to keep hidden elements of the truth. This leads to the critical question: Why would lawyers trying to clothe themselves with the aura of "Honest Abe" ever object in front of the jury?

Lawyers object for the same reason people fall down when they are shot: They believe that they should.[21] Law schools and many continuing-legal-education providers even teach students and lawyers how to object to evidence. They are, in reality, teaching hara-kiri.

Truth-givers do not object in front of the jury to the admission of evidence—facts cannot hurt a truth-giver. Skilled trial lawyers thus save their display of evidentiary knowledge for motions *in limine*, where the real battles shaping the trial should be fought. A lawyer should risk objecting in front of the jury to the admission of evidence *only* if the evidence is *both inadmissible* and a *case-loser*.

First, if the evidence is admissible, but not through the witness then testifying, an objection garners nothing but the jury's distrust—the evidence will come in eventually.

Second, the successful trial lawyer shapes the trial's theme so that it accounts for *all* facts, including those unfavorable facts that cannot be

---

[21] "Although the popular belief that many people fall down upon being shot is generally accurate, experts have determined that this occurs not for physiological reasons, but as a learned response. People who have been shot believe they are supposed to fall immediately to the ground, so they do." David Simon, HOMICIDE 413 (1993).

excluded by an order *in limine*. The skilled trial lawyer is a truth-giver who is not afraid to let it all hang out.[22]

Many lawyers tell me that they object in front of the jury to the admission of evidence in order to make their record. An objection that is overruled when it should be sustained, they argue, will give them fodder for an appeal. This is too slim a reed to justify giving jurors the impression that you are trying to hide something from them.

Professor Margaret A. Berger, original co-author of *Weinstein's Federal Evidence*, studied decisions issued by the United States courts of appeals and reported:

"Although more than twenty thousand cases a year were tried in the federal courts in the twenty-four month period between July 1, 1988 and June 30, 1990, I could find only thirty cases decided in 1990 in which a court of appeals stated in an officially reported opinion that its reversal was due to an evidentiary error at trial."[23]

Even this small number, however, she concluded, may overstate the extent of evidentiary reversals:

"Examination of the cases indicates (1) that some of the alleged errors are not really evidentiary errors, and (2) that in a number of cases an element other than evidentiary error may have accounted for the appellate court's response despite the court's stated reliance on an erroneous evidentiary ruling. These thirty cases suggest that an evidentiary error alone is not very likely to induce the reviewing court to term the error 'reversible' on the ground that the error affected a substantial right of a party."[24]

The United States Court of Appeals for the Seventh Circuit is even more direct: "Appellants who challenge evidentiary rulings of the district court are

---

[22] One of the silliest objections is "irrelevant." Why would anyone object if the opponent's evidence was irrelevant? No one wants to get the case over faster than the judge. Let the judge control the lawyer littering the trial with inconsequentia.

[23] M. A. Berger, *When, if Ever, Does Evidentiary Error Constitute Reversible Error?* 25 LOY. L.A. L. REV. 893, 894 (1992). Of the thirty cases, seventeen were civil and thirteen were criminal. *Ibid.*

[24] *Ibid.*

like rich men who wish to enter the Kingdom; their prospects compare with those of camels who wish to pass through the eye of a needle."[25]

Objections not only hurt the lawyer's status as the trial's truth-giver and provide little help on appeal, even when the trial judge is wrong, but they also can prevent the objecting lawyer from making a killer argument. Consider the following two examples. The first is from the criminal trial of Oliver North. The second, from the O.J. Simpson criminal trial.

Congressman Lee H. Hamilton is on the witness stand. He is questioned by John Keker, one of North's prosecutors.

> Q   Chairman Hamilton, in our system of government, is there any situation where it's all right just to go ahead and lie to the House intelligence committee?

Although this question went to the heart of North's public-interest defense, his lawyer, Brendan Sullivan, objected. The transcript, however, shows that Congressman Hamilton got his answer in first.

> A   No.
>
> Sullivan: Objection.
>
> The Court: Sustained.

By objecting and by having his objection sustained, Sullivan not only gave the jury the impression that he was afraid of Hamilton's response to Keker's question, but Sullivan also missed the opportunity to make the following argument on cross-examination.

Consistent with the techniques that we have already discussed, notice how in this hypothetical the answers are either compelled, because the witness knows what answers the jurors are expecting, or the answers do not matter because the jurors have already answered the question in favor of the examiner's argument. Again, the examiner is not seeking information; he is, rather, making his argument to the jury through the witness.

---

[25]   *United States v. Glecier*, 923 F.2d 496, 503 (7th Cir. 1991).

Q   Chairman Hamilton, very little that goes on in Congress can be kept secret for very long?

A   Yes, that's true, unfortunately.

Q   And even in your committee, no one can be absolutely, one-hundred percent positive, that something said during one of your secret sessions would not be leaked to the press, or to a staffer, or even a relative or a lover?

A   We do have strict rules for secrecy.

Q   Of course. But there really is no way to make absolutely certain that even your committee is one-hundred percent, positively, leak proof?

A   No, I guess not.

Q   Now, you testified on direct-examination that there is no situation where it is all right just to go ahead and lie to the House intelligence committee. Let's explore that for a moment. Imagine with me that it is early in 1944, and that your committee is in full operation, and is looking into the ongoing conduct of World War II.

A   Yes.

Q   And imagine that General Dwight Eisenhower has taken time from his command to bring you folks up to date.

A   Yes.

Q   And that one of your committee members, a congressman from, let's say, South Dakota, asks General Eisenhower if it is true, as he's heard, that D-Day is set for June of 1944 and that the attack will be at Normandy. Congressman, don't you think that it would be all right for General Eisenhower to lie to your committee?

It makes no difference what answer Hamilton gives. The jury has already answered "yes," and this answer is consistent with North's theme of defense.

Shifting to the Simpson criminal trial, Los Angeles police detective Philip Vannatter is on the witness stand. Prosecutor Brian Kelberg is asking him about when Vannatter and the other officers entered Simpson's house without a search warrant. Johnnie Cochran, like Sullivan, objects, rather than using Vannatter's response to make his own killer argument. First, the excerpt from the trial:

> Q   Detective Vannatter, bottom line, if you thought Mr. Simpson was a suspect when you first are going from Bundy to Rockingham, number one, would you have told that to this jury?
>
> Cochran: Objection.
>
> The Court: Overruled.
>
> A   You bet I would have.
>
> Q   Would you have told this to the judge at the preliminary hearing?
>
> A   Yes sir. You bet I would have.
>
> Q   Would you have told this to the grand jury?
>
> A   I would have told it to anybody that asked me.
>
> Q   Is there any reason in your mind why you would not have said that if that is in fact how you honestly felt at that particular time?
>
> Cochran: Objection. Self-serving.
>
> The Court: Overruled.
>
> A   That is not a true statement. I wouldn't say something like that. The truth of the matter is, Mr. Simpson was not a suspect. I went there to make an identification and disposition of two minor children. That was my purpose for going to that location.
>
> Q   And wouldn't you agree, sir, that it would have been very easy for you to say if you wanted to, that Mr. Suspect [sic] uh Mr. Simpson of course was a suspect? If you wanted to?
>
> Cochran: Objection.

The Court: Sustained. Speculation.

This is what Cochran *could* have done. Again, as with the North-trial hypothetical, it does not make any difference what Vannatter's answers are; the lawyer is making his argument through Vannatter to the jury.

Q   Detective Vannatter, you've been a police detective for a long time?

A   Yes.

Q   And during that time, you've investigated many, many crimes?

A   Yes.

Q   And you've heard of the Fourth Amendment?

A   Yes.

Q   And the Fourth Amendment essentially tells the police what they can and cannot do in investigating crimes?

A   The courts tell us that.

Q   Of course. They tell you what the Fourth Amendment says you can do or not do in investigating crimes?

A   Yes.

Q   And you would not want anyone to believe that you've violated people's rights under the Fourth Amendment?

A   Sir, I would not violate anyone's rights.

Q   And you would not want the judge or this jury to believe that you violated anyone's Fourth Amendment rights, even Mr. Simpson's?

A   That's right.

Q   And the Fourth Amendment essentially says that the police can't go into someone's home unless either they have a warrant or it is some sort of an emergency?

A   Yes.

Q   And a judge issues a search warrant to police officers if the officers can persuade the judge that there is a reason to believe that there is evidence of a crime in the place to be searched?

A   Yes.

Q   And if the police go into someone's home to look for evidence, and it is not an emergency and they do not have a warrant, whatever evidence they find will be kept out of court?

A   Yes.

Q   So if the police suspect that evidence will be in someone's home, but they don't get a search warrant from a judge first, they can jeopardize the case because whatever evidence they find could be kept out of court?

A   Mr. Simpson was not a suspect.

Q   I understand that's what you're telling us, Detective Vannatter, but you have a reason to tell us that because if you went into his house to look for evidence because you believed he was a suspect, and you did not have a warrant, which you did not, all the evidence that you found there — this whole table full of evidence — would have been kept out?

A   He was not a suspect.

Q   Detective Vannatter, you went into Mr. Simpson's house without a warrant?

A   Yes.

Q   And if you told this jury that you went into his house because you suspected him of these crimes and wanted to look for evidence, you would be concerned that all this evidence would not be admissible at this trial?

Again, it makes no difference what Vannatter's answer is. He certainly is not going to admit to testifying falsely. Yet, the jury will get the point that he had a *motive* to testify falsely, which was the door Kelberg opened and, inexplicably, Cochran tried so hard to close.

During the more than 350 jury trials over which I presided during my nine-year stint as a trial judge, I have seen many lawyers object to a line of questioning that was either killing their adversaries or opening the door to their own killer responses. But, like people who expect to fall down when they are shot, lawyers think it part of the routine of the trial to object. Law schools and many continuing-legal-education programs (some of which put the lawyer-registrants through elaborate "objection" exercises) perpetuate the myth. In fact, as I write this Judge Myron H. Bright of the United States Court of Appeals for the Eighth Circuit is travelling the lecture circuit giving a CLE course entitled: "Objections at Trial, 1997." One of the avowed purposes of the seminar is how to object at trial, and Judge Bright distributes what the promotional brochure for the seminar describes as a "take-to-trial pocketbook" on how to phrase objections—"It will help you find the objection law you need," the brochure boasts. The brochure reproduces the following excerpt from "Objections at Trial":

Question: What did the man who was standing at the corner tell you about the accident?

Objection: I object. Hearsay, your honor.

Ruling: Sustained.

Come on! What is any reasonable juror going to think the bystander said—something that helps or hurts you? And guess what? The evidence is probably admissible in any event. Let's consider the two alternatives: the witness is either an investigating police officer or a fact witness. Let's first assume that the witness is an investigating police officer. The trial judge has just sustained the "hearsay" objection, as Judge Bright's book predicts she will.

Q   Officer, how long have you been a police officer?

Q   And how many years have to been assigned to investigate accidents?

Q   Have you taken courses to help you evaluate what you see at accident scenes?

Q   Following your investigation, do you take official action based on what you determine to have been the cause of the accident?

Q   If you believe that someone is at fault, do you give that person a citation?

Q   Do you also write reports based on your investigations of accidents?

Q   Are you required to do so?

Q   Now, officer, in investigating accidents is it helpful or not helpful to get statements from people you find on the scene?

Q   And did you do so in this case?

Q   Is this just something that *you* do, or do other officers you know who investigate accidents also take into account statements from people who are the scene of an accident in determining what caused the accident?

Q   And based on those statements and the other evidence you find at the scene do you form a conclusion as to what caused the accident?

Q   And did you form an opinion based on your expertise and all the information that you gathered at the scene, including what that bystander might have told you, in forming your opinion about the cause of the accident in this case?

Q   And what is your opinion?

The officer, testifying as an expert, may give his opinion on the ultimate issue of causation. Rule 704 of the Federal Rules of Evidence and its state counterparts.[26] Moreover, in reaching his or her opinion, the expert witness

---

[26]   Rule 704 provides:

Opinion on Ultimate Issue

(a) Except as provided in subdivision (b), testimony in the form of an opinion or inference otherwise admissible is not objectionable because it embraces an ultimate issue to be decided by the trier of fact.

may rely on things that are *not* admissible as evidence. Rule 703 of the Federal Rules of Evidence and its state counterparts.[27] Additionally, if the officer has written a report, that report, which will probably have the bystander's statement, is admissible under Rule 803(8)(B) & (C) of the Federal Rules of Evidence and its state counterparts.[28]

If the witness is not an investigating officer, the proponent of the bystander's statement may be able to lay a foundation under the "excited

---

[27] (b) No expert witness testifying with respect to the mental state or condition of a defendant in a criminal case may state an opinion or inference as to whether the defendant did or did not have the mental state or condition constituting an element of the crime charged or of a defense thereto. Such ultimate issues are matters for the trier of fact alone.

Rule 703 of the Federal Rules of Evidence provides:

Bases of Opinion Testimony by Experts

The facts or data in the particular case upon which an expert bases an opinion or inference may be those perceived by or made known to the expert at or before the hearing. If of a type reasonably relied upon by experts in the particular field in forming opinions or inferences upon the subject, the facts or data need not be admissible in evidence.

[28] Rule 803(8) of the Federal Rules of Evidence provides:

Rule 803 Hearsay Exceptions.

Availability of Declarant Immaterial. The following are not excluded by the hearsay rule, even though the declarant is available as a witness:
. . .

(8) *Public records and reports.* Records, reports, statements, or data compilations, in any form, of public offices or agencies, setting forth

(A) the activities of the office or agency, or

(B) matters observed pursuant to duty imposed by law as to which matters there was a duty to report, excluding, however, in criminal cases matters observed by police officers and other law enforcement personnel, or

(C) in civil actions and proceedings and against the Government in criminal cases, factual findings resulting from an investigation made pursuant to authority granted by law, unless the sources of information or other circumstances indicate lack of trustworthiness.

utterance" exception to the rule against hearsay.[29] Again, we pick up the testimony at the point suggested by Judge Bright's book:

> *Question:* What did the man who was standing at the corner tell you about the accident?
>
> *Objection:* I object. Hearsay, your honor.
>
> *Ruling:* Sustained.
>
> Q Well, sir, did you talk to the man?
>
> A Yes.
>
> Q Did he seem calm or excited when you spoke to him?
>
> A Excited.
>
> Q Were you present when the accident happened?
>
> A I was around the corner.
>
> Q Did you hear the crash?
>
> A Yes.
>
> Q How soon after you heard the crash did you see what had happened?
>
> A Seconds. I had just turned the corner.

---

[29] Rule 803(2) of the Federal Rules of Evidence provides:

Rule 803 Hearsay Exceptions.

Availability of Declarant Immaterial. The following are not excluded by the hearsay rule, even though the declarant is available as a witness:
. . .

(2) *Excited utterance.* A statement relating to a startling event or condition made while the declarant was under the stress of excitement caused by the event or condition.

Q   Was the man you spoke to, the man we're talking about, was he there when you turned the corner?

A   Yes.

Q   You said that he seemed excited when you first saw him. How shook up was he?

Objection: Leading.

The Court: Sustained.

Q   How excited did seem to be?

A   Very.

Q   Did you say anything to him when you turned the corner, seconds after you heard the crash?

A   Yes.

Q   What did you say?

A   I asked what happened?

Q   And did he respond?

A   Yes.

Q   What was his tone of voice? Was it calm, excited, very excited, or something else?

A   It was very excited.

Q   What did he tell you?

Even if your opponent cannot get the evidence in, wouldn't you rather like to have a chance to deal with it than to have the jury assume the worse? Again we pick up the testimony at the point suggested by Judge Bright's book:

Question: What did the man who was standing at the corner tell you about the accident?

A   He said the red car went through the yellow light.

Then, on cross-examination:

Q   You did not see the accident?

A   No.

Q   You were around the corner when it happened?

A   Yes.

Q   There was a loud crash?

A   Yes.

Q   And then you turned the corner?

A   Yes.

Q   And the man you spoke to, he was there when you turned the corner?

A   Yes.

Q   And you didn't see him actually see the accident?

A   He said he did.

Q   Were you there when the accident happened?

A   No.

Q   So you didn't see the man see the accident?

A   No, I guess that's right.

Q   And you don't know what he was doing when you heard the crash, because you were around the corner at the time?

A   Yes, that's right.

Q That street corner is a pretty busy place. Lots of businesses in that area?

A Yes.

Q Lots of store windows?

A Yes.

Q Buses go on that street?

A Yes.

Q Trucks?

A Yes.

Q Pedestrians? People walking about?

A Yes.

Q Lots of distractions?

A You could say that?

Q Did you hear tires squealing before you heard the crash?

A No.

Q So everything happened pretty fast?

A Yes.

Q And you don't know what the man was doing before the accident happened? For all you know he could have been looking in one of the store windows?

A Yes.

Q Or looking at one of the pedestrians, perhaps a pretty woman?

A Yes.

Q   And, of course, you have no information that he knew that there would be an accident on that corner that day at that time?

A   No. Of course not.

Q   So he wouldn't be watching out for it?

Opposing Lawyer: Objection. Calls for speculation.

The Court: Sustained.

Q   Do you have any reason to believe that he was expecting the accident to happen?

A   No.

Q   So you have no idea at all how closely he was watching to spot where the cars collided, was examining the status of the traffic lights in that area, or anything else?

A   Yes, I guess that's right.

In my view, dealing with this evidence in this way is far better than letting the jurors think that you are afraid of the answer, and are invoking a "legal technicality" to keep them from hearing it.

As much as you might like to sound like a lawyer and strut your stuff, a trial is not an evidence test. It is a battleground where the lawyer whom the jury perceives as the trial's truth-giver will generally prevail. The lawyer who wants to win should do nothing that tarnishes his or her image as "Honest Abe," and that means not objecting in front of the jury to the admission of evidence.

XXV.
THE THREE FACES OF CROSS-EXAMINATION

On the first page of his insightful book on cross-examination, the third volume of his four-volume *Trying Cases to Win* series, former federal judge Herbert J. Stern, reminds us that: "'More cross examinations are suicidal rather than homicidal.'"[30] And so it is. Lawyers who try to emulate the movie and television Perry Masons will, more often than not, hoist themselves by their own petard.[31]

The cross-examination, like the direct-examination, is an argument by the lawyer to the jury through the witness. It is, as with the direct-examination, the lawyer's summation through the window of what the witness can give. Cross-examination has three sub-functions:

1. **To expose the limits of the witness's testimony.**

Cross-examination that limits the effect of the witness's testimony exposes the witness's lack of knowledge, the witness's lack of certainty, and the like. Consider the following simple example:

Q   Ms. Jones, before you heard the crash, were you expecting there to be an accident on the corner of Fifth and Main?

A   No.

Q   In fact, you were not studying that street corner, trying to remember everything as it was, just in case there would be an accident?

A   No, of course not.

Q   And you heard the sound of the crash first, before you saw anything?

A   Actually, I heard the screeching of brakes.

Q   Yes, and before you heard the screeching of brakes, you were not expecting an accident?

A   No.

---

[30] Herbert J. Stern, 3 *Trying Cases to Win* 1 (Wiley 1993) (quoting Emory Buckner, the United States Attorney for the Southern District of New York during the first part of the Twentieth Century).

[31] Blow themselves up with their own bomb. A petard was a bomb that those trying to break into a besieged, walled city would hang on the locked city gates to blow them open. Often, the person assigned to hang the petard on the gates was blown up by his bomb.

Q   And the sound of the crash came right after the sound of the screeching brakes?

A   Yes.

Q   And then you saw the cars entangled with one another?

A   Yes.

Q   And that was after the sound of the crash?

A   Yes.

Q   So the first time you saw both cars was after they had already crashed together, making that crash noise?

A   Yes.

Q   And so you did not see what the cars were doing before they crashed—before you heard the sound of the crash.

A   Yes, I guess that's right.

You must ask *some* questions on cross-examination, even if the witness has not hurt you. The jury will generally not understand this, and will believe that you are not asking questions on cross-examination because you have been so devastated by the witness's testimony that you have no rejoinder. This rule does not apply, however, if the direct-examiner has not established an element of his or her case that only this witness can provide. If that happens, say "I have no questions, Your Honor," thus avoiding a re-direct examination, and move to dismiss at the end of the plaintiff's or prosecution's case.

2. **To get help from the witness.**

Not every witness called by your adversary is there to hurt you. Most witnesses are disinterested, and are trying to be fair. You can use the window of what the cross-examined witness can give you to make your argument to the jury, in the same way you would do this with witnesses on direct-examination.

A well-executed example of this is illustrated by the Colin Ferguson criminal trial. Ferguson was convicted of shooting up a commuter train in Long Island, New York, and he acted as his own lawyer during the trial. He did a fairly good job, too, as his cross-examination of one of the persons on the train at the time of the shooting demonstrates. As you will see below, he argued to the jury that identification of the shooter was problematic because of the wide-spread panic and chaos.

Q   You did not experience any sudden trauma?

A   No. That's correct.

Q   And in your position, your testimony indicated that you still did not see anything. Am I correct?

A   Correct.   [HE WAS NOT SHOT, AND HE CAN'T SAY WHO DID THE SHOOTING.]

Q   And that was because of the situation that existed on the train. It made it impossible for you to see anything accurately. Am I correct?

A   Well, the . . . I intentionally avoided to see the source of the gunfire.

Q   And people around you were in a state of panic. People were screaming, according to your testimony, people were running.

A   Yes.

Q   Anything they could do to avoid contact with this particular movement or source of fire. Am I correct?

A   Yes.

Q   It was total chaos. People were out of their minds?

A   That's correct.

Q   It was a very difficult, shocking and traumatic experience. Am I correct?

A   Uh, yes.

[THIS ATTACKS THE ABILITY OF THOSE ENMESHED IN THE PANIC TO IDENTIFY THE SHOOTER.]

Q   No further questions.

Although an experienced and skillful lawyer would have made the ultimate point at this time, rather than saving it for summation, Ferguson's use of cross-examination to set a fence around the testimony of other witnesses is fairly well-done and sophisticated. The most striking thing about this excerpt, however, doesn't come across in the transcription: Ferguson *listens* to the witness before asking his next question. It is obvious that he is using the witness's answer to frame the next question. This is what every lawyer should do, and it the reason why written questions hinder, rather than help, effective trial lawyering.

3.   **To discredit the witness.**

This, of course, is the movie- and television-function of cross-examination—to make the witness out to be the liar he is. Indeed, every cross-examiner dreams of having a fact-finder come to this conclusion after his or her blistering cross:

> "Gorelick took the stand and attempted brazenly to lie to the court. During cross-examination, the crucible of truth, Gorelick continuously shifted uneasily in the chair, sweated like a trapped liar, and the glaze that come over his shifty eyes gave proof to his continuing perjury."[32]

You will rarely be so lucky. And this leads us to a fact of life in the courtroom. If you take on a witness in order to expose that witness as a liar, and the jury believes the witness, the jury will then believe that you are the liar. Seeking to discredit the witness on cross-examination is not a "nothing ventured, nothing gained" situation, it is "everything ventured, lose the farm" if you fail. This is what Buckner meant by "More cross examinations are suicidal rather than homicidal."

There are some circumstances, however, where you have to "bet the farm." In any case where it is the plaintiff's word against the defendant's word, or the complaining witness's word against the defendant's word, you have to destroy the other party's credibility, because if the jurors believe the opposing party they, necessarily, disbelieve your client. If that happens, the case is over.

---

[32] *Penthouse Int., Ltd. v. Dominion Federal S & L Assn.*, 665 F. Supp. 301, 307 (SDNY 1987), *aff'd in part and rev'd in part*, 855 F.2d 963 (2d Cir. 1988), *cert. denied*, 490 U.S. 1005.

There is one critical thing to remember: Irrespective of which sub-function of cross-examination you use (and, of course, you can use more than one with a witness), your cross-examination, like your direct-examination, must *advance your theme*, that is, *make your argument to the jury through the witness*.

XXVI.
CROSS-EXAMINING PROBLEM WITNESSES

Let's discuss some of the problems that lawyers face on cross-examination, and the techniques to deal with those problems.

1. **The witness who glides by your question and tosses in stuff that he or she thinks will hurt you.**

Attorney, journalist, and author Roger Parloff describes such a witness in his book about an innocent man who spent some two decades on death row before he was finally freed, *Triple Jeopardy*. Called often to give expert opinions in fire cases, the man revealed to Parloff how he's able to control the examination:

> "After decades as an expert witness, if you get really tired of a particular line of cross-examination, you can sometimes offer a response that is truthful and responsive but it's just slightly off target. And then hope that the cross-examiner follows you down that particular line so you can saw it off behind him."[33]

Mark Fuhrman used a variant of this technique to deflect questions asked by Gerald Uelman during the O.J. Simpson preliminary examination. Fuhrman not only mastered the body language of credibility (shrugs, smiles, and that special look and sound of candor that police officers develop after years of testifying), but he also was sharp enough to shift the focus of Uelman's examination to the area Fuhrman wanted to discuss.

The issue, as with the Vannatter excerpt we looked at earlier, concerns the warrantless entry by the officers into Simpson's house:

---

[33] Roger Parloff, *Triple Jeopardy* 247–248 (The American Lawyer/Little Brown & Co. 1996).

Q   Did you feel at that point you had probable cause that criminal activity had gone on at the Rockingham premises?

A   I think I was personally more concerned with somebody bleeding to death inside. I just came from the scene of an extremely brutal murder.

Q   All right. An extremely brutal murder six hours before.

A   Well, it was six hours before, but I just . . . I don't know how long it takes for someone to bleed to death.

Q   Well, did you hear anything from within the premises that gave you any reason to believe that there might be somebody bleeding to death inside the premises.

A   Yes. From all indications Mr. Simpson was not on a scheduled trip and there was supposed to be a live-in maid there all the time.

Let's look more closely at this paradigm example of a skillful witness leading a lawyer around by the nose:

Q   Did you feel at that point you had probable cause that criminal activity had gone on at the Rockingham premises?

[THIS IS A POOR QUESTION, BECAUSE IT DOES NOT START BACK EARLY ENOUGH. FUHRMAN CAN SAY "NO" AND GET AWAY WITH IT, JUST AS VANNATTER DID. BUT FUHRMAN IS AN EXTREMELY SKILLED WITNESS. HE DOES FAR MORE DAMAGE TO UELMAN THAN A SIMPLE "NO."]

A   I think I was personally more concerned with somebody bleeding to death inside. I just came from the scene of an extremely brutal murder.

[FUHRMAN DOESN'T ANSWER THE QUESTION. HE GLIDES OFF OF IT TO WHERE *HE* WANTS TO GO, AND UELMAN *FOLLOWS*.]

Q   All right. [UELMAN VALIDATES FUHRMAN'S RESPONSE WITH "ALL RIGHT."] An extremely brutal murder six hours before. [NOW UELMAN IS PLAYING FUHRMAN'S GAME.]

A   Well, it was six hours before, but I just . . . I don't know how long it takes for someone to bleed to death.

[FUHRMAN GLIDES AGAIN! THIS TIME HE LEADS UELMAN FURTHER DOWN THE ROAD FROM UELMAN'S ORIGINAL QUESTION, WHICH BY THIS TIME, EVERYONE, PROBABLY INCLUDING UELMAN, HAS FORGOTTEN.]

Q   Well, did you hear anything from within the premises that gave you any reason to believe that there might be somebody bleeding to death inside the premises.

[NOTE THAT UELMAN ASKS IF FUHRMAN "HEARD" ANYTHING FROM INSIDE SIMPSON'S HOUSE THAT INDICATED THAT IT MIGHT BE AN EMERGENCY, AND, THEREFORE, PERMIT THE OFFICERS TO ENTER WITHOUT A WARRANT. FUHRMAN IS NOT GOING TO BE SO LIMITED.]

A   Yes. From all indications Mr. Simpson was not on a scheduled trip and there was supposed to be a live-in maid there all the time.

[THIS IS A REMARKABLE PROPOSITION: BE AWAY FROM YOUR HOUSE, BUT NOT ON A SCHEDULED TRIP, HAVE A LIVE-IN MAID WHO IS OUT, LIVE SEVERAL MILES FROM WHERE A FORMER WIFE IS MURDERED, AND, *IPSO FACTO*, THERE IS REASON TO BELIEVE THAT SOMEONE IS BLEEDING TO DEATH IN YOUR HOUSE. YET, UELMAN NEVER CHALLENGED FUHRMAN ON THIS.]

What should have Uelman done? First, let me tell you what he should *not* have done (in addition to not doing what he actually did): He should not have, as most lawyers do, ask the judge for help. There are three reasons:

1. The judge may not be listening, and may ask the court reporter to read the question and answer. This interrupts your momentum and thread.

2. Whether listening or not, the judge may respond this way to your request for help:

    Counsel: Would the court please direct the witness to answer the question.

    The Court: I believe that he has answered the question, counselor. Please move on.

3. If the judge grants your request, you still lose. As part of your persona as the truth-giver in the courtroom, you need to appear to be in control. Those in control do not have to ask for help, they solve their own problems.

When faced with a witness who does not answer the question, or who decides to toss something over the transom that he or she believes will hurt your case, **just repeat the question word-for-word**; do not ask the court reporter to read it back (this takes too long, and court reporters do not read with the emphasis and authority that you should bring to the examination):

> Q   Did you feel at that point you had probable cause that criminal activity had gone on at the Rockingham premises?
>
> A   I think I was personally more concerned with somebody bleeding to death inside. I just came from the scene of an extremely brutal murder.
>
> Q   Did you feel at that point you had probable cause that criminal activity had gone on at the Rockingham premises?

Another example:

> Q   When you first saw the red car, it was waiting at the light?
>
> A   Yeah. And the driver, your client, was soused. I could see it.
>
> Q   When you first saw the red car, it was waiting at the light?

Experience shows that you may have to repeat the question *verbatim* two times before the witness finally either responds or omits the extraneous matters. All this time, the jury sees that the witness is being not only uncooperative, but is also a partisan for the other side. This helps you.

   2.   **The witness who equivocates.**

This happens all the time. A witness responds with "I don't really remember" to your question when it is clear that he or she should remember. Another example from the Simpson criminal trial. Johnnie Cochran is examining police detective Ronald Phillips:

> Q   You told Mr. Simpson, according to your statement, that uh ... you gave him your name, is that correct?
>
> A   Yes sir.
>
> Q   You told him that "we had to relate some bad information" to him. Is that correct?

A   That's correct.

Q   At that point, when you said you had to relate some bad information to him, did you preface it by saying "your children are all right, Mr. Simpson"? Remember saying that to him?

A   The children were brought up later in the conversation.

Q   No, I'm asking you now when you said "I've got some bad information for you, but your children are all right," did you say that in an early point in the conversation?

A   I don't recall that.

Q   Is it possible that you said "your children are all right," words to that effect?

A   It's extremely possible that I could have said it, I just don't recall saying it.

Q   All right. I understand, I understand. It's been some time, right?

Notice how, like Uelman, Cochran validates the detective's equivocation by saying "all right" and "I understand, I understand."

The solution to the problem of the equivocating witness is the following three-step, which I first learned from Steve Saltzburg:

1. Q   The car was red?

    A   I really don't remember?

2. Q   Well, was it red or not?

    A   I said that I don't remember.

3. Q   As you sit here today, are you prepared to swear under oath that the car was not red?

The witness must answer "no." The skeleton of the three-step is:

1. Q It was "A"?

2. Q Well was it "A" or "B"?

3. Q As you sit here today, are you prepared to swear under oath that it was not "A"?

Don't omit the critical second step ("Well was it 'A' or 'B'?") because this locks in the witness and compels the answer to the final question.

Let's apply the three-step to Cochran's cross-examination of Detective Phillips. I've put the added material in italics:

Q You told Mr. Simpson, according to your statement, that uh . . . you gave him your name, is that correct?

A Yes sir.

Q You told him that "we had to relate some bad information" to him. Is that correct?

A That's correct.

Q At that point, when you said you had to relate some bad information to him, did you preface it by saying "your children are all right, Mr. Simpson"? Remember saying that to him?

A The children were brought up later in the conversation.

Q No, I'm asking you now when you said "I've got some bad information for you, but your children are all right," did you say that in an early point in the conversation?

A I don't recall that.

Q *Well, did you say "I've got some bad information for you, but your children are all right" in the early part of that conversation or did you not say that in the early part of your conversation?*

A *I said that I don't remember.*

Q As you sit here today, are you prepared to swear under oath that you did not say that in the early part of the conversation?

A "no" answer is compelled, and the jury—believing that you *really know* what happened—will infer that the witness did say "I've got some bad information for you, but your children are all right."

3. **The witness who testifies contrary to what he or she has said in the past.**

This situation is the lawyer's dream, because it permits the lawyer to strut his or her stuff by impeaching a witness in front of an appreciative audience of clients, family, and friends. The problem is that most lawyers don't do it the right way. It's as if they are practicing law in the 19th Century, when the Rule in Queen Anne's case governed, and a lawyer could not impeach a witness with a prior inconsistent statement unless the lawyer first showed the statement to the witness. Rule 613(a) of the Federal Rules of Evidence and its state counterparts make this no longer necessary:

> Rule 613 **Prior Statements of Witnesses.**
> (a) *Examining witness concerning prior statement.* In examining a witness concerning a prior statement made by the witness, whether written or not, the statement need not be shown nor its contents disclosed to the witness at that time, but on request the same shall be shown or disclosed to opposing counsel.
>
> (b) *Extrinsic evidence of prior inconsistent statement of witness.* Extrinsic evidence of a prior inconsistent statement by a witness is not admissible unless the witness is afforded an opportunity to explain or deny the same and the opposite party is afforded an opportunity to interrogate the witness thereon, or the interests of justice otherwise require. This provision does not apply to admissions of a party opponent as defined in rule 801(d)(2).

Yet, lawyers routinely go through the following ritual when they impeach a witness with a prior inconsistent statement:

> Q Mr. Jones, on direct-examination you testified that the car was red. Now, do you remember giving a deposition in this case? Coming to my office, where we had a court reporter, like the

Q man sitting behind the machine here, and the plaintiff's lawyer and I asked you questions?

A Yes.

Q And do you remember that before we asked you questions, you raised your right hand and swore to tell the truth, as you did in this courtroom this morning?

A Yes.

Q And do you remember that I specifically told you that if you did not understand anything you should tell me, and that I would explain it to you?

A Yes.

Q Now, let me show you a copy of your deposition, and direct your attention to the open page, page 23, lines 15 through 20. Please read this to yourself and let me know when you are done.

As Herb Stern is fond of saying, the witness will stare at that page until he either dies or can think of some reason why he testified at the deposition that the car was green. Rule 613 and its state equivalents permit the following more streamlined and powerful approach:

Q Mr. Jones, today you testified that the car was red. Yet, when you appeared in my office for your deposition you testified under oath that the car was green. Your Honor, I offer page 23, lines 15 through 20 into evidence both to show that he is not telling the truth today, and to prove that the car was, as he earlier testified, green. I am handing a copy of that page to opposing counsel.

Let's analyze this powerful impeachment phrase by phrase.

1. Rule 613(a) permits the first sentence: "Mr. Jones, today you testified that the car was red. Yet, when you appeared in my office for your deposition you testified under oath that the car was green."

2. Rule 32(a) of the Federal Rules of Civil Procedure and its state counterparts permit the first part of the second

sentence: "Your Honor, I offer page 23, lines 15 through 20 into evidence . . ." This rule provides:

> **Rule 32. Use of Depositions in Court Proceedings.**
> (a) Use of Depositions. At the trial or upon the hearing of a motion or an interlocutory proceeding, any part or all of a deposition, so far as admissible under the rules of evidence applied as though the witness were then present and testifying, may be used against any party who was present or represented at the taking of the deposition or who had reasonable notice thereof, in accordance with any of the following provisions:
>
> (1) Any deposition may be used by any party for the purpose of contradicting or impeaching the testimony of deponent as a witness, or for any other purpose permitted by the Federal Rules of Evidence.

3. Rule 32(a) of the Federal Rules of Civil Procedure and its state counterparts permit the second part of the second sentence: "to show that he is not telling the truth today."

4. The witness's testimony at the deposition "was given under oath subject to the penalty of perjury at a . . . deposition." It is thus admissible for the substantive purpose of proving the truth of the assertion, by virtue of Rule 801(d)(1)(A) of the Federal Rules of Evidence and its state counterparts. This rule provides:

> Rule 801(d) *Statements which are not hearsay.* A statement is not hearsay if
> (1) *Prior statement by witness.* The declarant testifies at the trial or hearing and is subject to cross-examination concerning the statement, and the statement is
> (A) inconsistent with the declarant's testimony, and was given under oath subject to the penalty of perjury at a trial, hearing, or other proceeding, or in a deposition

Thus, the statement is admissible "to prove that the car was, as he earlier testified, green"

5. The examiner is entitled to have the prior inconsistent deposition testimony received for both purposes, and to have the jury instructed as to each purpose. First, a party is entitled to have the jury instructed about the applicable law. When evidence is admissible for several purposes, a party is entitled to have the jury told about the permissible purposes. Second, this is the underlying rationale of Rule 105 of the Federal Rules of Evidence and its state counterparts, even though these rules are usually invoked by opposing parties seeking to limit the scope of the jury's consideration of certain evidence. FRE 105 provides:

Rule 105 **Limited Admissibility.**
When evidence which is admissible as to one party or for one purpose but not admissible as to another party or for another purpose is admitted, the court, upon request, shall restrict the evidence to its proper scope and instruct the jury accordingly.

6. The last sentence, "I am handing a copy of that page to opposing counsel" more than satisfies the requirements of FRE 613(a) because opposing counsel is being given a copy without making the "request" anticipated by that rule.

If the prior inconsistent statement was not "given under oath subject to the penalty of perjury at a trial, hearing, or other proceeding, or in a deposition," it is not admissible as substantive non-hearsay under FRE 801(d)(1)(A), but—whether written or oral—can still come in for impeachment purposes, as is recognized by FRE 613.[34] If this is the case, the impeachment rubric is as follows:

Q   Mr. Jones, I show you what's been marked as Exhibit 45, a copy of which I am also giving to opposing counsel, and ask you whether it is a letter that you wrote to your landlord two and one half years ago?

A   Yes, it is.

---

[34] *See also* 3 Stephen A. Saltzburg, Michael M. Martin, & Daniel J. Capra *Federal Rules of Evidence Manual* 1227–1228 (Michie 6th ed. 1994) and the new edition, 3 Stephen A. Saltzburg, Michael M. Martin & Daniel L. Capra, *Federal Rules of Evidence Manual* 1136 (Lexis 7th ed. 1998).

Q   Now, Mr. Jones, today you testified that the car was red. Yet, you wrote in this letter to your landlord that the car was green. Your Honor, I offer that letter into evidence to show that he is not telling the truth today.

If you have an oral inconsistent statement by the witness, you offer the statement at the time the impeaching witness testifies:

Q   Mr. Rogers, you are Mr. Jones's landlord?

A   Yes.

Q   And shortly after the accident that took place in front of your building, you talked to him about the accident?

A   Yes.

Q   And did he say that the car that hit Susie was a red car or a green car?

A   He said it was a green car.

Q   Your Honor, Mr. Jones has testified that the car was red, and I offer Mr. Rogers's testimony that Mr. Jones told him that the car was green to prove that Mr. Jones is not telling the truth when he testified that the car was red.

As noted, FRE 105 requires the judge to instruct the jury about any limitations on their consideration of the evidence. In my view, this permits you to request that the prior inconsistent statement be received for impeachment purposes and that the jury be so told.

3. **The biased witness.**

Bias of a witness may always be shown; evidence of bias is never collateral.[35] To be really effective, however, the lawyer seeking to discredit a witness by proof of bias must lay the groundwork so that he or she can bring the jury aboard the train while it is still in the station.

---

[35]   *Davis v. Alaska*, 415 U.S. 308, 316–317 (1974).

For example, if you represent the plaintiff in a personal-injury action, and the defendant's insurance company has a stable of doctors whom they use to examine claimants, don't just point out that the physician is getting paid for both the examination and his or her testimony, but prove to the jury that the witness has a motive to shade that testimony.[36]

Let's look at the following scenario. Your client is seriously injured. The doctor retained by the insurance company says that the injuries are not as serious as you contend, and, what's more, that they were not caused by the accident. You take the physician's deposition and, among other things, you seek: 1) the number of times the doctor has been retained by the insurance company; 2) the total amount of money that the doctor has received from the insurance company; 3) the percentage of the doctor's total income that is attributable to the money the doctor has received from the insurance company. This evidence is all relevant to the doctor's bias, and you must fight any attempt by the insurance company's lawyer to prevent discovery on this issue.[37] Once you get the information you can use it at trial.

---

[36] As we have seen so far, lawyers do many things in the courtroom that hurt their cases, and they do them because, in essence, that's what everyone does. One of the great puzzlements is why any plaintiff's lawyer would refer to the examination of his or her client by the insurance company's doctor as an "independent medical examination," or, as lawyers love to refer to it, the "IME." I feel sorry for the clients of any lawyer who thus plants the imprimatur of "independence" on the opposing side's "hired gun."

Some jurisdictions permit a defendant's insurance company to be joined as a defendant. In those jurisdictions that do not permit the joinder of the defendant's insurance company, the bias of a witness paid by the insurance company may still be exposed if the jurisdiction follows Rule 411 of the Federal Rules of Evidence. This rule provides:

Rule 411 Liability Insurance.
Evidence that a person was or was not insured against liability is not admissible upon the issue whether the person acted negligently or otherwise wrongfully. This rule does not require the exclusion of evidence of insurance against liability when offered for another purpose, such as proof of agency, ownership, or control, *or bias or prejudice of a witness*. (Emphasis added.)

[37] Significantly, unless the doctor is employed by the insurance company, as opposed to being an independent contractor hired by the insurance company, the insurance company's lawyer cannot represent both the interests of the defendant and those of the doctor.

In doing the "probative value" versus "prejudice" balancing required by Rule 403 of the Federal Rules of Evidence and its state counterparts, the trial judge is limited to the issues in the lawsuit, and may not consider matters that only affect the doctor. If these matters (reputation, privacy, etc.) are important to the doctor, the doctor has a right to be heard, either by counsel or *pro se*. The lawsuit is between the plaintiff and the defendant, and bias of the doctor is a legitimate area of inquiry.

AN ILLUSTRATION:

Assume that over the last ten years, the doctor earned $450,000 from the insurance company. Last year, she earned $55,000. So far this year, she has received $35,000. Over the ten years, the money the doctor received from the insurance company amounted to thirty-five percent of her earned income. Last year, the figure was forty percent.

The defendant calls the doctor to the witness stand. You have two choices. First, you know that the defense lawyer is going to try to "remove the sting" by bringing out in his direct-examination how much the doctor received from the insurance company.

Your first choice is to wait until he does that, and then cross-examine on the issue.

The second choice is to try to let the judge permit you to *voir dire* on the bias issue. Once the defense lawyer either asks the court to declare the doctor an "expert," or asks a question that calls for an expert opinion, you have the right to *voir dire* the witness on her qualifications. If I were representing the plaintiff, I would try to include in the *voir dire* the following questions on the doctor's bias so as to exploit the power of primacy. The judge, of course, may not let you—it's a discretionary call. But you should, nevertheless, try.

The following are three ways to handle the issues of the doctor's bias. The first example is if you are permitted to do it on *voir dire*. The second example is if you are not. The third is the way I would bring out the facts surrounding the doctor's payment if I were the defense lawyer,

1. Q Doctor, in addition to your private practice, you also take referrals from the ABC insurance company?

    A I do independent medical examinations for them, yes.

Rule 403 of the Federal Rules of Evidence provides:

Rule 403 Exclusion of Relevant Evidence on Grounds of Prejudice, Confusion, or Waste of Time.

Although relevant, evidence may be excluded if its probative value is substantially outweighed by the danger of unfair prejudice, confusion of the issues, or misleading the jury, or by considerations of undue delay, waste of time, or needless presentation of cumulative evidence.

Q   You examine for the insurance company those people who have been hurt and whom the insurance company wants you to examine?

A   I do.

Q   You get paid for this?

A   Yes.

Q   Who pays you?

A   The insurance company.

Q   And the insurance company tries to pay as little money as it can?

A   I think they try to be fair.

Q   Well, they certainly don't want to have to pay out more than they have to?

A   That's right. That's why they send the people to me for me to examine them. To see if their claims are legitimate.

Q   The insurance company doesn't want to pay more out in claims than it has to?

A   Yes, that's right. That's why they want me to examine them.

Q   And how much the insurance company will ultimately have to pay may very well depend on what you have to say about how injured a person is and whether the jury believes your testimony?

A   Yes.

Q   How does that make your examination of Mr. Jones any more "independent" than the examinations of Mr. Jones by his family physician, or for that matter, expert physicians whom we have paid to examine Mr. Jones?

A   I try to be fair. [YOU DO NOT CARE WHAT HER ANSWER IS; YOU ARE MAKING YOUR ARGUMENT TO THE JURY.]

Q   Doctor, last year the insurance company paid you $55,000 to examine hurt people?

A   Yes. I'm entitled to make a living.

Q   And that $55,000 was forty percent of your income last year?

A   Yes.

Q   And over the last ten years the insurance company paid you $450,000?

A   Yes.

Q   And that $450,000 over the last ten years was thirty-five percent of your income?

A   Yes.

Q   So last year, you received more from the insurance company as a percentage of your total income than you did in each of the preceding ten years?

A   Yes.

Q   Doctor, when did you examine Mr. Jones, the plaintiff in this case?

A   Last year.

Q   That was the year the insurance company paid you forty percent of your income?

A   Yes.

Q   Doctor, do you like the money that the insurance company pays you?

A   I don't know what you mean "like." I work for a living and I like being paid.

Q   Well, doctor, would you rather have the money from the insurance company or would you rather not have it?

A   I'd rather have it, of course.

Q   Would you, or would you not, want to jeopardize that stream of income, which, as we've seen, last year amounted to forty percent of your income?

A   I call them as I see them.

Q   Would you, or would you not, want to jeopardize that stream of income, which, as we've seen, last year amounted to forty percent of your income?

A   I wouldn't shade my opinions just to get their money, no.

Q   Would you do anything to risk having that stream of income cut off?

A   I might, if they asked me to do anything unethical or illegal.

Q   How many injured people did you see last year under your arrangement with the insurance company?

A   Fifty or sixty.

Q   So you received approximately $1,000 for each injured person?

A   Yes, on the average.

Q   And you testified in court in how many of the fifty or sixty cases?

A   Twenty-one so far.

Q   There are other cases pending?

A   Yes.

Q   And in each of those twenty-one cases you testified that the injured person was not as seriously injured as he or she said?

A   Yes.

Q   All of them?

A   Yes.

Q   And I take it that you are going to tell this jury that Mr. Jones isn't as badly hurt as he says, either?

A   I think he's exaggerated his injuries.

Q   Have you ever testified in a case in which this insurance company was involved where you testified that the plaintiff did not exaggerate his or her injuries?

A   No.

Q   And that's because you have a stream of income, $55,000 last year, to protect? [OF COURSE, SHE'S GOING TO DENY THIS. BUT YOU DON'T CARE. YOU ARE MAKING YOUR ARGUMENT TO THE JURY (AND YOU HAVE A REASONABLE BASIS FOR ASKING THE QUESTION).]

A   Absolutely not.

Q   How much have they paid you this year, so far?

A $35,000.

Q   And, after you testify that Mr. Jones isn't as badly hurt as he says he is, there will be more money that the insurance company is going to pay you?

A   I resent that implication.

Q   Well, the insurance company paid you $55,000 last year, and this year you're only up to $35,000. Do you or do you not hope that the insurance company gives you more than $35,000 this year?

A   Yes, obviously I would like that.

Q   And you expect it?

A   I'm not a fortune teller.

Q   Do you expect to get more than $35,000 from the insurance company this year?

A   Yes.

Q   I have no further questions on *voir dire*, Your Honor.

If the judge does not permit you to ask questions about bias on *voir dire*, and the defense lawyer has already "removed the sting" before you can cross-examine, I suggest the following line of questions (I've left out the answers this time).

2. Q   Doctor, you admitted on direct-examination that last year the insurance company paid you $55,000 to examine hurt people?

    Q   And you admitted that that $55,000 was forty percent of your income last year?

    Q   So that means that the insurance company accounted for forty percent of your income last year?

    Q   And you further revealed that over the last ten years the insurance company paid you $450,000?

    Q   And that $450,000 over the last ten years was thirty-five percent of your income?

    Q   So, for the last ten years you've received thirty-five percent of your income from the insurance company?

    Q   In fact, you received more from the insurance company as a percentage of your total income last year than you did in the last ten years?

    Q   Doctor, do you like the money that the insurance company pays you?

    Q   Would you rather have the money from the insurance company or would you rather not have it?

Q   Would you, or would you not, want to jeopardize that stream of income, which, as we've seen, last year amounted to forty percent of your income?

Q   How many injured people did you see last year under your arrangement with the insurance company?

Q   And the insurance company tries to pay as little money as it can?

Q   And how much the insurance company will ultimately have to pay may very well depend on what you have to say about how injured a person is and whether a jury believes your testimony?

Et cetera. Although not as effective as if you could have gone first, this cross-examination builds off of the direct-examiner's "removal of the sting"—especially by the use of the concepts of "admit" and "reveal." Note: given the power of primacy, you should, of course, argue all of this in your opening statement, where you get to go first:

> Ladies and gentlemen, I am going to prove to you that the doctor they will bring in here to tell you that Mr. Jones is malingering has been on the insurance company's payroll for the last ten years. Indeed, she will admit to you that over the last ten years she's received thirty-five percent of her income from the insurance company. What's more, last year, the year she examined Mr. Jones on behalf of the insurance company, forty percent of her income was from the insurance company. Et cetera.

Now let's look at a way of handling this issue on direct-examination if you represent the defendant. We must do more than "remove the sting," which, typically, involves bringing out the fact of payment and, perhaps, the amount. I would first, of course, make the doctor a sympathetic person, in the ways that we've earlier discussed.

3. Q   Doctor, do you have a private practice?

    A   Yes.

    Q   Do you treat patients in that private practice?

    A   Yes.

Q   Do you also accept referrals from the ABC Insurance Company to examine people who claim that they've been injured in accidents?

A   Yes.

Q   How long have you accepted referrals from the ABC Insurance Company?

A   For the last ten years or so.

Q   Do you get paid for that?

A   Yes.

Q   Do you get paid when you treat patients in your private practice?

A   Yes.

Q   Having examined people who claim that they've been injured and have filed lawsuits, have you found some of the complaints legitimate?

A   Yes.

Q   Have some people been, in fact, very badly injured.

A   Yes.

Q   And in those cases have you told that to the ABC Insurance Company?

A   Yes. [THIS IS NOT INCONSISTENT WITH THE FACT THAT SHE HAS ALWAYS TESTIFIED AGAINST THE PLAINTIFF. THE INSURANCE COMPANY ONLY GOES TO COURT WHEN THEY BELIEVE THAT THE DAMAGES ARE OVERSTATED OR THERE IS NO LIABILITY.]

Q   Are you asked to testify in those cases?

A   No.

Q   In what cases are you asked to testify?

A   In those that I think the person is exaggerating his injuries or where the accident wasn't a cause of those injuries.

Q   So you have also examined people who, in your professional opinion, have exaggerated their injuries?

A   Yes.

Q   Based on your experience, doctor, how long will an insurance company be able to stay in business if it does not try to screen the valid claims from claims that might not be valid?

A   Not very long.

Q   Putting aside for a moment government programs that might step in to help, if an insurance company goes out of business will it be able to pay the legitimate claims?

A   No.

Q   As far as you know, are you the only doctor in this community who takes referrals from the ABC Insurance Company to examine and screen persons who claim to be injured?

A   I am not. There are others.

Q   How much did the ABC Insurance Company pay you last year to examine people who claimed to be injured?

A $55,000.

Q   And was that a high or a low percentage of your income?

A   It was forty percent of what I earned last year.

Q   Does that mean that if you did not receive any referrals from the ABC Insurance Company last year that you would have earned $55,000 less?

A   No. Not at all.

Q   Why is that?

A   On a per-hour basis, the insurance company cases pay less than I receive for private patients whom I treat.

Q   Would you have earned more or less money last year if you did not accept any cases from the ABC Insurance Company.

A   Oh more.

Q   Is that because there are only a limited number of hours in each day?

A   Yes. [LEADING? SURE. BUT SO WHAT? RULE 611(C) OF THE FEDERAL RULES OF EVIDENCE AND ITS STATE COUNTERPARTS PERMIT LEADING TO DEVELOP THE WITNESS'S TESTIMONY. TRUE A JUDGE MAY SUSTAIN THE OBJECTION. IF SO, YOU CAN ASK THE QUESTIONS AS SUGGESTED IN THE FOOTNOTE.][38]

Q   Then why, doctor, do you take the cases if you could earn more money if you did not take them?

A   The billing is simpler, and we get paid sooner than we would from most of my private patients' reimbursement plans.

Q   Is it a hassle to deal with those reimbursement plans?

A   Most of the time it is.

Q   Is it a hassle dealing with the ABC Insurance Company?

A   No.

---

[38]   Don't give in. Rather, back up, pick up the thread at an earlier point, and take the line to the question where the judge sustained the objection:

Q Doctor, how many hours are there in a day.

A Twenty-four.

Q Can there ever be more?

A No.

Q Are the number of hours in a day limited or unlimited?

Q Could you earn more money if you were willing to put up with the hassle of dealing with the reimbursement plans of your patients?

A Oh yes.

Q Why don't you?

A It's not worth the hassle.

Q Doctor, would you ever misrepresent a diagnosis or shade an opinion to remain in the good graces of the ABC Insurance Company?

A Absolutely not.

Q Has anyone over at the ABC Company ever, directly or indirectly, asked you to pull any punches, to shade an opinion, or testify to anything other than your honest opinion?

A No.

Q In fact, what did they tell you when you were first contacted ten years ago by them?

A "Call it like you see them." That's what they said.

Q Have you done that?

A Yes.

XXVII.
THE CROSS-EXAMINATION MAXIM

During my nine years as a trial judge, I repeatedly saw lawyers struggling with cross-examination. They'd badger the witnesses, as if to brow-beat them into agreeing with the lawyers' questions. More often than not, the lawyers would get flustered while the witnesses remained calm. All too frequently, the cross-examiner would just go over the witnesses' direct-examination testimony, thereby burnishing that testimony into the minds of the jurors. All in all, the cross-examination was usually pitiful. All this can be avoided if you follow this maxim:

The cross-examination of every witness must obey one of the following rules:

1. The jury knows the answer before the witness responds.

This is the same dynamic that we discussed in the chapters on direct-examination. The mechanisms are the same.

2. The answer cannot hurt you, even though you do not know what it is.

Lawyers are generally told to never ask a question the answer to which they do not know. This is silly. As we have seen, a lawyer in the courtroom is not seeking information—he or she is making an argument to the jury. There will be many questions that advance your argument irrespective of what the answers are. My favorite example comes from Herb Stern's *Trying Cases to Win* series.

The 19th Century British playwright Oscar Wilde was having an affair with Lord Alfred Douglas, the son of the most macho man in Victorian England, the Marquis of Queensbury, the boxing aficionado. Queensbury was upset about this, and sent to Wilde a note accusing him of homosexuality. Wilde got terrible legal advice. He sued Queensbury for criminal libel. Truth, of course, was a defense.

During the libel trial, Queensbury's lawyer, Edward Carson, asked Wilde on cross-examination whether he had ever kissed a young lad who had once worked for Wilde. The lawyer did not know the answer. But the answer, whether it was "yes" or "no," could not hurt. The answer, however, was a gem, and reflects one of those moments that reverberate through the ages—much like Willie Mays's great going-away catch. This was Wilde's answer: "Oh dear no. He was a peculiarly plain boy. He was unfortunately extremely ugly. I pitied him for it."[39]

---

[39] 3 Herbert J. Stern, *Trying Cases to Win* 3-15–3-16 (Wiley 1993).

3. You have material (deposition testimony, for example) that will punish the witness if the witness answers in a way other than you want.

We've discussed extensively the techniques of impeachment in the preceding chapter. The important point to remember with this and the other two rules of the cross-examination maxim is that you are making your argument through the witness to the jury—you're not trying to persuade the witness to agree with you. If the jury answers your question the way you want, it does not matter how the witness responds. Indeed, you should frame your questions so that they are **statements** ("You saw the car careen through the light?"); remember, the jury believes that you know what really happened. Avoid the *static words* of "right?" "isn't that correct?" "true?" and "isn't that right?" They add nothing, are annoying, and appear to be bullying.[40]

XXVIII.
WHY IRVING YOUNGER WAS WRONG

Before we look at an annotated cross-examination of Al Haig in the *Rock* file by St. Louis lawyer Ben Clark, let's spend a moment to discuss Irving Younger's *Ten Commandments of Cross-Examination*. When I was in New York, I met Younger several times. He was a scholarly state judge in New York, and was a charismatic teacher of trial-advocacy. Unfortunately for generations of disciples, he's wrong on some critical points.

These are Younger's famous "Ten Commandments", and I have placed check-marks next to those with which I agree, and +s next to those with which I disagree:

1.	Be Brief.	✓
2.	Use Plain Words.	✓
3.	Use Only Leading Questions.	+
4.	Be Prepared.	✓
5.	Listen.	✓

---

[40] The introductory phrase that is commonly used by some lawyers, "Will you agree with me . . . " plays off of the jurors' belief that the lawyer knows what actually happened. In my view, however, this phrase crosses the ethical line and *does* purport to express directly the lawyer's personal knowledge. I do not recommend it for that reason, although it can be powerful if sparingly used.

6.	Do Not Quarrel.		✓
7.	Avoid Repetition.		✓
8.	Disallow Witness Explanation.		+
9.	Limit Questioning.		+
10.	Save for Summation.[41]		+

The four commandments marked with a + are counterproductive at best and suicidal at worst. Let's see why.

Commandment Number Three, directs that the cross-examiner "Use Only Leading Questions." Younger is an absolutist on this—he brooks no dissent. This is how he puts it in the monograph: "The third commandment is that you should never ask anything but leading questions on cross-examination."[42]

This is bad advice. Although leading questions can be a useful tool on cross-examination, non-leading questions are often more effective, as we will see in the cross-examination of Al Haig done by Ben Clark. The important point is not whether to lead or not to lead, but to effectively make your argument to the jury through the witness. If you follow the **cross-examination maxim** discussed in Chapter XXVII, your cross-examination will be powerful and effective.

Commandment Numbers Eight, "Disallow Witness Explanation," and Nine, "Limit Questioning," say essentially the same thing (I suspect that Younger did this to reach the magic number "Ten"). If followed, they condemn you to the same result: advocacy suicide. To either gag the witness when he or she wants to explain, or not ask what Younger calls "the one question too many," undercuts your position in the courtroom as the truth-giver. Think about it, if there is either an explanation or an answer to that "one question too many" it will certainly come out on re-direct. Wouldn't you rather hear the explanation or answer when you are standing and can deal with it, rather than when you are sitting down?

Younger's example in support of this advice reveals the folly of these commandments. He writes:

---

[41] Irving Younger, *The Art of Cross-Examination* 21–32 (A.B.A. 1976)

[42] *Id.* at 23.

"A classic story illustrates the one-question-too-many problem. The case is a criminal prosecution for atrocious assault or assault in the first degree. The theory of the prosecution is that the defendant and the victim got into a fight. In the course of the fight, the defendant got his teeth around the victim's nose and bit it off. Horrible, but it is possible. The teeth are very sharp, the jaws the strongest voluntary muscle in the body and the nose is only cartilage. One can bite it off.

"The prosecution rests upon the testimony of an eyewitness who testifies that it happened just that way. The defense lawyer cross-examines:

Question: Where were the defendant and the victim when the fight broke out?

Answer: In the middle of a field.

Question: Where were you?

Answer: On the edge of the field.

Question: What were you doing?

Answer: Bird watching.

Question: Where were the birds?

Answer: In the trees.

Question: Where were the trees?

Answer: On the edge of the field.

Question: Were you looking at the birds?

Answer: Yes.

Question: So your back was to the people fighting?

Answer: Yes.

"Now what do you do? You stop and sit down. And what will you argue in summation? He could not have seen it. His back was to them. You have challenged perception. Instead, you ask one question too many:

> Question: Well, if your back was to them, how can you say that the defendant bit off the victim's nose?

And the answer: Well, I saw him spit it out.

"That is the kind of answer you will get every time you ask the one question too many."[43]

Do you really believe that the prosecutor is not going to ask that question on re-direct if you do not elicit it on cross-examination? And where will you want to hide when she does?

Younger's other example in support of these two commandments similarly displays the foolishness of his advice. He relates the story of how Abraham Lincoln, representing a young man accused of killing the victim during a fight, had established that the eyewitness was in a thick stand of beech trees at 11:00 p.m. and was one-hundred and fifty feet from the fight:

> "Question: Did you have a candle?
>
> Answer: No, what would I want a candle for?
>
> Question: How could you see from distances of a hundred and fifty feet or more without a candle at eleven o'clock at night?
>
> Answer: The moon was shining real bright."

Younger's Eighth and Ninth Commandments dictate that you not ask the last question. But, again, wouldn't you prefer to deal with the explanation during cross-examination than have it elicited on re-direct, irrespective of whether or not there was a moon that night? As with the nose-bite-off case, what credibility would you have as the truth-giver in the courtroom after you sat down in the face of such an obvious explanation without bringing it out yourself?[44]

---

[43] *Id.* at 30-31.

[44] Younger relates the legend that Lincoln saved the day by producing a counterfeit almanac to show that there was no moon that night. *Id.* at 28–30.

Commandment Number Ten, "Save for Summation," decrees obscurity rather than clarity, and assumes that jurors have the interest, tenacity, and clarity of purpose to not only keep an open mind until the end of the case but also to remember some obscure point until you explain its significance. This flies in the face of all reason and common sense. This is how Younger explains his rationale:

> "You have worked out the mode of cross-examination so that it is elegant and artistic, buttressed by brief leading questions. The argument is overwhelming. There is only one element to be added to the picture. You are reasonably confident that when you ask that one question, you will know what is happening, but the jury will not know. The jury will not understand the significance of the question. Why? That is the way you want it to be. Why? They will pay attention. They will wonder about the question for the rest of the trial. If they wonder about it, they will remember it; if they remember it, you are halfway toward persuading them.
>
> "The temptation, however, is to explain it all on the cross-examination. How do you explain it? By asking the witness the one question too many, and the force of the impeachment will disappear. You must save it [for summation]."[45]

This ignores the most important tools of persuasion: primacy, clarity, simplification, and repetition; it ignores common sense. If the jury does "not understand the significance of the question," the jury will remember neither the question nor the answer. When the "clever" lawyer finally explains the mystery in summation it will be too late because the jurors will have already made up their minds.

XXIX.
CROSS-EXAMINATION: AN ANNOTATED DEMONSTRATION

The following is a transcription of a skillful cross-examination by St. Louis lawyer Ben Clark at the Trial Advocacy Institute at the University of Virginia program. It is the *Rock* file again, and Ben is cross-examining Al Haig. Notice how hardly any of Clark's questions are "leading" in the traditional sense. Yet, they are controlling. Haig, who is played by a lawyer

---

[45] *Id.* at 31.

attending the Institute, must answer the way he does, and he does so begrudgingly, because he knows that the jurors already know the answers—he must conform his testimony to what they know.

This is the excerpt from Clark's longer cross-examination.

Q   Mr. Rock had nearly three times as much postal experience as Ms. Climber? Correct?

[THERE IS NO NEED FOR THE "CORRECT." IT IS MORE EFFECTIVE TO MAKE STATEMENTS, USING THE INFLECTION IN YOUR VOICE TO INDICATE THAT IT IS A QUESTION. BY MAKING STATEMENT-QUESTIONS, YOU ARE MAKING YOUR ARGUMENT TO THE JURORS IN ITS MOST FORCEFUL FORM, AND YOU AVOID THE "STATIC" OF "RIGHT?" "ISN'T THAT CORRECT?" "TRUE?" AND "ISN'T THAT RIGHT?"]

A   Yes, that's correct.

Q   He had eleven years more experience?

[THIS IS THE WAY THAT IT SHOULD BE PHRASED.]

A   Approximately.

Q   Who had had more different positions within the postal service, Mr. Rock or Ms. Climber?

[THIS QUESTION IS NOT "LEADING." YET, THE ANSWER IS COMPELLED, BECAUSE CLARK HAS THE POSTAL SERVICE FORMS TO BRING HAIG TO HEEL IF HE TRIES TO STRAY.]

A   Mr. Rock had. I'm not entirely certain that some of those positions still exist, with restructuring and the like.

[NOW HAIG IS "SELLING" AND IS HURTING HIS CASE.]

Q   They existed at the time he held them?

A   Yes.

Q   In fact, he held three times as many different postal positions than Ms. Climber during his career, did he not?

A   Yes.

Q   He was a General Supervisor of Mails?

A   Yes, at the time he applied for the position. He still is.

Q   What was he before that?

A   Prior to that he was a Supervisor of Mails.

Q   How about before that?

A   A foreman for Platform Operations.

Q   And before that?

A   A foreman for Mails.

Q   And before that?

A   Well, a Distribution Clerk.

Q   And before that?

A   A regular clerk.

[THIS IS A GREAT SERIES OF NON-"LEADING" QUESTIONS, FORCING HAIG TO LIST NORMAN ROCK'S POSITIONS AND EXPERIENCE.]

Q   This was all on the face of the 991, which you considered? Correct?

A   Yes, it is.

[THE INFERENCE HERE IS THAT HAIG IGNORED ALL OF THIS, EVEN THOUGH HE HAD IT IN FRONT OF HIM. IN A FEW QUESTIONS, CLARK WILL HAMMER THE POINT HOME.]

Q   Had he ever been detailed into other job assignments during his career with the postal service?

A   Yes. He had been detailed as a General Supervisor of Mails and a Supervisor of Mails, two positions he was later promoted to. Rather like Ms. Climber in this case.

Q   And before that . . . strike that. Which of the two had more supervisory experience?

A   Mr. Rock.

Q   For that matter, which of the two had more non-supervisory experience?

A   Mr. Rock.

Q   Does the 991 have a place to list training received at governmental facilities?

A   Yes, it does.

Q   Who had more of that sort of training, Mr. Rock or Ms. Climber?

A   Uh, Mr. Rock had approximately one month more.

Q   He had twice as much more, didn't he?

A   Yes.

Q   Does the form 991, which you considered, have a place for education?

A   Yes, it does.

Q   Had either Mr. Rock or Ms. Climber concluded a college degree?

A   Mr. Rock has a completed college degree. A Bachelor of Arts in Business Administration.

Q   And Ms. Climber has not? Has she?

A   She is working toward a degree in communications and is three-quarters of the way.

Q   Has she completed it?

A   She will.

[AGAIN, HAIG IS "SELLING."]

Q   Had she completed it at the time she applied for Tour Superintendent?

A   No, she had not.

Q   In your opinion, as a person who interviews for these posts, is a person's experience important in determining whether they should be promoted.

A   It's one of many factors.

Q   Is a person's experience important in determining whether they should be promoted?

A   It's one of many factors.

Q   Is it an important factor?

A   Not as important as some others.

Q   Is their training important?

A   Training is important. Basically, it depends first off what the position they are applying for is. Not every position has the same job description.

Q   Are you suggesting that experience and training are not important for some positions within the postal service?

A   No, they are important for some positions. (Laughter)

[THE AUDIENCE AT THE INSTITUTE APPRECIATED THE BOX INTO WHICH CLARK PUT HAIG.]

Q   Can you name a position that they're not important for?

[GREAT QUESTION! DOES CLARK REALLY CARE WHAT THE ANSWER IS? OF COURSE NOT. THIS IS ONE OF THOSE QUESTIONS THE ANSWER TO WHICH CANNOT HURT AND THE MERE ASKING ADVANCES YOUR ARGUMENT. THE LAWYER PLAYING THE ROLE OF HAIG PAUSED A LONG TIME BEFORE HE WAS ABLE TO COME UP WITH A RESPONSE TO THIS QUESTION. JURORS SEE THAT AND CONSIDER IT.]

A   They are more important for some positions than others.

Q   How about Tour Superintendent?

A   For Tour Superintendent, it is important to have a wide variety of skills. Particularly the ability to communicate well, the ability to manage crises with quick, definitive solutions at a moment's notice. Particularly on the late night tour, when the higher administrative personnel like myself are not in the office, and the Tour Superintendent is the highest-ranking person at the postal building.

Q   That's where experience and training comes to bear, doesn't it?

A   It also . . . that is part of it, yes.

[GOTCHA! BUT, HERE AGAIN, IT DOES NOT MATTER WHAT THE ANSWER IS. CLARK HAS ASKED A QUESTION SO POWERFUL IN THIS CONTEXT THAT NO ANSWER CAN HURT HIM.]

Q   Was education important in determining who should be promoted?

A   It depends on specifics types of education. Not every degree is helpful for every type of job.

Q   How about business administration in running a business?

A   It's helpful in running a business.

Q   Is the postal service a business?

A   Yes, but he wasn't running it.

Q   Well, had he been promoted to Tour Superintendent, he would have had a better shot at running it, wouldn't he?

A   Are you assuming more promotions?

Q   Let me ask you this. In all of these three areas: education, training, and experience, you could tell from the face of the 991 that Mr. Rock had a superior list of credentials, could you not? In those three areas.

A   Mr. Rock had more training. Mr. Rock had been with the postal service longer.

Ben Clark has made his points cleanly, powerfully, and efficiently. This a classic example of how to argue your case to the jury through the witness.

XXX.
SUMMATION

The summation, or the closing argument as it is also called, is, along with the cross-examination, a Hollywood favorite. It permits the screenwriter to condense a plot line in a dramatic, grabbing oration. Lawyers, too, love closing arguments. It permits them to wax eloquent about justice and injustice, about messages that need to be sent, and about the flag, apple pie, and the American way. More latitude is given to lawyers during closing-argument than during any other part of the trial. Thus, lawyers can reminisce with the jury about their childhood, their favorite teacher, their first love, almost anything. And trial lawyers, frustrated actors all, love it.

Lawyers' love of the closing argument is only one reason that this part of the trial is so popular. It's also popular because most lawyers believe that closing arguments change jurors' minds. Thus, these lawyers believe that one side can be losing—the evidence has persuaded the jurors that the other side should win—and a compelling closing argument will save the day. Indeed, we have seen that no lesser light than Irving Younger put so much stock in the power of the closing argument that he advised lawyers to keep their trial evidence—at least the point they are making on cross-examination—muddy and unclear. Respectfully, Younger and the others are wrong.

People credit closing arguments with so much power because that's what jurors focus on when they are interviewed after a trial. Jurors hear closing arguments last. Thus, under the psychological mechanism of "recency" they will naturally remember closing arguments the best. Additionally, closing arguments are more interesting than any other part of the trial.

Critical to our analysis, jurors will credit the winning lawyer's closing argument with having carried the day because *they were receptive to that argument before they even heard it.* In a word, they were already convinced by the opening statements and the evidence, and they embraced the closing argument that supported their conviction; it validated the conclusion they had already reached. This is the same psychology that we see at political conventions and rallies—a candidate's partisans will *love* their candidate's speech, and will actually report that they were persuaded by it. In fact, of course, they were persuaded by it because it reinforced their own conclusions.

Does all this mean that the closing argument is not important? No. Not at all. The closing argument is very important. But it is important for reasons that are different than those advanced by the conventional wisdom.

The closing argument is important because it gives to a lawyer's partisans on the jury—those jurors who are *already* persuaded by that lawyer's case—tools with which to persuade the other jurors once they start deliberations. This is why the burden of proof is so meaningful during the closing-argument stage of the trial, especially in criminal cases. It permits those jurors who believe that the defendant is innocent to argue to those jurors who believe that he or she is guilty that the government has not proven guilt beyond a reasonable doubt. But, and this is important, jurors will not make this argument unless they believe the defendant to be innocent.

One year, when I delivered the closing-argument lecture at the Trial Advocacy Institute in Virginia, I decided to try an experiment. For five days, the lawyers attending the program had heard faculty demonstrations on the *Rock* file. They were now going to hear a closing argument on behalf of Norman Rock (there was no closing argument for the postal service). I asked those in the group who would, at that moment, find for Rock to raise their hands. About half in the audience did. Then I asked those who would find for the postal service to raise their hands. Again, about half did.

After the vote, Robert Weinberg, a superb lawyer with the Washington, D.C., law firm of Williams & Connelly, delivered one of the most stirring closing arguments I have heard anywhere—either in the courtroom or on the silver screen. After Weinberg's incredible performance, I took another vote. The audience split as before. I then asked those who had changed their minds to raise their hands. Out of approximately 150 lawyers, fewer than five did.

Later, I talked with some of the lawyers and asked them about Weinberg's closing argument. Those who were predisposed to Rock loved it. Those who favored the postal service thought that it was clever rhetoric, but were not persuaded. We believe what we want to believe.

We know that if we took similar votes after closing arguments but before juries retired to deliberate, that we would, most often, find splits. It is a rare jury that walks into the jury room unanimous for one side or the other. Yet, we also know that hung juries are the exception—some five percent of juries nation-wide cannot reach a decision. Something happens in the jury room that transforms a divided jury into one with sufficient votes to return a verdict. What happens is that jurors on one side persuade the others.

I often used alternate jurors during my nine years as a trial judge. These alternates sat through the entire trial. Just before the start of deliberations, the clerk would select by lot those who were to be excused. The lawyers routinely questioned these alternate jurors in an attempt to get some feel for where the deliberating jury was heading. Routinely, and I cannot think of an exception, the alternates' prediction of which side would win was wrong! Clearly, minds get changed in the jury room.

Several years ago, a police officer in Detroit was tried for murder in connection with the death of a citizen. Prior to the return of a verdict convicting the officer of second-degree murder, the eleven jurors favoring that decision confronted the lone holdout. According to an Associated Press dispatch, one of the jurors later recalled to a reporter for WXYZ-TV in Detroit what they told the holdout:

> "'We have 11 of us that believe that Walter Butzyn was guilty of second-degree. You believe he's guilty of something, involuntary manslaughter. If you want us to come across to what you believe then you're going to have to prove it to us. We said the ball is in your court, Now it's up to you to prove it to us.'"

When a juror in one of your cases is so confronted, you want that juror to have the means to "prove" why you should win. This is the purpose of closing argument.

XXXI.
THE FUNCTION OF CLOSING ARGUMENT

The closing-argument stage of the trial is like the legendary old west—there is no law; judges will rarely, if ever, intervene. The following is what generally happens when one side objects to the other side's restatement of the evidence:

> So, ladies and gentlemen, you will recall that Loretta Adams testified that Sam Smith's car went through the red light and a stop sign before hitting little Jimmie.
>
> > Counsel: I object. That misstates the evidence.
> >
> > The Court: The jurors will decide the facts of this case based on their recollection of the evidence. I remind you, ladies and gentlemen, that you are the sole

judges of the facts of this case, and
your memory of what the evidence is
must govern your decision.

Of course, if the other side *is* misstating the evidence, you must object, so that the jury, which you hope still sees you as the truth-giver, will not be misled by your silence.

You have two jobs to do during your closing argument.

1. Validate the decision of those jurors who believe that your side should win.

2. Give those jurors the tools with which to persuade the others.

The skillful lawyer knows that he or she accomplishes both of these jobs by recapitulating the evidence in its most persuasive order. In this sense, the closing argument is like an opening statement. Unlike the opening statement, however, you now have concrete evidence rather than promises of proof. Although your persona as the truth-giver was critical at the opening-statement part of the trial, before the jury had heard or seen any of the evidence, that persona shares the stage with that evidence during closing argument. This means that you must show that evidence to the jury, and, if you are fortunate enough to have transcripts of the trial, read to the jury important portions of the testimony.

Advice to show evidence to the jury during the closing arguments seems pretty obvious. Yet, I rarely saw that done. Typically, a lawyer would say to the jury: "When you get into the jury room, look at Exhibit 48, and you'll see that it supports our contention that the defendant promised to deliver 5,000 widgets every Friday." What the lawyer should have done, of course, was to blow it up and show the document to the jury. Lawyers also routinely undercut themselves when, in recounting the evidence, they remind the jury that "what I'm telling you is not evidence, and if your recollection of the evidence differs from mine, you must credit yours." Huh? Why would you want to tell the jury that you, the truth-giver in the courtroom, might not remember the evidence accurately? Yet, lawyers do this all the time.

Judges from around the country tell me that my experience with the way most lawyers handle their closing arguments coincides with their perceptions as well. Indeed, those of you who have read Jonathan Harr's gripping story of mass-tort litigation, *A Civil Action*, may remember that one of the jurors favoring the plaintiffs had to do the work in the jury room that the plaintiffs' lawyers should have done: "She announced one morning that she intended to go through the evidence piece by piece until she found proof of dumping on Beatrice's [Beatrice Foods] land between 1968 and 1979."[46] The date of dumping was critical to the case; indeed, the verdict form asked specifically about dates. Yet, the plaintiffs' lawyers did not marshall for the jury the evidence necessary for a plaintiffs' verdict. Don't make the same mistake.

Another tool you can use to help your partisans on the jury persuade the others is the burden of proof. As we noted earlier, "Yes, but the government has not proven her guilty beyond a reasonable doubt" is something a juror who believes the defendant to be innocent will say *as an arguing point* to one who believes that the defendant is guilty. Thus, in framing the structure of your closing argument, you should stress your client's innocence, but use the burden of proof so that it's there for the *jurors to use*:

> Ladies and gentlemen, when we started this trial, I told you that I would prove that Ms. Jones is falsely accused, that she is innocent. I believe that I have done that, and that the evidence proves her an innocent person. But, as His Honor has told you, we don't have the burden of proof. Before you may vote to find Ms. Jones guilty, the judge has told you that you must find that the government has proven her guilty beyond a reasonable doubt. The judge has also told you that a "reasonable doubt" is "a doubt based on common sense," that it is a "doubt for which a reason can be given." Well, folks, there are lots of reasons why Ms. Jones is not guilty. [Then argue the evidence.]

A similar closing argument can be made by a defendant in a civil case:

> Ladies and gentlemen, when we started this trial, I told you that I would prove that Ms. Jones was not negligent. I believe that I have done that, and that the evidence proves clearly that she exercised ordinary care while driving her car that day. But, as Her Honor has told you, we don't have the burden of proof. Before you may vote to find that Ms. Jones was negligent the judge has told you that you must find that the plaintiff has proven her negligent by a

---

[46] Jonathan Harr, *A Civil Action* 386 (Vintage 1996).

preponderance of the evidence. Well, folks, more than a preponderance of the evidence demonstrates that she was not negligent. [Then argue the evidence.]

If you have the burden of proof, on the other hand, you must embrace it:

Ladies and gentlemen, the court has told you that before you may find the defendant guilty, we had to prove guilt beyond a reasonable doubt. By any fair view of the evidence, we have done that. [Then argue the evidence.]

Similarly, for the plaintiff in a civil case:

Ladies and gentlemen, the court has told you that before you may find that the defendant negligently caused this accident, we had to prove by a preponderance of the evidence that she was negligent. Although, as the judge told you, preponderance of the evidence means just more than half, we have proved without question that the defendant was negligent and that she caused this accident. [Then argue the evidence.]

XXXII.
A "Test Yourself" Practice Session
(including the answers)

See if you can do a direct-examination better than Johnnie Cochran!

PART ONE

For this exercise, we turn again to the O.J. Simpson criminal trial. The following is the first part of the July 11, 1995, direct-examination by Johnnie Cochran of Denise Pilnak, a woman who lived in the same neighborhood as Nicole Brown.

The point of Pilnak's testimony was to establish circumstantially the time of the murder by trying to pin-point the time she heard a dog bark in the neighborhood. The prosecution had presented witnesses who said that they had heard a dog bark at a time when Simpson would have been able to commit the murders before returning to his home and going to the airport for a late-night flight to Chicago.

According to the prosecution theory, the dog barked furiously when it saw Nicole Brown and Ronald Goldman killed. The defense hope was that Pilnak's testimony would establish that the dog barked later than the prosecution contended, and that it would have, therefore, been physically impossible for Simpson to have killed Brown and Goldman, return home, and get to the airport in time for his flight.

Read the Cochran examination, and decide how *you* would **argue the defense theory to the jury through the window of what this witness can give you.** You should make a list of points that you want to cover. Then, use the points to frame your questions. Apply Occam's Razor and cut out the inconsequentia, and do not ask "what happened next"—type questions. You should also try to make the witness a three-dimensional person with whom the jury will empathize. In this regard, feel free to supplement the witness's personal background, as long as it is not inconsistent with the facts as they are revealed by the Cochran examination. All the other facts must, of course, track Pilnak's actual testimony.

Although you would never again use written questions in court, write out these questions (aware, of course, that the dynamics of the trial court may lead to others), so that you can compare what you've done with Part Three of this exercise, which sets out how I would do it.

COCHRAN'S EXAMINATION OF DENISE PILNAK:

Q: Good afternoon, Miss Pilnak.

A: Good afternoon.

Q: Miss Pilnak, do you presently reside in the 900 block of south Bundy? I won't give your exact address.

A: Yes.

Q: And back in the month of June of 1994, did you live in the 900 block of south Bundy?

A: Yes.

Q: What line of work are you generally in, Miss Pilnak?

A: I've been in the high tech publishing business for about the last 10 years.

Q: All right. Now, I'd like to direct your attention back to the date of June 12th of 1994. Do you recall that particular day?

A: Yes, I do.

Q: And was that a Sunday?

A: Yes.

Q: And as a result of your work in the publishing field, have you--do you have any specific--strike that. As a result of your work in the publishing field, are you kind of a stickler for time?

A: I've been in sales for 20 years. So I have to account for my time.

Q: And so you're kind of used to accounting for your time?

A: Yes, sir.

Q: Now, with regard to that date, June 12th, 1994, do you know the various things you did on that particular date?

A: Yes, I do.

Q: And let's start with the morning. What were you doing at about 8:30 that morning?

A: I had to go over to my girlfriend's house and feed her dog. She was out of town.

Q: All right. And what did you do after you fed your girlfriend's dog?

A: I met a bunch of friends. We meet every Sunday at 9:00 o'clock and run, and I ran 11 miles.

Q: All right. You're a runner, are you?

A: Long distance, yes.

Q: And you ran 11 miles that Sunday?

A: Uh-huh.

Q: You've got to answer out--you've got to say yes or no.

A: Yes.

Q: All right. And do you run most days or many days?

A: Every day.

Q: Did you know who Miss Nicole Brown Simpson was?

A: Yes, I did.

Q: And you knew where she lived prior to June 12th, 1994?

A: No, I didn't.

Q: How did you know who she was before that?

A: I used to see her running with her girlfriend Cora several times a week. But I just knew her--just living in Brentwood, you know everyone.

Q: All right. And you've lived in Brentwood for a period of time, have you?

A: Yes, I have.

Q: Now, that--let's shift to the afternoon. We won't go through your entire day. Let's shift to the afternoon. What were you doing around 5:30 on that day?

A: Went to church.

Q: Is that a church in that area?

A: St. Martins of Tours on Sunset.

Q: All right. And after that, did you have occasion to do something else?

A: Yes. My mother was in from the midwest with her husband and they were staying at my sister's. They came over and we ended up having dinner.

Q: All right. And you took them to some restaurant for dinner?

A: Yes. To Louise's.

Q: And that Louise's located where?

A: It's on San Vicente. I don't know what the little side street is. It's right across from Toscana.

Q: All right. Now, with regard to the times that evening, what time did you finish dinner at Louise's, if you know and what time did you arrive back home?

A: Umm, we finished dinner sometime around--close to 9:30 and got home just a couple minutes after. It only takes about 3 minutes.

Q: To get home from Louise's?

A: Yes.

Q: All right. What street is Louise's on if you recall?

A: It is on San Vicente Boulevard.

Q: All right. Now, you then returned home. Did you return home in the company of anyone else?

A: Yes.

Q: And who was that?

A: My girlfriend was over, Judy Telander. She had joined us for dinner. She had been over all day.

Q: So how many people went to dinner? Four?

A: Four.

Q: It was Judy Telander, yourself, your mom and--

A: And her husband Nick.

Q: Nick. All right. Now, at some point after you returned home from dinner with Judy Telander, did your mom and Nick have occasion to leave your residence on the 900 block of south Bundy?

A: Yes, they did.

Q: Can you tell the jury and--the Court and jury about what time they left your residence that evening?

A: Umm, when they came back, they just came in for about five minutes. So it was around 9:45 to 10 to 10:00.

Q: And they were going someplace at that time?

A: They were staying at my sister's house in Torrance. So they were driving back to her home.

Q: Okay. Now, after they left, did you have occasion to see what time it was after that as you looked toward obtaining some messages from your machine? [WOW! DO YOU BELIEVE THIS QUESTION?]

A: Umm, I did look at the clock because my girlfriend had been over all day using my computer.

Q: And again, now, what girlfriend are we talking about?

A: Judy Telander.

Q: Okay. What time was that that you looked at the clock?

A: 10:18.

Q: All right. And are you sure it was that time?

A: I am a stickler with time. I don't go anywhere without two watches when it's important.

Q: For the record, your Honor, she has--

Q: Do you have two watches on today?

A: Yeah. My running watch, which is very accurate, and my other watch which isn't.

Q: All right. So you keep two watches at all times?

A: Well, not at all times. When it's real important.

Q: All right. I appreciate your being on time here today.

A: Yes.

Q: Thank you. Now, you were about to tell us that your friend, Judy Telander, had been over pretty much all day using your computer. And so you had occasion to look at a clock or something to determine the time, and it was 10:18?

A: Yes.

Q: Okay. What happened at 10:18, please?

A: Umm, Judy had been over all day and I noticed the digital time. I said--I said to her, "Judy, it's 10:18. You've been here all day and I'm going out of town in a couple days. You're going to have to leave." So--

Q: Well, you said--let's see now. You said that she's a friend, right?

A: She's a friend.

Q: You said that in a nice way?

A: In a nice way.

Q: All right. So you said that, "You have to leave now," or, "It's time to go home," right?

A: Yeah. Well, "It's time to go home," and I said, "Let's just print out your report and you can look at it tomorrow, and any changes, I'd be happy to make tomorrow."

Q: All right.

A: But I had things I had to get done.

Q: Okay. I understand. Did you at that time assist her in printing out anything for her before she left?

A: Yes.

Q: What did you print out for Judy Telander?

A: I printed out a letter that she had been working on all day, and actually it's two pages and then about two lines on the third page. And I printed out two copies. I wasn't sure if it was one or two. I think it was two.

Q: All right. Did you give that to her?

A: Yes, I did.

Q: All right. And so you parted company at about what time?

A: 10:21.

Q: All right. And again, you're pretty sure about that time?

A: Well, I re-timed everything. My little speech to her took about 45 seconds and the printing out was a minute and 25 seconds for each three-page copy. So that's--that's right about 3 minutes.

Q: All right. So after the fact, you went back and redid these things yourself; is that right?

A: Uh-huh. Uh-huh.

Q: Uh-huh means yes?

A: Yes. I'm sorry.

Q: Okay. All right. So how did you--did you escort her out or tell us what you did when Judy Telander was leaving?

A: Whenever my girlfriends leave my home, I always turn off the porch light, stand on the porch, watch until they get in their car and take off.

Then I make them call me when they get home just so we know they're safe.

Q: All right.

A: And I did exactly that.

Q: All right. Did you--with regard--let's back up for a moment. When your mom and Nick left, did you see them outside also?

A: Yes, I did.

Q: Okay. And did you make arrangements also for your mom to call when she got home?

A: I didn't ask my mother to call. I told her I'd call her later.

Q: But you made arrangements for Judy Telander to call?

A: Yes.

Q: Now, when you walked out and you're out on the porch with Judy Telander, can you describe for the jury the condition of Bundy drive that particular night, that Sunday evening?

A: That Sunday evening, it was exceptionally quiet. As long as I've lived in that home, I never remember a night when it was absolutely still. There wasn't a sound to be heard.

Q: All right. Now, what time is this that it's exceptionally quiet?

A: It was about--Judy and I were outside talking probably between 10:21 and about 10:25.

Q: During that time, you were out on your porch; is that correct?

A: Yes.

Q: And how long had you lived at that location at that point?

A: Umm, four years.

Q: So in the four years you lived there, you had never heard Bundy so quiet; is that right?

A: Yes.

Q: So that we're clear--I want to show you People's 26 for identification.

Q: If I might approach, your Honor.

THE COURT: Yes.

Q: And I'm going to give you a pointer and ask if you would familiarize yourself. And you've seen this diagram before; have you not?

A: Yes.

Q: And I want to indicate to you and counsel that the red here is the Nicole Brown condo--Nicole Brown Simpson condo. And I want you to look--this is Dorothy and this would be Darlington (Indicating), and I would like for you to point and show the jury where you live approximately.

A: Right about--right in the middle of this block (Indicating).

Q: All right.

A: On the east side.

Q: All right. Your Honor, for the record, of People's 26, Miss Pilnak is indicating for the record she lives between Dorothy and Darlington on the east side of Bundy.

Q: Is that correct?

A: Yes.

Q: And so that we're clear, you--have you had occasion to measure the distance from the corner there of Dorothy to your residence?

A: It's about 75 yards.

Q: All right. So you know generally where you are at that location?

A: I'm a distance runner.

Q: Okay. And so you're on the east side of the street, right?

A: Yes.

Q: And so your porch is there where you and Judy Telander stood before she left; is that correct?

A: Yes.

Q: Okay. And at that time, it was about 10:25 P.M. on June 12th, 1994, right?

A: Yes.

Q: And it was quieter than you could ever remember it; is that correct?

A: Yes.

Q: Do you remember seeing any people walking around at that point?

A: No.

Q: See people walking? Do you remember seeing anybody walking dogs at that point?

A: No.

Q: Do you remember hearing any dogs barking at that point at 10:25?

A: No.

Q: All right. Now, after you saw Judy Telander off, did you have occasion to come back in and do something at that time at about 10:25 P.M.?

A: Umm, the minute Judy left, I picked up the telephone and called my mother to make sure she got home safely.

Q: Now, your mother had left I recall at about 9:45 to 9:50?

A: Yes.

Q: And she had to go to Gardena or Torrance or something?

A: Torrance. Uh-huh.

Q: As I understand your testimony, your mom and Nick had left at something like 9:45 to 9:50; is that correct?

A: Yes.

Q: And after Judy Telander left, you then called your mom at some location; is that correct?

A: Yes.

Q: Okay. And what time was it that you called your mother?

A: 10:25.

Q: And you have provided us with a phone bill which I would like to show to counsel, mark it as our next exhibit.

(Discussion held off the record between the Deputy District Attorney and Defense counsel.)

Q: Counsel has it, your Honor. May I mark this Defendant's next in order, your Honor?

THE COURT: 1237.

Q: We'll mark this as Defendant's exhibit 1237.

(Deft's 1237 for id = phone bill)

Q: And I want to approach you, Miss Pilnak, and I want to ask you what Defendant's 1237 is. Will you look at that, please?

A: Yes.

Q: Okay. Tell us--tell the jury what that is.

A: That's my phone bill.

Q: All right. That's your phone bill? And what's the date of that phone bill?

A: The date of the phone bill--well, the bill date is July 10th, but it includes calls from June 10th through June 15th on this page.

Q: You have a phone call about June 12th, 1994 at about 10:25 P.M.?

A: Yes, I do.

Q: And where is that call to?

A: It's to my sister's house.

Q: Is that where your mom was?

A: Yes.

Q: And did you connect with your mom that she made it?

A: Yes, I did.

Q: And so this phone bill indicates the time that you called your mother at 10:25 P.M., says Gardena on it with a phone number; is that correct?

A: Yes.

Q: You talked to her for about three minutes, did you?

A: Yes.

Q: All right. Now, I'm not going to put this on the Elmo [a projection device] your Honor, because I don't want to block out all these numbers.

Q: But this is an accurate copy of your phone bill that you received after June 12th, 1994; is that right?

A: Yes.

Q: The one you got on July 10th?

A: Yes.

Q: Okay. Is that right? So that reflects the fact that for about three minutes, is that accurate, that you talked to your mom?

MS. CLARK: Objection. Leading.

THE COURT: Sustained.

Q: Well, let me rephrase that, your Honor.

Q: Look at that phone bill and tell us how long you talked at 10:25 on the phone.

A: Three minutes.

Q: And is that about accurate?

A: Yes.

Q: All right. And after that--now, that would make it about 10:28; is that correct?

A: Yes.

Q: All right. And tell us then what happened after you placed this phone call to your mother.

A: Well, actually while I was speaking with my mother--it was a portable phone--I washed four glasses and put them away, crystal glasses, and I washed my face, brushed my teeth, flossed, and--and then I went into the kitchen to bring a bunch of newspapers and reading material into my bedroom and put those in the bedroom and then I went back into the bathroom.

Q: All right. Now, these--you have a habit about collecting reading materials and keeping papers until you throw them away?

A: I don't throw anything away until I've read it.

Q: All right. So you collected up--what did you do? You collected up a number of papers and things?

A: Yes.

Q: All right. And ultimately, you took those things and gathered them up and you took them someplace in your house?

A: Yes. Into my bedroom because I--

Q: All right. Now, up to that time, ma'am, up to the time that you picked these newspapers up and you brushed your teeth and flossed and everything, had you heard any loud dogs barking at that time?

A: No.

Q: It was still very quiet out?

A: I wasn't outside, but it was--I didn't hear any noises from outside.

Q: You couldn't hear anything from inside; is that correct?

A: Correct.

Q: When you had been out on your porch and Judy Telander had left, it had been very, very quiet?

A: Extremely quiet.

Q: All right. Now, at some point thereafter, did you hear a dog or dogs start barking?

A: When I went back into the bathroom, I was drying my hands and I heard a dog barking.

Q: All right. And to the best of your recollection, what time was that that you heard this dog barking at that point, your best recollection?

A: About 10:35.

Q: All right. Nearest you can tell, that was the earliest it was?

A: It could be 10:33 because I've re-timed those activities.

Q: All right. Between 10:30, 10:35; is that correct?

A: Yes.

Q: All right. And you never came outside to check that dog, did you?

A: No.

Q: All right. You just heard the dog barking?

A: Yes.

Q: And did they--did you hear this sound of barking, did it continue for a period of time?

A: It continued for a long time.

Q: All right. Do you recall what time you went to sleep that night?

A: Yes.

Q: What time did you approximately fall off to sleep?

A: Well, I closed the lights off at 12:30 A.M.

Q: All right. You closed the lights off at 12:30. How soon after that did you go to sleep, if you know?

A: Probably right afterward.

Q: All right. And at some point, did the dog--this dog stop barking?

A: Yes.

Q: All right. Were you able to tell whether or not during that time frame of about 10:35 until you turned the lights off at 12:30, you ever heard more than one dog barking?

A: I'm not sure. I heard one continuous bark for a very long time.

Q: All right. You can't tell us whether or not it was one dog or a different dog or whatever, but you heard a continuous bark; is that correct?

A: Yes.

Q: All right. And so when you finally got ready to fall asleep, did the dog--did the barking stop at some point?

A: The barking had stopped.

Q: And that would have been at about 12:30 the barking stopped?

A: No. It had stopped before then.

Q: Okay. Do you know when it had stopped approximately?

A: Approximately--it was a long time. I would have guessed that it--from the time it started barking, it had to be about 45 minutes or so. But I don't know precisely.

Q: All right. You didn't write anything down about that, did you?

A: No. That I didn't.

Q: All right. Now, with regard to the time of 10:15, at which time you've indicated you were still in your house, did you hear a dog barking at all at that time?

A: No.

Q: And when you came out on that porch with Judy Telander--and that was I think you've told us between 10:21 and 10:25--you didn't hear any dogs barking at that time, did you?

A: No. We commented on how quiet it was.

Q: When you say "We," you're talking about you and Judy?

A: Judy and I commented.

PART TWO

Now is your turn. Jot down the points you want to argue to the jury. Write out the questions that you would ask, and the answers you expect. You should draw your questions from the notes. You would not, of course, use written questions during an actual examination. The notes should be the guide for your written questions, just as they would be the guide for your oral questions in court. After you are finished, compare what you have written with Part Three.

Q _____

A _____

Q _____

A _____

Q _____

A _____

Q _____

A _____

Q _____

A _____

Q _____

A _____

Q _____

A _____

Q _____

A _____

Q _____

A _____

Q _____

A _____

PART THREE

In my mock direct-examination, I have added details that, **although not inconsistent** with Pilnak's testimony, may not accurately reflect her life. Accordingly, the witness is named Cooper, and her friend is Jane Rogers.

Q Good afternoon, Ms. Cooper.

A Good afternoon.

Q I'm going to ask you a few questions about the night Nicole Brown and Ronald Goldman were killed, and what you heard that night. All right? [LET THE JURY KNOW WHAT YOU'RE DOING AND WHERE THE EXAMINATION IS HEADED.]

Q Do you live near where Nicole Brown lived?

A Yes.

Q Do you know how far your house is from her house?

A Yes. [THIS ESTABLISHES THE REQUISITE FOUNDATION UNDER RULE 602 OF THE FEDERAL RULES OF EVIDENCE AND ITS STATE COUNTERPARTS. YOU DO NOT NEED ANYTHING MORE. WHAT'S MORE, IT EITHER IS OR IS NOT SEVENTY-FIVE FEET. YOU WOULD HAVE MEASURED IT BEFORE THE TRIAL.][47]

Q How far?

A Seventy-five feet.

---

[47] **Rule 602 Lack of Personal Knowledge.**
A witness may not testify to a matter unless evidence is introduced sufficient to support a finding that the witness has personal knowledge of the matter. *Evidence to prove personal knowledge may, but need not, consist of the witness' own testimony.* This rule is subject to the provisions of rule 703, relating to opinion testimony by expert witnesses. (Emphasis added.)

Q Did you know Nicole Brown personally?

A No.

Q Did you see her occasionally?

A Yes.

Q Where?

A On the street. I'm a runner and so was she.

Q Do you run a lot?

A Yes. Every day.

Q How far do you run every day?

A Ten, eleven miles.

Q Where do you work, Ms. Cooper?

A The ABC Publishing Company.

Q What do you do for them?

A I'm in sales?

Q How long have you been in sales?

A Ten years for ABC, and then ten years before that for another company.

Q Do you get a salary or are you paid on commission?

A Commission.

Q Does that mean time is important or not important to you?

A Important. If I'm not selling, I'm not earning.

Q Are you married?

A   No. [SOME JURORS WILL WANT TO KNOW.]

Q   Now you told us that you're a runner. Are you active in any running groups?

A   Yes. One.

Q   Which one?

A   The Brentwood Breakers.

Q   Was Nicole Brown a member of that group?

A   No. [I ASK THIS BECAUSE THE JURY WILL BE CURIOUS, INASMUCH AS NICOLE WAS A RUNNER TOO. MOREOVER, I WANT THE JURY TO SEE THIS WITNESS AS DISINTERESTED. IF NICOLE BROWN WAS EITHER A FRIEND OR A MEMBER OF THE SAME CLUB, THAT FACT MIGHT LEAD SOME JURORS TO PERCEIVE A BIAS.]

Q   Do you have any position of responsibility with the group or are you just a member?

A   I'm vice-president in charge of events.

Q   Is that fairly time-consuming?

A   Yes, especially before a race. But I love running and I want to help out. [SHE'S SKILLED AT WHAT SHE DOES, SHE'S A "GOOD PERSON" (DEVOTING HER VALUABLE TIME FOR THE GOOD OF THE GROUP), AND, AS WE HAVE SEEN, HAS A STABLE POSITION OF RESPONSIBILITY.]

Q   Let's talk a little bit about the evening that Nicole Brown and Ron Goldman were murdered, Sunday June 12, 1994. [A TRANSITION QUESTION.]

A   OK.

Q   Do you remember that day?

A   Yes.

Q   Why is that? [YOU MUST EXPLAIN TO THE JURY WHY SHE WOULD REMEMBER DAY A YEAR EARLIER.]

A   Well, after they found the bodies, there was a good deal of commotion.

Q   Do you remember where you were at 10:00 p.m. that evening?

A   Yes.

Q   Where were you?

A   At home.

Q   Were you with someone?

A   Yes.

Q   Who?

A   Jane Rogers.

Q   Who is she?

A   She's a friend of mine. She was using my computer that day.

Q   Does she live with you?

A   No. She was visiting, to use the computer.

Q   She was still there at ten O'Clock?

A   Yes. [NO NEED TO GO INTO ALL OF THE TEDIOUS RECOUNTING OF ALL THE NON-RELEVANT THINGS SHE DID THAT DAY—FROM AFTERNOON ON. THOSE FACTS JUST CLUTTER UP THE EXAMINATION, ADD NOTHING, AND DO NOT HELP YOUR ARGUMENT THAT THE DOG DID NOT BARK BEFORE 10:33 P.M.]

Q   At ten o'clock that evening, did you want her to stay longer, or were you eager that she go home? [NOT LEADING BECAUSE IT HAS TO BE ONE OR THE OTHER. THE WITNESS HAS A CHOICE.]

A   Well, it was pretty late and I had things to do, so I suggested that maybe it was time for her to leave.

Q   Do you remember when that evening you suggested that to her?

A   Yes. It was 10:18.

Q   How do you remember that?

A   It was a digital clock, and that's what it said.

Q   Is there any other reason why you remember the reading on the digital clock that evening?

A   Yes. Cops and investigators began asking me to recall specific times, and the 10:18 just stuck in my head. [YOU MUST EXPLAIN TO THE JURY WHY SHE WOULD REMEMBER THIS DETAIL ON A DAY A YEAR EARLIER.]

Q   Well, let's talk about that. Did you hear a dog bark that evening?

A   Yes. [THIS IS NOT LEADING. THE EXAMINER IS MERELY ALERTING THE WITNESS TO THE SUBJECT MATTER. THE QUESTION IS NEUTRAL, AND THE ANSWER CAN BE JUST AS EASILY "NO" AS "YES." IF A JUDGE ERRONEOUSLY SUSTAINS A "LEADING" OBJECTION, SLIP INTO: "TELL ME WHETHER OR NOT YOU HEARD A DOG BARK THAT EVENING."]

Q   Can you tell us when you heard a dog bark?

A   Yes. It was around 10:35 p.m., perhaps as early as 10:33.

Q   No earlier than 10:33?

A   No.

Q   All right, let's see how you know that. [A TRANSITION.] When did your friend Jane leave your house?

A   At around 10:20.

Q   Did you stay in your house or did you walk out with her?

A   I walked her out. I always like to see my friends to their cars.

Q   When you were outside with Jane, did you hear a dog bark?

A   No, actually it was quite quiet out there.

Q   Do you know when you went back inside your house?

A   Yes.

Q   When was that?

A   No later than 10:25 p.m.

Q   How do you know that?

A   Because that's when I called my mother.

Q   I show you what's been marked as Defense Exhibit 1237. Is this your telephone bill for the month of June, 1994?

A   Yes.

Q   Does it reflect your call to your mother?

A   Yes.

Q   Did you look at this bill before you came to court today in order to refresh your memory as to when you called your mother?

A   Yes. [A WITNESS CAN REFRESH HIS OR HER RECOLLECTION WITH ANYTHING. THE "ANYTHING" NEED NOT BE ADMISSIBLE INTO EVIDENCE. THE BILL CONTEMPORANEOUSLY CORROBORATES HER TESTIMONY ABOUT HER PHONE CALL TO HER MOTHER. THE BILL NEED NOT BE OFFERED INTO EVIDENCE. THE JURY SEES IT, AND KNOWS THAT THE OTHER SIDE WOULD SCREAM IF THE BILL DID NOT SUPPORT THE WITNESS'S TESTIMONY.]

Q   Between the time that you left your house with Jane and when you returned and called your mother at 10:25, did you hear a dog bark?

A   No.

Q   Now, you testified a moment ago that the earliest time you heard a dog bark that night was 10:33?

A   Yes.

Q   Did you look at a clock when the dog barked?

A   No. [AGAIN, THIS TESTIMONY HAS TO "RING TRUE." MAKING THE WITNESS A CONTINUAL CLOCK-WATCHER WILL NOT "RING TRUE." THERE MUST BE SOME OTHER EXPLANATION WHY SHE REMEMBERED THE TIME. HERE IT COMES.]

Q   Are you estimating that the earliest you heard the dog bark that night was 10:33, or are your fairly certain?

A   I'm pretty certain.

Q   All right, let's look at that. How long did you talk to your mother that night?

A   Three minutes.

Q   Did you look at the bill, Exhibit 1237, before you testified today to help you remember how long you talked to your mother?

A   Yes.

Q   So, if you called her at 10:25 and talked for three minutes, that means that you hung up at 10:28?

A   Yes.

Q   Do you remember what you did after you finished talking to your mother?

A   Yes.

Q   What did you do?

A   I washed my face, brushed my teeth, flossed, and--and then I went into the kitchen to bring a bunch of newspapers and reading material into my bedroom and put those in the bedroom and then I went back into the bathroom. [NOW'S THE TIME FOR THIS. WHEN THE JURORS HEARD IT DURING COCHRAN'S DIRECT-EXAMINATION OF PILNAK, MOST OF THEM MUST HAVE FADED OUT WHEN SHE DESCRIBED ALL THIS ACTIVITY (AS THEY DID WITH THE DETAILS OF THE DINNER AND THE CHURCH VISIT). NOW, THESE THINGS MAKE SOME SENSE.]

Q   Do you know how long that took?

A   Yes.

Q   How do you know? [A LOGICAL QUESTION, THE ANSWER TO WHICH THE JURY WILL WANT TO KNOW.]

A   I did all those things again and timed it?

Q   As an experiment?

A   Yes.

Q   Why? [A LOGICAL QUESTION, THE ANSWER TO WHICH THE JURY WILL WANT TO KNOW.]

A   Because everyone was interested in when I heard the dog bark, and I wanted to get it as exact as I could. [THIS "RINGS TRUE."]

Q   Is that how you came up with the 10:33 time?

A   Yes.

Q   By the way, when you heard a dog bark that night, was the barking a one-shot deal, or did the barking last for a while?

A   It lasted for a while, for forty-five minutes or so.

Q   Was that continuous or sporadic?

A   Continuous.

Q   Is a continually barking dog in your neighborhood usual or unusual?

A   Unusual. Very unusual.

Notice that we make the witness a sympathetic person by making her three-dimensional along the lines we've discussed earlier. Also, we eliminated all of the stuff that cluttered up the examination. There is only one reason this witness was called: To establish that the dog did not bark earlier than 10:33 that night. We made this point to the jury by building on facts that "rang true." How did you do?

Don't let this exercise be your last practice of the techniques that you have now learned. You can easily hone your skills until they become second nature for you. Dig out your old trial and deposition transcripts. Read them, and, as you do, think about how you would reframe the themes, structure, and questions in light of what you now know. Spend less than thirty minutes a day, and the powerful and winning techniques will be yours forever.

XXXIII.
How To Know the Rules of Evidence Cold

In the course of this book, I've referred to some of the rules of evidence. Although a trial is not an evidence test, the rules of evidence are critical to your preparation and theme development. Yet, very few lawyers (and judges, for that matter) know the rules of evidence well. But there is an easy way: read the rules—less than thirty seconds a night, one rule at a time (or, for the longer rules, part of one rule), every day, and then repeat the process. Sounds simple, but it works. To help you, an up-to-date copy of the Federal Rules of Evidence is reprinted in Appendix A. Read the rules. Then, read Appendix B, which analyzes the Federal Rules of Evidence by their purpose and function so you can see how the rules relate and work with one another. After six months or so, you will know the rules cold—by the number. And, because you will understand how the rules work, you will be able to use them as a powerful tool to win your trials. What's more, judges will, more likely than not, defer to you if you know the rules so well that you can cite them off the top of your head and by the number.

XXXIV.
Voir Dire

A word about *voir dire*. There is a whole industry that caters to lawyers' desire for the golden, magic key to victory. Pick the right jury, lawyers are told, and you can win in a walk. It is not that easy.

First, although a lawyer can get a sense of a juror's mind-set from his or her demographics, lawyers and jury experts are often wrong. Ross P. Laguzza, a vice-president of the highly respected trial-consulting firm *DecisionQuest* points out that "[e]laborate studies of jurors show that the factors most easily observed in the courtroom — demographics, nonverbal cues — are the least predictive of juror decision-making."[48] And how could it be otherwise? As Dr. Laguzza explains:

---

[48] R.P. Laguzza *Voodoo Jurynomics* (Los Angeles Daily Journal, April 9, 1997).

"The goal during jury selection is to predict future behavior of a complete stranger, not just a few minutes after the prediction, but often days, weeks, even months later. This would be hard enough to do if the object of the prediction were a spouse or close friend or relative. How many of us have struggled to predict or even explain the behavior of someone we have lived with for years?

"The only clue available for making this prediction is behavior produced by this stranger in an unfamiliar setting in the presence of many other strangers, a judge, sometimes representatives of the media, and besuited trial attorneys and their assistants. And these clues are only available for a short period of time. To complicate matters further, the lawyer must predict the degree to which one stranger's future behavior will coincide with the future behavior of as many 11 other strangers, which must also be accurately predicted."[49]

Many years ago, I was asked to keynote a convention of jury consultants. The president of the organization sent to me a tape of a television program that showed his firm advising California personal-injury lawyers in the selection of a jury for an important trial. Jury selection lasted several days, and the program showed the jury consultants pouring over lists of potential jurors, the various demographic studies they had done, as well as the responses made by the potential jurors to the court's questionnaire. It was all very interesting, but, oddly, the program did not mention what had happened at the trial. When I returned the tape, I asked him how the case turned out. "We lost," was his two-word, muted response.

Second, I believe that a good lawyer can win with *any* jury that does not have persons on it who are so obviously out of the main stream that their bizarre traits would be immediately apparent to anyone. Several years ago, a skilled lawyer in Atlanta won a several-million dollar verdict in a medical malpractice case involving a baby born damaged on which he kept a juror who, during *voir dire*, had excoriated the legal profession for driving doctors out of business. Soon, the juror complained, the lawyers will have to deliver babies.

Third, many judges, most in the federal system, permit little, if any, *voir dire* by the lawyers. Additionally, the scope of peremptory challenges has been narrowed by decisions that prevent lawyers from striking jurors for racial and

---

[49] R.P. Laguzza *Voodoo Jurynomics* (Los Angeles Daily Journal, April 9, 1997).

other reasons. In my view, we will soon see a system where there is little *voir dire*, and little control by the lawyers over whom is selected to sit on juries.

Where *voir dire* is permitted, however, the opportunity can be used to give mini-opening statements and inculcate the jury panel with your theory of the case. Consider the following examples.

1. Let us assume that you represent the plaintiff in a medical malpractice case. One of the prospective jurors is the husband of a physician. The conventional wisdom suggests that the plaintiff's lawyer strike this person from the panel. I disagree, and would ask the following questions on *voir dire*:

Q   Sir, where does you wife work?

A   St. Joseph's Hospital.

Q   How long has she been a physician?

A   Thirteen years.

Q   And she knows lots of doctors?

A   Yes.

Q   And over the past thirteen years, she's worked with lots of doctors?

A   Yes.

Q   And, I am certain that she knows doctors who are very good at what they do?

A   Yes.

Q   And she either knows or knows of some doctors who are not as good?

A   Yes, unfortunately.

Q   And if she had her druthers, I am sure, no patient would ever have to be treated by a doctor who wasn't any good?

A   Yes.

Q   Do you believe that too?

A   Yes.

There is, obviously, no other way for the man to answer these questions. Having him on the panel of prospective jurors gives the lawyer an opportunity to ask these questions—making an argument to this potential juror and, through him, to the others on the panel. In my view, he would sign on to a plaintiff's verdict if he can be convinced that the defendant doctor committed malpractice. Given that you wouldn't have taken the case unless *you* were so convinced, why strike him?

2. Assume that your client is accused of robbing a grocery-store clerk. He denies it. The case rests on the clerk's identification. Although substantial research shows that identification evidence is less trustworthy than most of us would suppose, courts generally do not allow expert witnesses to so testify. What do you do? Well, you can use *voir dire* to make that point for you, over and over again, with each potential juror. Consider the following questions:

Q   Has anyone on the panel ever had the embarrassing moment of thinking that you recognized someone, running over to that person on the street, tapping them on the shoulder, only to have it be a complete stranger?

The odds are the someone in the group will answer that question "yes." Follow up and contrast the conditions under which the potential juror made the mistake with the conditions when the clerk saw the robber.

Q   Did it happen to you once or more than once?

Q   Let's talk about the first time. How long ago?

Q   Was it during the day or at night?

Q   Were you outside or inside?

Q   How far away were you when you first saw the person you thought was your friend?

Q How close did you have to get before you realized that it was not your friend?

Q By the way, how long did you know your friend before that day when you thought you saw him on the street but it turned out to be someone else?

Q Would you generally see your friend monthly, weekly, or more often?

Q If you had not caught up with the person you thought was your friend, you would have thought that you had seen him that day?

Q And, in fact, if that later became important—if, let's say, the outcome of a lawsuit depended on where your friend was that day, and you hadn't caught up with the person whom you thought was your friend, you would think that he was on that street that day?

Q And, in fact, if called to court to testify about it, you'd testify that you saw him there that day?

Q And you'd be testifying in good faith based on what you saw and on what you believed?

I won't belabor the point here. But *you* should on *voir dire*, for as long as the judge allows you to do it. And you should ask similar questions of each and every potential juror who says that he or she has had a similar experience.

If no potential jurors have ever had this experience, some of them will, undoubtedly, be familiar with the phenomenon.

Q Has anyone on the panel ever heard of someone being embarrassed by thinking that they recognized someone, but finding out that it was a complete stranger?

If anyone answers this question "yes," you can make your point through additional questions as before. The simple fact is that you have a right to this information. Courts everywhere recognize that jurors may bring with them into the jury room their life's experiences, and you need to know about those experiences so you can exercise intelligently your for-cause and peremptory challenges.

One additional point about *voir dire*. Defense lawyers in criminal cases often ask prospective jurors whether they will stand their ground and hang the jury if they find themselves in the minority during deliberations. This type of question is silly and counterproductive. Not only does it seek a commitment that jurors won't honor, but it also sends the message that the lawyer, whom the jurors believe knows the truth, is looking for someone to hang the jury. Why would a lawyer who knows that his or her client is innocent want the jury to hang?

XXXV.
WIN VICTORIES, NOT PRAISE

One final word. There is a story, most likely apocryphal, about a new newspaper editor conducting a survey to determine the best local lawyers. Only jurors who had served during the preceding five years were polled.

When published, the results of the poll shocked the legal community. A long-time and very active criminal-defense lawyer who had never lost a case in twenty years not only did not place first, he did not even make the list of the top ten criminal-defense lawyers. Stricken and heartbroken, the lawyer sulked for a couple of weeks. Finally, he had to get a haircut. As he was sitting in the chair, he asked the barber if he had been surveyed because the man had served on two of the lawyer's juries, which acquitted both times. The barber replied that he had filled out the survey but didn't think about putting the lawyer's name down.

"Why?" the lawyer asked.

"Hell, you're the luckiest sonofabitch alive. All your clients were innocent."

That, my friends, is the essence of being an effective, and winning, trial lawyer. Hide your art so that everyone who watches will think that you are incredibly lucky because you got the "easy" cases, the ones that could not be lost. Follow the precepts in this book, and you will. They will lead you down the "royal road" to winning trial-advocacy. Your clients will be grateful.

Appendix A

Federal Rules of Evidence

(specially formatted for ease of reference)

Table of Contents

Article	Page
Article I: General Provisions	198
Article II: Judicial Notice	200
Article III: Presumptions	200
Article IV: Relevancy	201
Article V: Privileges	208
Article VI: Witnesses	208
Article VII: Opinions	214
Article VIII: Hearsay	216
Article IX: Authentication	224
Article X: Writings	227
Article XI: Miscellaneous	230

Article I: General Provisions

Rule 101 Scope

These rules govern proceedings in the courts of the United States and before United States bankruptcy judges and United States magistrate judges, to the extent and with the exceptions stated in rule 1101.

Rule 102 Purpose and Construction

These rules shall be construed to secure fairness in administration, elimination of unjustifiable expense and delay, and promotion of growth and development of the law of evidence to the end that the truth may be ascertained and proceedings justly determined.

Rule 103 Rulings on Evidence

(a) *Effect of erroneous ruling.* Error may not be predicated upon a ruling which admits or excludes evidence unless a substantial right of the party is affected, and

>(1) *Objection.* In case the ruling is one admitting evidence, a timely objection or motion to strike appears of record, stating the specific ground of objection, if the specific ground was not apparent from the context; or

>(2) *Offer of proof.* In case the ruling is one excluding evidence, the substance of the evidence was made known to the court by offer or was apparent from the context within which questions were asked.

(b) *Record of offer and ruling.* The court may add any other or further statement which shows the character of the evidence, the form in which it was offered, the objection made, and the ruling thereon. It may direct the making of an offer in question and answer form.

(c) *Hearing of jury.* In jury cases, proceedings shall be conducted, to the extent practicable, so as to prevent inadmissible evidence from being suggested to the jury by any means, such as making statements or offers of proof or asking questions in the hearing of the jury.

(d) *Plain error.* Nothing in this rule precludes taking notice of plain errors affecting substantial rights although they were not brought to the attention of the court.

Rule 104 Preliminary Questions

(a) *Questions of admissibility generally.* Preliminary questions concerning the qualification of a person to be a witness, the existence of a privilege, or the admissibility of evidence shall be determined by the court, subject to the provisions of subdivision (b). In making its determination it is not bound by the rules of evidence except those with respect to privileges.

(b) *Relevancy conditioned on fact.* When the relevancy of evidence depends upon the fulfillment of a condition of fact, the court shall admit it upon, or subject to, the introduction of evidence sufficient to support a finding of the fulfillment of the condition.

(c) *Hearing of jury.* Hearings on the admissibility of confessions shall in all cases be conducted out of the hearing of the jury. Hearings on other preliminary matters shall be so conducted when the interests of justice require, or when an accused is a witness and so requests.

(d) *Testimony by accused.* The accused does not, by testifying upon a preliminary matter, become subject to cross-examination as to other issues in the case.

(e) *Weight and credibility.* This rule does not limit the right of a party to introduce before the jury evidence relevant to weight or credibility.

Rule 105 Limited Admissibility

When evidence which is admissible as to one party or for one purpose but not admissible as to another party or for another purpose is admitted, the court, upon request, shall restrict the evidence to its proper scope and instruct the jury accordingly.

Rule 106 Remainder of or Related Writings or Recorded Statements

When a writing or recorded statement or part thereof is introduced by a party, an adverse party may require the introduction at that time of any other part or any other writing or recorded statement which ought in fairness to be considered contemporaneously with it.

Article II. Judicial Notice

Rule 201 Judicial Notice of Adjudicative Facts

(a) *Scope of rule.* This rule governs only judicial notice of adjudicative facts.

(b) *Kinds of facts.* A judicially noticed fact must be one not subject to reasonable dispute in that it is either

  (1) generally known within the territorial jurisdiction of the trial court or

  (2) capable of accurate and ready determination by resort to sources whose accuracy cannot reasonably be questioned.

(c) *When discretionary.* A court may take judicial notice, whether requested or not.

(d) *When mandatory.* A court shall take judicial notice if requested by a party and supplied with the necessary information.

(e) *Opportunity to be heard.* A party is entitled upon timely request to an opportunity to be heard as to the propriety of taking judicial notice and the tenor of the matter noticed. In the absence of prior notification, the request may be made after judicial notice has been taken.

(f) *Time of taking notice.* Judicial notice may be taken at any stage of the proceeding.

(g) *Instructing jury.* In a civil action or proceeding, the court shall instruct the jury to accept as conclusive any fact judicially noticed. In a criminal case, the court shall instruct the jury that it may, but is not required to, accept as conclusive any fact judicially noticed.

Article III. Presumptions in Civil Actions and Proceedings

Rule 301 Presumptions in General in Civil Actions and Proceedings.

In all civil actions and proceedings not otherwise provided for by Act of Congress or by these rules, a presumption imposes on the party against whom it is directed the burden of going forward with evidence to rebut or meet the presumption, but does not shift to such party the burden of proof in the sense of the risk of nonpersuasion, which remains throughout the trial upon the party on whom it was originally cast.

Rule 302 Applicability of State Law in Civil Actions and Proceedings.

In civil actions and proceedings, the effect of a presumption respecting a fact which is an element of a claim or defense as to which State law supplies the rule of decision is determined in accordance with State law.

ARTICLE IV. RELEVANCY AND ITS LIMITS

Rule 401 Definition of "Relevant Evidence."

"Relevant evidence" means evidence having any tendency to make the existence of any fact that is of consequence to the determination of the action more probable or less probable than it would be without the evidence.

Rule 402 Relevant Evidence Generally Admissible; Irrelevant Evidence Inadmissible.

All relevant evidence is admissible, except as otherwise provided by the Constitution of the United States, by Act of Congress, by these rules, or by other rules prescribed by the Supreme Court pursuant to statutory authority. Evidence which is not relevant is not admissible.

Rule 403 Exclusion of Relevant Evidence on Grounds of Prejudice, Confusion, or Waste of Time.

Although relevant, evidence may be excluded if its probative value is substantially outweighed by the danger of unfair prejudice, confusion of the issues, or misleading the jury, or by considerations of undue delay, waste of time, or needless presentation of cumulative evidence.

Rule 404 Character Evidence Not Admissible To Prove Conduct; Exceptions; Other Crimes.

(a) *Character evidence generally.* Evidence of a person's character or a trait of character is not admissible for the purpose of proving action in conformity therewith on a particular occasion, except:

(1) *Character of accused.* Evidence of a pertinent trait of character offered by an accused, or by the prosecution to rebut the same;

(2) *Character of victim.* Evidence of a pertinent trait of character of the victim of the crime offered by an accused, or by the prosecution to rebut the same, or evidence of a character trait of peacefulness of the victim offered by the prosecution in a homicide case to rebut evidence that the victim was the first aggressor;

(3) *Character of witness.* Evidence of the character of a witness, as provided in rules 607, 608, and 609.

(b) *Other crimes, wrongs, or acts.* Evidence of other crimes, wrongs, or acts is not admissible to prove the character of a person in order to show action in conformity therewith. It may, however, be admissible for other purposes, such as proof of motive, opportunity, intent, preparation, plan, knowledge, identity, or absence of mistake or accident, provided that upon request by the accused, the prosecution in a criminal case shall provide reasonable notice in advance of trial, or during trial if the court excuses pretrial notice on good cause shown, of the general nature of any such evidence it intends to introduce at trial.

Rule 405 Methods of Proving Character.

(a) *Reputation or opinion.* In all cases in which evidence of character or a trait of character of a person is admissible, proof may be made by testimony as to reputation or by testimony in the form of an opinion. On cross-examination, inquiry is allowable into relevant specific instances of conduct.

(b) *Specific instances of conduct.* In cases in which character or a trait of character of a person is an essential element of a charge, claim, or defense, proof may also be made of specific instances of that person's conduct.

Rule 406 Habit; Routine Practice.

Evidence of the habit of a person or of the routine practice of an organization, whether corroborated or not and regardless of the presence of eyewitnesses, is relevant to prove that the conduct of the person or organization on a particular occasion was in conformity with the habit or routine practice.

Rule 407 Subsequent Remedial Measures.

When, after an injury or harm allegedly caused by an event, measures are taken that, if taken previously, would have made the injury or harm less likely to occur, evidence of the subsequent measures is not admissible to prove negligence, culpable conduct, a defect in a product, a defect in a product's design, or a need for a warning or instruction.

Rule 408 Compromise and Offers to Compromise.

Evidence of (1) furnishing or offering or promising to furnish, or (2) accepting or offering or promising to accept, a valuable consideration in compromising or attempting to compromise a claim which was disputed as to either validity or amount, is not admissible to prove liability for or invalidity of the claim or its amount. Evidence of conduct or statements made in compromise negotiations is likewise not admissible. This rule does not require the exclusion of any evidence otherwise discoverable merely because it is presented in the course of compromise negotiations. This rule also does not require exclusion when the evidence is offered for another purpose, such as proving bias or prejudice of a witness, negativing a contention of undue delay, or proving an effort to obstruct a criminal investigation or prosecution.

Rule 409 Payment of Medical and Similar Expenses.

Evidence of furnishing or offering or promising to pay medical, hospital, or similar expenses occasioned by an injury is not admissible to prove liability for the injury.

Rule 410 Inadmissibility of Pleas, Plea Discussions, and Related Statements.

Except as otherwise provided in this rule, evidence of the following is not, in any civil or criminal proceeding, admissible against the defendant who made the plea or was a participant in the plea discussions:

(1) a plea of guilty which was later withdrawn;

(2) a plea of nolo contendere;

(3) any statement made in the course of any proceedings under Rule 11 of the Federal Rules of Criminal Procedure or comparable state procedure regarding either of the foregoing pleas; or

(4) any statement made in the course of plea discussions with an attorney for the prosecuting authority which do not result in a plea of guilty or which result in a plea of guilty later withdrawn. However, such a statement is admissible

>(i) in any proceeding wherein another statement made in the course of the same plea or plea discussions has been introduced and the statement ought in fairness be considered contemporaneously with it, or

>(ii) in a criminal proceeding for perjury or false statement if the statement was made by the defendant under oath, on the record and in the presence of counsel.

Rule 411 Liability Insurance.

Evidence that a person was or was not insured against liability is not admissible upon the issue whether the person acted negligently or otherwise wrongfully. This rule does not require the exclusion of evidence of insurance against liability when offered for another purpose, such as proof of agency, ownership, or control, or bias or prejudice of a witness.

Rule 412 Sex Offense Cases; Relevance of Alleged Victim's Past Sexual Behavior or Alleged Sexual Predisposition.

(a) *Evidence generally inadmissible.* The following evidence is not admissible in any civil or criminal proceeding involving alleged sexual misconduct except as provided in subdivisions (b) and (c):

>(1) Evidence offered to prove that any alleged victim engaged in other sexual behavior.

>(2) Evidence offered to prove any alleged victim's sexual predisposition.

(b) *Exceptions.*

>(1) In a criminal case, the following evidence is admissible, if otherwise admissible under these rules:

>>(A) evidence of specific instances of sexual behavior by the alleged victim offered to prove that a person other than the accused was the source of semen, injury or other physical evidence;

(B) evidence of specific instances of sexual behavior by the alleged victim with respect to the person accused of the sexual misconduct offered by the accused to prove consent or by the prosecution; and

(C) evidence the exclusion of which would violate the constitutional rights of the defendant.

(2) In a civil case, evidence offered to prove the sexual behavior or sexual predisposition of any alleged victim is admissible if it is otherwise admissible under these rules and its probative value substantially outweighs the danger of harm to any victim and of unfair prejudice to any party. Evidence of an alleged victim's reputation is admissible only if it has been placed in controversy by the alleged victim.

(c) *Procedure to determine admissibility.*

(1) A party intending to offer evidence under subdivision (b) must—

(A) file a written motion at least 14 days before trial specifically describing the evidence and stating the purpose for which it is offered unless the court, for good cause requires a different time for filing or permits filing during trial; and

(B) serve the motion on all parties and notify the alleged victim or, when appropriate, the alleged victim's guardian or representative.

(2) Before admitting evidence under this rule the court must conduct a hearing in camera and afford the victim and parties a right to attend and be heard. The motion, related papers, and the record of the hearing must be sealed and remain under seal unless the court orders otherwise.

Rule 413 Evidence of Similar Crimes in Sexual Assault Cases

(a) In a criminal case in which the defendant is accused of an offense of sexual assault, evidence of the defendant's commission of another offense or offenses of sexual assault is admissible, and may be considered for its bearing on any matter to which it is relevant.

(b) In a case in which the Government intends to offer evidence under this rule, the attorney for the Government shall disclose the evidence to the defendant, including statements of witnesses or a summary of the substance of any testimony that is expected to be offered, at least fifteen days before the scheduled date of trial or at such later time as the court may allow for good cause.

(c) This rule shall not be construed to limit the admission or consideration of evidence under any other rule.

(d) For purposes of this rule and Rule 415, "offense of sexual assault" means a crime under Federal law or the law of a State (as defined in section 513 of title 18, United States Code) that involved—

> (1) any conduct proscribed by chapter 109A of title 18, United States Code;
>
> (2) contact, without consent, between any part of the defendant's body or an object and the genitals or anus of another person;
>
> (3) contact, without consent, between the genitals or anus of the defendant and any part of another person's body;
>
> (4) deriving sexual pleasure or gratification from the infliction of death, bodily injury, or physical pain on another person; or
>
> (5) an attempt or conspiracy to engage in conduct described in paragraphs (1)-(4).

Rule 414 Evidence of Similar Crimes in Child Molestation Cases

(a) In a criminal case in which the defendant is accused of an offense of child molestation, evidence of the defendant's commission of another offense or offenses of child molestation is admissible, and may be considered for its bearing on any matter to which it is relevant.

(b) In a case in which the Government intends to offer evidence under this rule, the attorney for the Government shall disclose the evidence to the defendant, including statements of witnesses or a summary of the substance of any testimony that is expected to be offered, at least fifteen days before the scheduled date of trial or at such later time as the court may allow for good cause.

(c) This rule shall not be construed to limit the admission or consideration of evidence under any other rule.

(d) For purposes of this rule and Rule 415, "child" means a person below the age of fourteen, and "offense of child molestation" means a crime under Federal law or the law of a State (as defined in section 513 of title 18, United States Code) that involved—

(1) any conduct proscribed by chapter 109A of title 18, United States Code, that was committed in relation to a child;

(2) any conduct proscribed by chapter 110 of title 18, United States Code;

(3) contact between any part of the defendant's body or an object and the genitals or anus of a child;

(4) contact between the genitals or anus of the defendant and any part of the body of a child;

(5) deriving sexual pleasure or gratification from the infliction of death, bodily injury, or physical pain on a child; or

(6) an attempt or conspiracy to engage in conduct described in paragraphs (1)-(5).

Rule 415 Evidence of Similar Acts in Civil Cases Concerning Sexual Assault or Child Molestation

(a) In a civil case in which a claim for damages or other relief is predicated on a party's alleged commission of conduct constituting an offense of sexual assault or child molestation, evidence of that party's commission of another offense or offenses of sexual assault or child molestation is admissible and may be considered as provided in Rule 413 and Rule 414 of these rules.

(b) A party who intends to offer evidence under this Rule shall disclose the evidence to the party against whom it will be offered, including statements of witnesses or a summary of the substance of any testimony that is expected to be offered, at least fifteen days before the scheduled date of trial or at such later time as the court may allow for good cause.

(c) This rule shall not be construed to limit the admission or consideration of evidence under any other rule.

Article V. Privileges

Rule 501 General Rule.

Except as otherwise required by the Constitution of the United States or provided by Act of Congress or in rules prescribed by the Supreme Court pursuant to statutory authority, the privilege of a witness, person, government, State, or political subdivision thereof shall be governed by the principles of the common law as they may be interpreted by the courts of the United States in the light of reason and experience. However, in civil actions and proceedings, with respect to an element of a claim or defense as to which State law supplies the rule of decision, the privilege of a witness, person, government, State, or political subdivision thereof shall be determined in accordance with State law.

Article VI. Witnesses

Rule 601 General Rule of Competency.

Every person is competent to be a witness except as otherwise provided in these rules. However, in civil actions and proceedings, with respect to an element of a claim or defense as to which State law supplies the rule of decision, the competency of a witness shall be determined in accordance with State law.

Rule 602 Lack of Personal Knowledge.

A witness may not testify to a matter unless evidence is introduced sufficient to support a finding that the witness has personal knowledge of the matter. Evidence to prove personal knowledge may, but need not, consist of the witness' own testimony. This rule is subject to the provisions of rule 703, relating to opinion testimony by expert witnesses.

Rule 603 Oath or Affirmation

Before testifying, every witness shall be required to declare that the witness will testify truthfully, by oath or affirmation administered in a form calculated to awaken the witness' conscience and impress the witness' mind with the duty to do so.

Rule 604 Interpreters.

An interpreter is subject to the provisions of these rules relating to qualification as an expert and the administration of an oath or affirmation to make a true translation.

Rule 605 Competency of Judge as Witness.

The judge presiding at the trial may not testify in that trial as a witness. No objection need be made in order to preserve the point.

Rule 606 Competency of Juror as Witness.

(a) *At the trial.* A member of the jury may not testify as a witness before that jury in the trial of the case in which the juror is sitting. If the juror is called so to testify, the opposing party shall be afforded an opportunity to object out of the presence of the jury.

(b) *Inquiry into validity of verdict or indictment.* Upon an inquiry into the validity of a verdict or indictment, a juror may not testify as to any matter or statement occurring during the course of the jury's deliberations or to the effect of anything upon that or any other juror's mind or emotions as influencing the juror to assent to or dissent from the verdict or indictment or concerning the juror's mental processes in connection therewith, except that a juror may testify on the question whether extraneous prejudicial information was improperly brought to the jury's attention or whether any outside influence was improperly brought to bear upon any juror. Nor may a juror's affidavit or evidence of any statement by the juror concerning a matter about which the juror would be precluded from testifying be received for these purposes.

Rule 607 Who May Impeach.

The credibility of a witness may be attacked by any party, including the party calling the witness.

Rule 608 Evidence of Character and Conduct of Witness.

(a) *Opinion and reputation evidence of character.* The credibility of a witness may be attacked or supported by evidence in the form of opinion or reputation, but subject to these limitations:

(1) the evidence may refer only to character for truthfulness or untruthfulness, and

(2) evidence of truthful character is admissible only after the character of the witness for truthfulness has been attacked by opinion or reputation evidence or otherwise.

(b) *Specific instances of conduct.*

Specific instances of the conduct of a witness, for the purpose of attacking or supporting the witness' credibility, other than conviction of crime as provided in rule 609, may not be proved by extrinsic evidence. They may, however, in the discretion of the court, if probative of truthfulness or untruthfulness, be inquired into on cross- examination of the witness

(1) concerning the witness' character for truthfulness or untruthfulness, or

(2) concerning the character for truthfulness or untruthfulness of another witness as to which character the witness being cross-examined has testified. The giving of testimony, whether by an accused or by any other witness, does not operate as a waiver of the accused's or the witness' privilege against self-incrimination when examined with respect to matters which relate only to credibility.

Rule 609 Impeachment by Evidence of Conviction of Crime.

(a) *General rule.* For the purpose of attacking the credibility of a witness,

(1) evidence that a witness other than an accused has been convicted of a crime shall be admitted, subject to Rule 403, if the crime was punishable by death or imprisonment in excess of one year under the law under which the witness was convicted, and evidence that an accused has been convicted of such a crime shall be admitted if the court determines that the probative value of admitting this evidence outweighs its prejudicial effect to the accused; and

(2) evidence that any witness has been convicted of a crime shall be admitted if it involved dishonesty or false statement, regardless of the punishment.

(b) *Time limit.* Evidence of a conviction under this rule is not admissible if a period of more than ten years has elapsed since the date of the conviction or of the release of the witness from the confinement imposed for that conviction, whichever is the later date, unless the court determines, in the interests of justice, that the probative value of the conviction supported by specific facts and circumstances substantially outweighs its prejudicial effect. However, evidence of a conviction more than 10 years old as calculated herein, is not admissible unless the proponent gives to the adverse party sufficient advance written notice of intent to use such evidence to provide the adverse party with a fair opportunity to contest the use of such evidence.

(c) *Effect of pardon, annulment, or certificate of rehabilitation.* Evidence of a conviction is not admissible under this rule if

(1) the conviction has been the subject of a pardon, annulment, certificate of rehabilitation, or other equivalent procedure based on a finding of the rehabilitation of the person convicted, and that person has not been convicted of a subsequent crime which was punishable by death or imprisonment in excess of one year, or

(2) the conviction has been the subject of a pardon, annulment, or other equivalent procedure based on a finding of innocence.

(d) *Juvenile adjudications.* Evidence of juvenile adjudications is generally not admissible under this rule. The court may, however, in a criminal case allow evidence of a juvenile adjudication of a witness other than the accused if conviction of the offense would be admissible to attack the credibility of an adult and the court is satisfied that admission in evidence is necessary for a fair determination of the issue of guilt or innocence.

(e) *Pendency of appeal.* The pendency of an appeal therefrom does not render evidence of a conviction inadmissible. Evidence of the pendency of an appeal is admissible.

Rule 610 Religious Beliefs or Opinions.

Evidence of the beliefs or opinions of a witness on matters of religion is not admissible for the purpose of showing that by reason of their nature the witness' credibility is impaired or enhanced.

Rule 611 Mode and Order of Interrogation and Presentation.

(a) *Control by court.* The court shall exercise reasonable control over the mode and order of interrogating witnesses and presenting evidence so as to

(1) make the interrogation and presentation effective for the ascertainment of the truth,

(2) avoid needless consumption of time, and

(3) protect witnesses from harassment or undue embarrassment.

(b) *Scope of cross-examination.* Cross-examination should be limited to the subject matter of the direct examination and matters affecting the credibility of the witness. The court may, in the exercise of discretion, permit inquiry into additional matters as if on direct examination.

(c) *Leading questions.* Leading questions should not be used on the direct examination of a witness except as may be necessary to develop the witness' testimony. Ordinarily leading questions should be permitted on cross-examination. When a party calls a hostile witness, an adverse party, or a witness identified with an adverse party, interrogation may be by leading questions.

Rule 612 Writing Used to Refresh Memory

Except as otherwise provided in criminal proceedings by section 3500 of title 18, United States Code, if a witness uses a writing to refresh memory for the purpose of testifying, either

(1) while testifying, or

(2) before testifying, if the court in its discretion determines it is necessary in the interests of justice, an adverse party is entitled to have the writing produced at the hearing, to inspect it, to cross-examine the witness thereon, and to introduce in evidence those portions which relate to the testimony of the witness.

If it is claimed that the writing contains matters not related to the subject matter of the testimony the court shall examine the writing in camera, excise any portions not so related, and order delivery of the remainder to the party entitled thereto. Any portion withheld over objections shall be preserved and made available to the appellate court in the event of an appeal. If a writing is not produced or delivered pursuant to order under this rule, the court shall make any order justice requires, except that in criminal cases when the prosecution elects not to comply, the order shall be one striking the testimony or, if the court in its discretion determines that the interests of justice so require, declaring a mistrial.

Rule 613 Prior Statements of Witnesses.

(a) *Examining witness concerning prior statement.* In examining a witness concerning a prior statement made by the witness, whether written or not, the statement need not be shown nor its contents disclosed to the witness at that time, but on request the same shall be shown or disclosed to opposing counsel.

(b) *Extrinsic evidence of prior inconsistent statement of witness.* Extrinsic evidence of a prior inconsistent statement by a witness is not admissible unless the witness is afforded an opportunity to explain or deny the same and the opposite party is afforded an opportunity to interrogate the witness thereon, or the interests of justice otherwise require. This provision does not apply to admissions of a party opponent as defined in rule 801(d)(2).

Rule 614 Calling and Interrogation of Witnesses by Court.

(a) *Calling by court.* The court may, on its own motion or at the suggestion of a party, call witnesses, and all parties are entitled to cross-examine witnesses thus called.

(b) *Interrogation by court.* The court may interrogate witnesses, whether called by itself or by a party.

(c) *Objections.* Objections to the calling of witnesses by the court or to interrogation by it may be made at the time or at the next available opportunity when the jury is not present.

Rule 615 Exclusion of Witnesses.

At the request of a party the court shall order witnesses excluded so that they cannot hear the testimony of other witnesses, and it may make the order of its own motion. This rule does not authorize exclusion of

(1) a party who is a natural person, or

(2) an officer or employee of a party which is not a natural person designated as its representative by its attorney, or

(3) a person whose presence is shown by a party to be essential to the presentation of the party's cause.

ARTICLE VII: OPINIONS AND EXPERT TESTIMONY

Rule 701 Opinion Testimony by Lay Witnesses

If the witness is not testifying as an expert, the witness' testimony in the form of opinions or inferences is limited to those opinions or inferences which are

(a) rationally based on the perception of the witness and

(b) helpful to a clear understanding of the witness' testimony or the determination of a fact in issue.

Rule 702 Testimony by Experts.

If scientific, technical, or other specialized knowledge will assist the trier of fact to understand the evidence or to determine a fact in issue, a witness qualified as an expert by knowledge, skill, experience, training, or education, may testify thereto in the form of an opinion or otherwise.

Rule 703 Bases of Opinion Testimony by Experts.

The facts or data in the particular case upon which an expert bases an opinion or inference may be those perceived by or made known to the expert at or before the hearing. If of a type reasonably relied upon by experts in the particular field in forming opinions or inferences upon the subject, the facts or data need not be admissible in evidence.

Rule 704 Opinion on Ultimate Issue.

(a) Except as provided in subdivision (b), testimony in the form of an opinion or inference otherwise admissible is not objectionable because it embraces an ultimate issue to be decided by the trier of fact.

(b) No expert witness testifying with respect to the mental state or condition of a defendant in a criminal case may state an opinion or inference as to whether the defendant did or did not have the mental state or condition constituting an element of the crime charged or of a defense thereto. Such ultimate issues are matters for the trier of fact alone.

Rule 705 Disclosure of Facts or Data Underlying Expert Opinion.

The expert may testify in terms of opinion or inference and give reasons therefor without first testifying to the underlying facts or data, unless the court requires otherwise. The expert may in any event be required to disclose the underlying facts or data on cross-examination.

Rule 706 Court Appointed Experts.

(a) *Appointment.* The court may on its own motion or on the motion of any party enter an order to show cause why expert witnesses should not be appointed, and may request the parties to submit nominations. The court may appoint any expert witnesses agreed upon by the parties, and may appoint expert witnesses of its own selection. An expert witness shall not be appointed by the court unless the witness consents to act. A witness so appointed shall be informed of the witness' duties by the court in writing, a copy of which shall be filed with the clerk, or at a conference in which the parties shall have opportunity to participate. A witness so appointed shall advise the parties of the witness' findings, if any; the witness' deposition may be taken by any party; and the witness may be called to testify by the court or any party. The witness shall be subject to cross-examination by each party, including a party calling the witness.

(b) *Compensation.* Expert witnesses so appointed are entitled to reasonable compensation in whatever sum the court may allow. The compensation thus fixed is payable from funds which may be provided by law in criminal cases and civil actions and proceedings involving just compensation under the fifth amendment. In other civil actions and proceedings the compensation shall be paid by the parties in such proportion and at such time as the court directs, and thereafter charged in like manner as other costs.

(c) *Disclosure of appointment.* In the exercise of its discretion, the court may authorize disclosure to the jury of the fact that the court appointed the expert witness.

(d) *Parties' experts of own selection.* Nothing in this rule limits the parties in calling expert witnesses of their own selection.

ARTICLE VIII: HEARSAY

Rule 801 Definitions. The following definitions apply under this article:

(a) *Statement*. A "statement" is

(1) an oral or written assertion or

(2) nonverbal conduct of a person, if it is intended by the person as an assertion.

(b) *Declarant*. A "declarant" is a person who makes a statement.

(c) *Hearsay*. "Hearsay" is a statement, other than one made by the declarant while testifying at the trial or hearing, offered in evidence to prove the truth of the matter asserted.

(d) *Statements which are not hearsay*. A statement is not hearsay if

(1) *Prior statement by witness*. The declarant testifies at the trial or hearing and is subject to cross-examination concerning the statement, and the statement is

(A) inconsistent with the declarant's testimony, and was given under oath subject to the penalty of perjury at a trial, hearing, or other proceeding, or in a deposition, or

(B) consistent with the declarant's testimony and is offered to rebut an express or implied charge against the declarant of recent fabrication or improper influence or motive, or

(C) one of identification of a person made after perceiving the person; or

(2) *Admission by party opponent*. The statement is offered against a party and is

(A) the party's own statement in either an individual or a representative capacity or

(B) a statement of which the party has manifested an adoption or belief in its truth, or

(C) a statement by a person authorized by the party to make a statement concerning the subject, or

(D) a statement by the party's agent or servant concerning a matter within the scope of the agency or employment, made during the existence of the relationship, or

(E) a statement by a coconspirator of a party during the course and in furtherance of the conspiracy.

The contents of the statement shall be considered but are not alone sufficient to establish the declarant's authority under subdivision (C), the agency or employment relationship and scope thereof under subdivision (D), or the existence of the conspiracy and the participation therein of the declarant and the party against whom the statement is offered under subdivision (E).

Rule 802 Hearsay Rule.

Hearsay is not admissible except as provided by these rules or by other rules prescribed by the Supreme Court pursuant to statutory authority or by Act of Congress.

Rule 803 Hearsay Exceptions.

Availability of Declarant Immaterial. The following are not excluded by the hearsay rule, even though the declarant is available as a witness:

(1) *Present sense impression.* A statement describing or explaining an event or condition made while the declarant was perceiving the event or condition, or immediately thereafter.

(2) *Excited utterance.* A statement relating to a startling event or condition made while the declarant was under the stress of excitement caused by the event or condition.

(3) *Then existing mental, emotional, or physical condition.* A statement of the declarant's then existing state of mind, emotion, sensation, or physical condition (such as intent, plan, motive, design, mental feeling, pain, and bodily health), but not including a statement of memory or belief to prove the fact remembered or believed unless it relates to the execution, revocation, identification, or terms of declarant's will.

(4) *Statements for purposes of medical diagnosis or treatment.* Statements made for purposes of medical diagnosis or treatment and describing medical history, or past or present symptoms, pain, or sensations, or the inception or general character of the cause or external source thereof insofar as reasonably pertinent to diagnosis or treatment.

(5) *Recorded recollection.* A memorandum or record concerning a matter about which a witness once had knowledge but now has insufficient recollection to enable the witness to testify fully and accurately, shown to have been made or adopted by the witness when the matter was fresh in the witness' memory and to reflect that knowledge correctly. If admitted, the memorandum or record may be read into evidence but may not itself be received as an exhibit unless offered by an adverse party.

(6) *Records of regularly conducted activity.* A memorandum, report, record, or data compilation, in any form, of acts, events, conditions, opinions, or diagnoses, made at or near the time by, or from information transmitted by, a person with knowledge, if kept in the course of a regularly conducted business activity, and if it was the regular practice of that business activity to make the memorandum, report, record, or data compilation, all as shown by the testimony of the custodian or other qualified witness, unless the source of information or the method or circumstances of preparation indicate lack of trustworthiness. The term "business" as used in this paragraph includes business, institution, association, profession, occupation, and calling of every kind, whether or not conducted for profit.

(7) *Absence of entry in records kept in accordance with the provisions of paragraph (6).* Evidence that a matter is not included in the memoranda reports, records, or data compilations, in any form, kept in accordance with the provisions of paragraph (6), to prove the nonoccurrence or nonexistence of the matter, if the matter was of a kind of which a memorandum, report, record, or data compilation was regularly made and preserved, unless the sources of information or other circumstances indicate lack of trustworthiness.

(8) *Public records and reports.* Records, reports, statements, or data compilations, in any form, of public offices or agencies, setting forth

    (A) the activities of the office or agency, or

(B) matters observed pursuant to duty imposed by law as to which matters there was a duty to report, excluding, however, in criminal cases matters observed by police officers and other law enforcement personnel, or

(C) in civil actions and proceedings and against the Government in criminal cases, factual findings resulting from an investigation made pursuant to authority granted by law, unless the sources of information or other circumstances indicate lack of trustworthiness.

(9) *Records of vital statistics.* Records or data compilations, in any form, of births, fetal deaths, deaths, or marriages, if the report thereof was made to a public office pursuant to requirements of law.

(10) *Absence of public record or entry.* To prove the absence of a record, report, statement, or data compilation, in any form, or the nonoccurrence or nonexistence of a matter of which a record, report, statement, or data compilation, in any form, was regularly made and preserved by a public office or agency, evidence in the form of a certification in accordance with rule 902, or testimony, that diligent search failed to disclose the record, report, statement, or data compilation, or entry.

(11) *Records of religious organizations.* Statements of births, marriages, divorces, deaths, legitimacy, ancestry, relationship by blood or marriage, or other similar facts of personal or family history, contained in a regularly kept record of a religious organization.

(12) *Marriage, baptismal, and similar certificates.* Statements of fact contained in a certificate that the maker performed a marriage or other ceremony or administered a sacrament, made by a clergyman, public official, or other person authorized by the rules or practices of a religious organization or by law to perform the act certified, and purporting to have been issued at the time of the act or within a reasonable time thereafter.

(13) *Family records.* Statements of fact concerning personal or family history contained in family Bibles, genealogies, charts, engravings on rings, inscriptions on family portraits, engravings on urns, crypts, or tombstones, or the like.

(14) *Records of documents affecting an interest in property.* The record of a document purporting to establish or affect an interest in property, as

proof of the content of the original recorded document and its execution and delivery by each person by whom it purports to have been executed, if the record is a record of a public office and an applicable statute authorizes the recording of documents of that kind in that office.

(15) *Statements in documents affecting an interest in property.* A statement contained in a document purporting to establish or affect an interest in property if the matter stated was relevant to the purpose of the document, unless dealings with the property since the document was made have been inconsistent with the truth of the statement or the purport of the document.

(16) *Statements in ancient documents.* Statements in a document in existence twenty years or more the authenticity of which is established.

(17) *Market reports, commercial publications.* Market quotations, tabulations, lists, directories, or other published compilations, generally used and relied upon by the public or by persons in particular occupations.

(18) *Learned treatises.* To the extent called to the attention of an expert witness upon cross-examination or relied upon by the expert witness in direct examination, statements contained in published treatises, periodicals, or pamphlets on a subject of history, medicine, or other science or art, established as a reliable authority by the testimony or admission of the witness or by other expert testimony or by judicial notice. If admitted, the may be read into evidence but may not be received as exhibits.

(19) *Reputation concerning personal or family history.* Reputation among members of a person's family by blood, adoption, or marriage, or among a person's associates, or in the community, concerning a person's birth, adoption, marriage, divorce, death, legitimacy, relationship by blood, adoption, or marriage, ancestry, or other similar fact of personal or family history.

(20) *Reputation concerning boundaries or general history.* Reputation in a community, arising before the controversy, as to boundaries of or customs affecting lands in the community, and reputation as to events of general history important to the community or State or nation in which located.

(21) *Reputation as to character*. Reputation of a person's character among associates or in the community.

(22) *Judgment of previous conviction*. Evidence of a final judgment, entered after a trial or upon a plea of guilty (but not upon a plea of nolo contendere), adjudging a person guilty of a crime punishable by death or imprisonment in excess of one year, to prove any fact essential to sustain the judgment, but not including, when offered by the Government in a criminal prosecution for purposes other than impeachment, judgments against persons other than the accused. The pendency of an appeal may be shown but does not affect admissibility.

(23) *Judgment as to personal, family, or general history, or boundaries*. Judgments as proof of matters of personal, family or general history, or boundaries, essential to the judgment, if the same would be provable by evidence of reputation.

(24) [Transferred to Rule 807]

Rule 804 Hearsay Exceptions. *Declarant Unavailable*.

(a) *Definition of unavailability*. "Unavailability as a witness" includes situations in which the declarant

(1) is exempted by ruling of the court on the ground of privilege from testifying concerning the subject matter of the declarant's statement; or

(2) persists in refusing to testify concerning the subject matter of the declarant's statement despite an order of the court to do so; or

(3) testifies to a lack of memory of the subject matter of the declarant's statement; or

(4) is unable to be present or to testify at the hearing because of death or then existing physical or mental illness or infirmity; or

(5) is absent from the hearing and the proponent of a statement has been unable to procure the declarant's attendance (or in the case of a hearsay exception under subdivision (b)(2), (3), or (4), the declarant's attendance or testimony) by process or other reasonable means. A declarant is not unavailable as a witness if exemption, refusal, claim of lack of memory, inability, or absence is due to the procurement or wrongdoing of the

proponent of a statement for the purpose of preventing the witness from attending or testifying.

(b) *Hearsay exceptions.* The following are not excluded by the hearsay rule if the declarant is unavailable as a witness:

(1) *Former testimony.* Testimony given as a witness at another hearing of the same or a different proceeding, or in a deposition taken in compliance with law in the course of the same or another proceeding, if the party against whom the testimony is now offered, or, in a civil action or proceeding, a predecessor in interest, had an opportunity and similar motive to develop the testimony by direct, cross, or redirect examination.

(2) *Statement under belief of impending death.* In a prosecution for homicide or in a civil action or proceeding, a statement made by a declarant while believing that the declarant's death was imminent, concerning the cause or circumstances of what the declarant believed to be impending death.

(3) *Statement against interest.* A statement which was at the time of its making so far contrary to the declarant's pecuniary or proprietary interest, or so far tended to subject the declarant to civil or criminal liability, or to render invalid a claim by the declarant against another, that a reasonable person in the declarant's position would not have made the statement unless believing it to be true. A statement tending to expose the declarant to criminal liability and offered to exculpate the accused is not admissible unless corroborating circumstances clearly indicate the trustworthiness of the statement.

(4) *Statement of personal or family history.*

> (A) A statement concerning the declarant's own birth, adoption, marriage, divorce, legitimacy, relationship by blood, adoption, or marriage, ancestry, or other similar fact of personal or family history, even though declarant had no means of acquiring personal knowledge of the matter stated; or

> (B) a statement concerning the foregoing matters, and death also, of another person, if the declarant was related to the other by blood, adoption, or marriage or was so intimately associated with the other's family as to be likely to have accurate information concerning the matter declared.

(5) [Transferred to Rule 807]

(6) *Forfeiture by wrongdoing.* A statement offered against a party that has engaged or acquiesced in wrongdoing that was intended to, and did, procure the unavailability of the declarant as a witness.

Rule 805 Hearsay Within Hearsay.

Hearsay included within hearsay is not excluded under the hearsay rule if each part of the combined statements conforms with an exception to the hearsay rule provided in these rules.

Rule 806 Attacking and Supporting Credibility of Declarant.

When a hearsay statement, or a statement defined in Rule 801(d)(2)(C), (D), or (E), has been admitted in evidence, the credibility of the declarant may be attacked, and if attacked may be supported, by any evidence which would be admissible for those purposes if declarant had testified as a witness. Evidence of a statement or conduct by the declarant at any time, inconsistent with the declarant's hearsay statement, is not subject to any requirement that the declarant may have been afforded an opportunity to deny or explain. If the party against whom a hearsay statement has been admitted calls the declarant as a witness, the party is entitled to examine the declarant on the statement as if under cross-examination.

Rule 807 Residual Exception.

A statement not specifically covered by Rule 803 or 804 but having equivalent circumstantial guarantees of trustworthiness, is not excluded by the hearsay rule, if the court determines that

(A) the statement is offered as evidence of a material fact;

(B) the statement is more probative on the point for which it is offered than any other evidence which the proponent can procure through reasonable efforts; and

(C) the general purposes of these rules and the interests of justice will best be served by admission of the statement into evidence.

However, a statement may not be admitted under this exception unless the proponent of it makes known to the adverse party sufficiently in advance of the trial or hearing to provide the adverse party with a fair opportunity to prepare to meet it, the proponent's intention to offer the statement and the particulars of it, including the name and address of the declarant.

ARTICLE IX: AUTHENTICATION AND IDENTIFICATION

Rule 901 Requirement of Authentication or Identification.

(a) *General provision.* The requirement of authentication or identification as a condition precedent to admissibility is satisfied by evidence sufficient to support a finding that the matter in question is what its proponent claims.

(b) *Illustrations.* By way of illustration only, and not by way of limitation, the following are examples of authentication or identification conforming with the requirements of this rule:

(1) *Testimony of witness with knowledge.* Testimony that a matter is what it is claimed to be.

(2) *Nonexpert opinion on handwriting.* Nonexpert opinion as to the genuineness of handwriting, based upon familiarity not acquired for purposes of the litigation.

(3) *Comparison by trier or expert witness.* Comparison by the trier of fact or by expert witnesses with specimens which have been authenticated.

(4) *Distinctive characteristics and the like.* Appearance, contents, substance, internal patterns, or other distinctive characteristics, taken in conjunction with circumstances.

(5) *Voice identification.* Identification of a voice, whether heard firsthand or through mechanical or electronic transmission or recording, by opinion based upon hearing the voice at any time under circumstances connecting it with the alleged speaker.

(6) *Telephone conversations.* Telephone conversations, by evidence that a call was made to the number assigned at the time by the telephone company to a particular person or business, if

(A) in the case of a person, circumstances, including self-identification, show the person answering to be the one called, or

(B) in the case of a business, the call was made to a place of business and the conversation related to business reasonably transacted over the telephone.

(7) *Public records or reports.* Evidence that a writing authorized by law to be recorded or filed and in fact recorded or filed in a public office, or a purported public record, report, statement, or data compilation, in any form, is from the public office where items of this nature are kept.

(8) *Ancient documents or data compilation.* Evidence that a document or data compilation, in any form,

(A) is in such condition as to create no suspicion concerning its authenticity,

(B) was in a place where it, if authentic, would likely be, and

(C) has been in existence 20 years or more at the time it is offered.

(9) *Process or system.* Evidence describing a process or system used to produce a result and showing that the process or system produces an accurate result.

(10) *Methods provided by statute or rule.* Any method of authentication or identification provided by Act of Congress or by other rules prescribed by the Supreme Court pursuant to statutory authority.

Rule 902 Self-authentication.

Extrinsic evidence of authenticity as a condition precedent to admissibility is not required with respect to the following:

(1) *Domestic public documents under seal.* A document bearing a seal purporting to be that of the United States, or of any State, district, Commonwealth, territory, or insular possession thereof, or the Panama Canal Zone, or the Trust Territory of the Pacific Islands, or of a political

subdivision, department, officer, or agency thereof, and a signature purporting to be an attestation or execution.

(2) *Domestic public documents not under seal.* A document purporting to bear the signature in the official capacity of an officer or employee of any entity included in paragraph (1) hereof, having no seal, if a public officer having a seal and having official duties in the district or political subdivision of the officer or employee certifies under seal that the signer has the official capacity and that the signature is genuine.

(3) *Foreign public documents.* A document purporting to be executed or attested in an official capacity by a person authorized by the laws of a foreign country to make the execution or attestation, and accompanied by a final certification as to the genuineness of the signature and official position

> (A) of the executing or attesting person, or
>
> (B) of any foreign official whose certificate of genuineness of signature and official position relates to the execution or attestation or is in a chain of certificates of genuineness of signature and official position relating to the execution or attestation. A final certification may be made by a secretary of an embassy or legation, consul general, consul, vice consul, or consular agent of the United States, or a diplomatic or consular official of the foreign country assigned or accredited to the United States. If reasonable opportunity has been given to all parties to investigate the authenticity and accuracy of official documents, the court may, for good cause shown, order that they be treated as presumptively authentic without final certification or permit them to be evidenced by an attested summary with or without final certification.

(4) *Certified copies of public records.* A copy of an official record or report or entry therein, or of a document authorized by law to be recorded or filed and actually recorded or filed in a public office, including data compilations in any form, certified as correct by the custodian or other person authorized to make the certification, by certificate complying with paragraph (1), (2), or (3) of this rule or complying with any Act of Congress or rule prescribed by the Supreme Court pursuant to statutory authority.

(5) *Official publications.* Books, pamphlets, or other publications purporting to be issued by public authority.

(6) *Newspapers and periodicals.* Printed materials purporting to be newspapers or periodicals.

(7) *Trade inscriptions and the like.* Inscriptions, signs, tags, or labels purporting to have been affixed in the course of business and indicating ownership, control, or origin.

(8) *Acknowledged documents.* Documents accompanied by a certificate of acknowledgment executed in the manner provided by law by a notary public or other officer authorized by law to take acknowledgments.

(9) *Commercial paper and related documents.* Commercial paper, signatures thereon, and documents relating thereto to the extent provided by general commercial law.

(10) *Presumptions under Acts of Congress.* Any signature, document, or other matter declared by Act of Congress to be presumptively or prima facie genuine or authentic.

Rule 903 Subscribing Witness' Testimony Unnecessary.

The testimony of a subscribing witness is not necessary to authenticate a writing unless required by the laws of the jurisdiction whose laws govern the validity of the writing.

ARTICLE X: CONTENTS OF WRITINGS, RECORDINGS AND PHOTOGRAPHS

Rule 1001 Definitions.

For purposes of this article the following definitions are applicable:

(1) *Writings and recordings.* "Writings" and "recordings" consist of letters, words, or numbers, or their equivalent, set down by handwriting, typewriting, printing, photostating, photographing, magnetic impulse, mechanical or electronic recording, or other form of data compilation.

(2) *Photographs.* "Photographs" include still photographs, X-ray films, video tapes, and motion pictures.

(3) *Original.* An "original" of a writing or recording is the writing or recording itself or any counterpart intended to have the same effect by a person executing or issuing it. An "original" of a photograph includes the negative or any print therefrom. If data are stored in a computer or similar device, any printout or other output readable by sight, shown to reflect the data accurately, is an "original".

(4) *Duplicate.* A "duplicate" is a counterpart produced by the same impression as the original, or from the same matrix, or by means of photography, including enlargements and miniatures, or by mechanical or electronic re-recording, or by chemical reproduction, or by other equivalent techniques which accurately reproduces the original.

Rule 1002 Requirement of Original.

To prove the content of a writing, recording, or photograph, the original writing, recording, or photograph is required, except as otherwise provided in these rules or by Act of Congress.

Rule 1003 Admissibility of Duplicates.

A duplicate is admissible to the same extent as an original unless

(1) a genuine question is raised as to the authenticity of the original or

(2) in the circumstances it would be unfair to admit the duplicate in lieu of the original.

Rule 1004 Admissibility of Other Evidence of Contents.

The original is not required, and other evidence of the contents of a writing, recording, or photograph is admissible if

(1) *Originals lost or destroyed.* All originals are lost or have been destroyed, unless the proponent lost or destroyed them in bad faith; or

(2) *Original not obtainable.* No original can be obtained by any available judicial process or procedure; or

(3) *Original in possession of opponent.* At a time when an original was under the control of the party against whom offered, that party was put on notice, by the pleadings or otherwise, that the contents would be a subject

of proof at the hearing, and that party does not produce the original at the hearing; or

(4) *Collateral matters*. The writing, recording, or photograph is not closely related to a controlling issue.

Rule 1005 Public Records.

The contents of an official record, or of a document authorized to be recorded or filed and actually recorded or filed, including data compilations in any form, if otherwise admissible, may be proved by copy, certified as correct in accordance with rule 902 or testified to be correct by a witness who has compared it with the original. If a copy which complies with the foregoing cannot be obtained by the exercise of reasonable diligence, then other evidence of the contents may be given.

Rule 1006 Summaries. The contents of voluminous writings, recordings, or photographs which cannot conveniently be examined in court may be presented in the form of a chart, summary, or calculation. The originals, or duplicates, shall be made available for examination or copying, or both, by other parties at reasonable time and place. The court may order that they be produced in court.

Rule 1007 Testimony or Written Admission of Party.

Contents of writings, recordings, or photographs may be proved by the testimony or deposition of the party against whom offered or by that party's written admission, without accounting for the nonproduction of the original.

Rule 1008 Functions of Court and Jury.

When the admissibility of other evidence of contents of writings, recordings, or photographs under these rules depends upon the fulfillment of a condition of fact, the question whether the condition has been fulfilled is ordinarily for the court to determine in accordance with the provisions of rule 104. However, when an issue is raised

(a) whether the asserted writing ever existed, or

(b) whether another writing, recording, or photograph produced at the trial is the original, or

(c) whether other evidence of contents correctly reflects the contents,

the issue is for the trier of fact to determine as in the case of other issues of fact.

ARTICLE XI:
MISCELLANEOUS RULES

Rule 1101 Applicability of Rules.

(a) *Courts and judges.* These rules apply to the United States district courts, the District Court of Guam, the District Court of the Virgin Islands, the District Court for the Northern Mariana Islands, the United States courts of appeals, the United States Claims Court, and to United States bankruptcy judges and United States magistrates, in the actions, cases, and proceedings and to the extent hereinafter set forth. The terms "judge" and "court" in these rules include United States bankruptcy judges and United States magistrate judges.

(b) *Proceedings generally.* These rules apply generally to civil actions and proceedings, including admiralty and maritime cases, to criminal cases and proceedings, to contempt proceedings except those in which the court may act summarily, and to proceedings and cases under title 11, United States Code.

(c) *Rule of privilege.* The rule with respect to privileges applies at all stages of all actions, cases, and proceedings.

(d) *Rules inapplicable.* The rules (other than with respect to privileges) do not apply in the following situations:

(1) *Preliminary questions of fact.* The determination of questions of fact preliminary to admissibility of evidence when the issue is to be determined by the court under rule 104.

(2) *Grand jury.* Proceedings before grand juries.

(3) *Miscellaneous proceedings.* Proceedings for extradition or rendition; preliminary examinations in criminal cases; sentencing, or granting or revoking probation; issuance of warrants for arrest, criminal summonses, and search warrants; and proceedings with respect to release on bail or otherwise.

(e) *Rules applicable in part.* In the following proceedings these rules apply to the extent that matters of evidence are not provided for in the statutes which govern procedure therein or in other rules prescribed by the Supreme Court pursuant to statutory authority: the trial of minor and petty offenses by United States magistrate judges; review of agency actions when the facts are subject to trial de novo under section 706(2)(F) of title 5, United States Code; review of orders of the Secretary of Agriculture under section 2 of the Act entitled "An Act to authorize association of producers of agricultural products" approved February 18, 1922 (7 U.S.C. 292), and under sections 6 and 7(c) of the Perishable Agricultural Commodities Act, 1930 (7 U.S.C. 499f, 499g(c)); naturalization and revocation of naturalization under sections 310-318 of the Immigration and Nationality Act (8 U.S.C. 1421-1429); prize proceedings in admiralty under sections 7651-7681 of title 10, United States Code; review of orders of the Secretary of the Interior under section 2 of the Act entitled "An Act authorizing associations of producers of aquatic products" approved June 25, 1934 (15 U.S.C. 522); review of orders of petroleum control boards under section 5 of the Act entitled "An Act to regulate interstate and foreign commerce in petroleum and its products by prohibiting the shipment in such commerce of petroleum and its products produced in violation of State law, and for other purposes", approved February 22, 1935 (15 U.S.C. 715d); actions for fines, penalties, or forfeitures under part V of title IV of the Tariff Act of 1930 (19 U.S.C. 1581-1624), or under the Anti-Smuggling Act (19 U.S.C. 1701-1711); criminal libel for condemnation, exclusion of imports, or other proceedings under the Federal Food, Drug, and Cosmetic Act (21 U.S.C. 301-392); disputes between seamen under sections 4079, 4080, and 4081 of the Revised Statutes (22 U.S.C. 256-258); habeas corpus under sections 2241-2254 of title 28, United States Code; motions to vacate, set aside or correct sentence under section 2255 of title 28, United States Code; actions for penalties for refusal to transport destitute seamen under section 4578 of the Revised Statutes (46 U.S.C. 679); actions against the United States under the Act entitled "An Act authorizing suits against the United States in admiralty for damage caused by and salvage service rendered to public vessels belonging to the United States, and for other purposes," approved March 3, 1925 (46 U.S.C. 781-790), as implemented by section 7730 of title 10, United States Code.

Rule 1102 Amendments

Amendments to the Federal Rules of Evidence may be made as provided in section 2072 of title 28 of the United States Code.

Rule 1103 Title.

These rules may be known and cited as the Federal Rules of Evidence.

APPENDIX B

THE FEDERAL RULES OF EVIDENCE

A Functional Analysis Outline

(bolding of key words added for ease of reference)

1. *An Overview*: The overriding goal of the Rules of Evidence is the **just determination** of contested proceedings.[1] The concept of "justness," however, requires a balancing of three occasionally competing interests: (a) **truth**, (b) **expense**, and (c) **privilege**—the protection from exposure of certain matters society deems worthy of keeping confidential.

The rules of evidence start with an all-encompassing net. "The need to develop all relevant facts in the adversary system is both fundamental and comprehensive." *United States v. Nixon*, 418 U.S. 683, 709 (1974). Not every fact, however, bears on, or is "consequential," to the dispute that is the subject of the litigation. Additionally, some evidence, although seemingly consequential, either lacks sufficient probative value to be **relevant**, or that probative value is outweighed by other important interests. Finally, there are considerations of necessity and expense as well as the law's policy-determinations that some matters should be kept confidential. Looked at in this way, the law of evidence can be analogized to an ever-narrowing funnel: a potential torrent of facts is ultimately reduced to a stream of admissible evidence. The narrowing occurs in five main stages:

- **Relevance**: Is the evidence of **consequence** to the dispute?

- **Capability**: Does the evidence have the **ability to be relevant**.

- **Necessity and Expense**: Whether, and to what extent, a party should be relieved of the burden of presenting certain evidence.

---

[1] "These rules shall be construed to secure fairness in administration, elimination of unjustifiable expense and delay, and promotion of growth and development of the law of evidence to the end that the truth may be ascertained and proceedings justly determined." FRE 102.

- **Exclusion**: Will a party or the process be unduly affected adversely by the admission of relevant evidence?

- **Privilege**: Should the truth-ascertaining function of the trial bow to other interests?

2. *Relevance—the main gate of admissibility*.

    - *The Substantive Rules*:

        - All "**relevant evidence**" is admissible, except when it is not. FRE 402.

        - Evidence is "**relevant**" if it is **consequential**; that is, if it has "any tendency to make the existence of any fact that is of consequence to the determination of the action more probable or less probable than it would be without the evidence." FRE 401.

    - *The Procedural Rules*:

        - The party seeking admission of evidence must demonstrate that the evidence is **relevant**. Normally, whether evidence is relevant will be self-evident; if not, the party seeking admission must make an offer-of-proof. FRE 103(a)(2).

        - The judge decides whether the evidence is within the scope of Rule 401. FRE 104(a).

3. *Capability*.

    - *The Substantive Rules—Witnesses*:

        - All persons have the legal ability to testify about that which they have **personal knowledge**. FRE 601, 602.

        - Persons with **specialized knowledge** may testify within the scope of that knowledge "in the form of an opinion or otherwise." FRE 702. The opinion may embrace the "**ultimate issue**" to be decided, except in a criminal case when that ultimate issue concerns "whether the defendant did or did not have the mental state or condition constituting an element of the crime charged or of a defense thereto." FRE 704.

- Persons **without specialized knowledge** may give their opinions or inferences about what they know as long as the opinions or inferences are both "rationally based" on their perceptions and "helpful to a clear understanding" of their testimony. FRE 701.

- *The Procedural Rules—Witnesses*:

    - The party proffering a person to testify as a witness must demonstrate that the witness is capable of testifying about the subject matter of the proposed testimony. FRE 602; FRE 702. With fact-witnesses this will normally be self-evident; if not, the party seeking admission must make an offer-of-proof. FRE 103(a)(2).

    - The judge decides whether the witness is qualified to give the proposed testimony. FRE 104(a).

- *The Substantive Rules—Evidence*:

    - Unless proffered evidence is what the proponent claims it to be, that evidence is not legally capable of making the fact to which it is addressed more or less probable; it is not "relevant." Accordingly, the proponent of that evidence, whether tangible or not, must persuade the judge that a reasonable trier of fact could find that evidence is what it is claimed to be. FRE 901.

- *The Procedural Rules—Evidence*:

    - When there is a question of whether certain evidence is what its proponent claims, the evidence is admitted if the judge determines that a reasonable trier of fact could so find. FRE 104(b).

4. *Necessity and Expense.*

- *The Substantive Rules—<u>Necessity</u>:*

  - Some facts are difficult to prove or to disprove, but usually flow from predicate conditions (a letter mailed is generally received, for example). When that happens, the law—as a matter of policy—gives the proponent a bye *via* a **presumption**. FRE 301. If the opponent, however, offers evidence to disprove the fact, the presumption disappears (the "bursting bubble") and the proponent must satisfy the otherwise applicable burden of proof. FRE 301.

  - Conduct of a person or organization at a particular time may be proved by the person's **habit** or the organization's **routine practice**, whether corroborated or not. FRE 406.

  - Although the truth-ascertaining function of the rules of evidence requires that either the **original**, or **duplicate original**, of a "writing, recording, or photograph" be produced in order to prove their contents, secondary evidence may be used if no original or duplicate original is available. FRE 1004(1), (2), & (3).

  - "A memorandum or record concerning a matter about which a witness once had knowledge but now has **insufficient recollection** to enable the witness to testify fully and accurately" about the matter, may be received into evidence if it was either made or adopted by the witness "when the matter was fresh in the witness's memory" so that it **accurately reflects** the witness's knowledge at that time. FRE 803(5).

  - There are times when a person with knowledge relevant to a material issue is "**unavailable**" as a witness, because:

    - He or she "is **exempted** by ruling of the court on the ground of **privilege** from testifying concerning the subject matter" of the out-of-court statement, FRE 804(a)(1);

- He or she "**refuses to testify** concerning the subject matter" of the out-of-court statement, FRE 804(a)(2);

- He or she "testifies to a **lack of memory** of the subject matter" of the out-of-court statement, FRE 804(a)(3);

- He or she "is unable to be present or to testify at the hearing because of **death** or then existing **physical or mental illness or infirmity**, FRE 804(a)(4);

- He or she "is **absent** from the hearing and the proponent of a statement" contained in the person's earlier testimony (as limited by FRE 804(b)(1)) has been **unable to procure the person's attendance or testimony**, FRE 804(a)(5);

- He or she "is **absent** from the hearing and the proponent of a statement" made under the speaker's belief that his or her **death was imminent** if the statement concerns the cause or circumstances of what the person believed was his or her impending death, has been **unable to procure the person's attendance or testimony**, FRE 804(a)(5);

- He or she "is **absent** from the hearing and the proponent of a statement" made against the person's "**pecuniary or proprietary interest**" (as limited by FRE 804(b)(3)), has been **unable to procure the person's attendance or testimony**, FRE 804(a)(5).

- He or she "is **absent** from the hearing and the proponent of a statement" made concerning that person's "**personal or family history**" (as limited by FRE 804(b)(4)) has been **unable to procure the person's attendance or testimony**, FRE 804(a)(5);

- He or she "is **absent** from the hearing and the proponent of a statement" that has "**equivalent circumstantial guarantees of trustworthiness**" to the exceptions in FRE 803 & 804 (as limited by

FRE 807) has been **unable to procure the person's attendance or testimony**, FRE 804(a)(5);

Under these circumstances, the following hearsay statements may be admitted:

- The person's testimony, given "at **another hearing** of the same or a different proceeding, or in a **deposition** taken in compliance with law in the course of the same or another proceeding, if the party against whom the testimony is now offered, or, in a civil action or proceeding, a predecessor in interest, had an opportunity and similar motive to develop the testimony by direct, cross, or redirect examination," FRE 804(b)(1);

- In a civil case, or in a criminal prosecution for homicide, a person's statement "concerning the cause or circumstances" of what the person believed was his or her **impending death**, so long as the statement was made while the person believed death was imminent, FRE 804(b)(2);

- A statement that, at the time it was made, was so contrary to the person's "**pecuniary or proprietary interest**," so tended to subject the person to **civil or criminal liability**, or so tended to **render invalid the person's claim**, that a reasonable person would not have made the statement unless he or she believed it to be true. FRE 804(b)(4). *Caveat*: "A statement tending to expose [the person whose out-of-court statement is proffered] to criminal liability and offered to exculpate the accused is not admissible unless corroborating circumstances clearly indicate the trustworthiness of the statement," FRE 804(b)4);

- A statement of **personal or family history**, or the history of a family with whom the person "was so intimately associated" that the person is likely toave knowledge about the subject matter of the statement, FRE 804(b)(4);

- A statement that has "**equivalent circumstantial guarantees of trustworthiness**" to the exceptions in FRE 803 & 804, if it "is offered as evidence of a material fact," "is more probative on the point for which it is offered than any other evidence which the proponent can procure through reasonable efforts," and if the "interests of justice" would be served by its admission. FRE 807.

- "A statement offered against a party that has engaged or acquiesced in wrongdoing that was intended to, and did, procure the unavailability of the declarant as a witness." FRE 804(b)(6).

■ The following out-of-court assertions are admitted because their **probative value cannot be replicated by in-court testimony**:

- Out-of-court assertions made by an **in-court witness** who is subject to cross-examination concerning the assertion:

    o An out-of-court **statement given under oath** that is **inconsistent** with the witness's in-court testimony, FRE 801(d)(1)(A);

    o An out-of-court assertion that is **consistent** with the witness's in-court testimony and is probative "to rebut an express or implied charge" of "recent fabrication or improper influence or motive" concerning the witness's in-court testimony, FRE 801(d)(1)(B);

    o An out-of-court assertion that is "one of **identification** of a person made after perceiving the person," FRE 801(d)(1)(C).

- Out-of-court assertions for which the **opposing party** is responsible:

    o The opposing party's **own statement**, FRE 801(d)(2)(A);

- o A statement about which the opposing party "has manifested an **adoption or belief in its truth**," FRE 801(d)(2)(B);

- o A statement by the opposing party's **spokesman**, FRE 801(d)(2)(C);

- o A statement made by the opposing party's **agent or employee** "concerning a matter within the scope of the agency or employment, and during the existence of the relationship," FRE 801(d)(2)(D);

- o A statement made by the opposing party's **co-conspirator** "during the course and in furtherance of the conspiracy," FRE 801(d)(2)(E).

- A contemporaneous statement "**describing or explaining an event or condition**," FRE 803(1).

- "A statement relating to a **startling event or condition** made while the person was "under the stress of excitement caused by the event or condition." FRE 803(2).

- A statement that describes the person's "**then existing state of mind, emotion, sensation, or physical condition** ... but not including a statement or memory or belief to prove the fact remembered or believed unless it relates to the execution, revocation, identification or terms" of the person's will. FRE 803(3).

- "Statements made for purposes of **medical diagnosis or treatment**" that relate to the person's medical condition "insofar as reasonably pertinent to diagnosis or treatment." FRE 803(4).

- *The Procedural Rules—<u>Necessity</u>:*

    - Unless some other rule applies, a party invoking a **presumption** must establish the predicate fact.

- "In civil actions and proceedings, the effect of a **presumption** respecting a fact which is an element of a claim or defense as to which State law supplies the rule of decision is determined in accordance with State law." FRE 302.

- The party introducing secondary evidence of a non-available "writing, recording, or photograph" must demonstrate that the item is not available. The judge decides under Rule 104(a) whether the secondary evidence will be received, except when the preliminary question requires a determination of "(a) whether the sserted writing ever existed, or (b) whether another writing, recording, or photograph produced at the trial is the original, or (c) whether other evidence of contents correctly reflects the contents"; if so, the responsibility for the determination is vested in the trier of fact, and the judge merely decides whether a reasonable jury could so find. FRE 1008.

- A party introducing a memorandum or record under Rule 803(5) *in lieu* of a witness's oral testimony must establish that the witness's memory is such that he or she cannot testify accurately about the subject matter of the memorandum or record, and that the memorandum or record was either made or adopted by the witness at a time when his or her recollection was fresh so that the memorandum or record accurately reflects the witness's now-forgotten knowledge. FRE 803(5). The judge decides these issues under Rule 104(a).

- A party introducing an out-of-court statement under Rules 801(d) and 803(1) through (4) must establish the predicate elements thereunder. The judge decides these matters under Rule 104(a).

- A party introducing an out-of-court statement made by a person who is not available to testify in court must demonstrate unavailability and the substantive elements of the exceptions under Rules 804(b)(1) through (6).[2] Additionally, if the statement is sought to be admitted under Rule 807, the proponent must give the requisite advance notice, show that the statement "is offered as evidence of a material fact," show that "the statement is more probative on the point for which it is offered than any other evidence which the proponent can procure through reasonable efforts," and show that the "interests of justice" would be served by its admission. FRE 807. The judge decides these matters under Rule 104(a).

- *The Substantive Rules—Expense:*

  - Some facts are either difficult or expensive to prove by direct evidence. The rules, therefore, provide mechanisms for proof by second-hand evidence—generally *via* **judicial notice** or **hearsay**.

  - A judge may take **judicial notice** of "adjudicative facts" that are "not subject to reasonable dispute" because they are generally known in the trial court's "territorial jurisdiction" or because they are "capable of accurate and ready determination by resort to sources whose accuracy cannot reasonably be questioned." FRE 201.

  - The following exceptions to the rule against hearsay permit proof of facts by second-hand evidence rather than put the proponent to the expense of producing witnesses with personal knowledge:

    - FRE 803(6) (statements in **business records**);

    - FRE 803(7) (**absence of entry in business records**);

    - FRE 803(8) (statements in **public records and reports**);

---

[2] Former FRE 804(b)(5) is now found at FRE 807.

- FRE 803(9) (statements in records of **vital statistics**);

- FRE 803(10) (**absence of entry in public records**);

- FRE 803(11) (statements in records of **religious organizations**);

- FRE 803(12) (statements in **marriage, baptismal, and similar certificates**);

- FRE 803(13) (statements in **family records**);

- FRE 803(14) (statements in **records of documents affecting interests in property**);

- FRE 803(15) (statements in **documents affecting interests in property**);

- FRE 803(16) (statements in **documents more than twenty years old**);

- FRE 803(17) (statements in **market reports, directories, and other publications that are generally relied upon** by either the public or persons in particular occupations);

- FRE 803(18) (statements in "**learned treatises**");

- FRE 803(19) (a person's **reputation** among family members, associates, or in the community concerning his or her **personal or family history**);

- FRE 803(20) (**reputation** in a community **concerning land boundaries or customs within that community**, or reputation concerning "**events of general history important to the community or State or nation** in which located");

- FRE 803(22) (evidence of a **final judgment of conviction** for a crime punishable by death or for imprisonment in excess of one year "to prove any fact essential to sustain the judgment" except when offered by the government in a criminal case either for purposes other than impeachment or against persons other than the accused);

- FRE 803(23) (**judgments as proof of personal, family, or general history, or boundaries**);

- FRE 807 (hearsay statements that have "**equivalent circumstantial guarantees of trustworthiness**" to the exceptions in FRE 803 & 804(b), if the proponent gives the requisite advance notice, shows that the statement "is offered as evidence of a material fact," shows that "the statement is more probative on the point for which it is offered than any other evidence which the proponent can procure through reasonable efforts," and shows that the "interests of justice" would be served by its admission).

- Parties need not establish independently the **authenticity** of certain types of documents that are deemed to be **self-authenticating**. FRE 902.

- Unless required by the jurisdiction whose laws govern the validity of a writing, the testimony of a **subscribing witness** is not a predicate to the authentication of the writing. FRE 903.

- A party may present **summaries** of voluminous writings, recordings, or photographs. FRE 1006

- A party may prove the **contents of writings, recordings, or photographs** by the opposing party's testimony (at trial or by deposition) or admission. FRE 1007

- *The Procedural Rules—<u>Expense</u>*:

    - A party seeking to have the court take **judicial notice** must supply to the court the information necessary from which judicial notice can be taken. FRE 201(d).

- A party seeking the admission of evidence under the exceptions to the rule against **hearsay** that apply irrespective of the availability of the out-of-court declarant, must establish the various substantive predicates. If the statement is sought to be dmitted under **Rule 807**, the proponent must give the requisite advance notice. Under **Rules 803(6), 803(7), and 803(8)**, the evidence will be excluded even if the substantive predicates to admission are shown if the opponent establishes that either the source of the information or "other circumstances" "indicate lack of trustworthiness." The judge decides under Rule 104(a) whether the hearsay will be admitted.

- A party introducing a document under the self-authenticating provisions of **Rule 902** must establish the various substantive predicates. The judge decides under Rule 104(a) whether the document will be admitted.

- A party that contends that under **Rule 903** the testimony of a subscribing witness is necessary to authenticate a writing must demonstrate that such testimony is required by the jurisdiction whose laws govern the writing's validity. FRE 903.

5. *Exclusion of Relevant Evidence.*

    - *The Substantive Rules*:

        - Evidence may be excluded even though it is relevant if: "its probative value is **substantially outweighed** by the danger of **unfair prejudice, confusion of the issues**, or **misleading the jury**, or by considerations of **undue delay, waste of time, or needless presentation of cumulative evidence**. FRE 403.

        - "Evidence of a person's **character or a trait of character** is not admissible for the purpose of proving **action in conformity therewith** on a particular occasion," FRE 404(a), 404(b), subject to the following exceptions:

            - "Evidence of a **pertinent trait of character** offered by an **accused**, or by the **prosecution** to rebut the same," FRE 404(a)(1);

- "Evidence of a **pertinent trait of character** of the **victim** of the crime offered by an **accused**, or by the **prosecution** to rebut the same," FRE 404(a)(2);

- "[E]vidence of a **character trait of peacefulness of the victim** offered by the prosecution in a homicide case to rebut evidence that the victim was the first aggressor," FRE 404(a)(2);

- **Specific instances of a person's conduct** are admissible when that conduct is relevant to the person's "**character or trait of character**" when "character trait of character" is "an **essential element of a charge, claim, or defense**," FRE 405(b);

- Although **specific instances of a person's conduct** may not be used to prove the person's "character" inorder to "**show action in conformity** there with, "they "may, however, be admissible for other purposes, such as proof of **motive, opportunity, intent, preparation, plan, knowledge, identity, or absence of mistake or accident**," and the like, FRE 404(b);

- When a person's **character trait** is sufficiently routinized to be that person's "**habit**," evidence of habit is admissible "to prove that the conduct of the person . . . on a particular occasion was in conformity with the habit." FRE 406.

- A defendant charged with sexual assault may introduce evidence (if it is "otherwise admissible" under the Federal Rules of Evidence):

    o "specific instances of sexual behavior by the alleged victim offered to prove that a person other than the accused was the source of semen, injury or other physical evidence";

    o "specific instances of sexual behavior by the alleged victim with respect to the person accused of the sexual misconduct offered by the accused to prove consent or by the prosecution";

- ○ if exclusion "would violate the constitutional rights of the defendant." FRE 412(b)(1)

- When a defendant in a criminal case is accused of "an offense of sexual assault" (as defined by FRE 413(d)), the prosecution may introduce the "defendant's commission of another offense or offenses of sexual assault." FRE 413(a).

- When a defendant in a criminal case is accused of "an offense of child molestation" (as defined by FRE 414(d)), the prosecution may introduce the "defendant's commission of another offense or offenses of child molestation." FRE 414(a).

- When a person is seeking "damages or other relief" in a civil case "predicated" on another's "alleged commission of conduct constituting an offense of sexual assault or child molestation" (as defined by FRE 413(d) and 414(d)), the party seeking the damages or other relief may introduce evidence of that other person's "commission of another offense or offenses of sexual assault or child molestation." FRE 415(a).

- Evidence of **remedial measures** taken after "an injury or harm allegedly caused by an event" that, "if taken previously, would have made the injury or harm less likely to occur . . . is not admissible to prove negligence, culpable conduct, a defect in a product, a defect in a product's design, or a need for a warning or instruction." FRE 407.

- "Evidence of furnishing or offering or promising to pay medical, hospital, or similar **expenses occasioned by an injury** is not admissible to prove **liability** for the injury." FRE 409.

- Pleas or statements encompassed by Rule 410 (**plea bargaining**) are not admissible in a civil or criminal proceeding against the defendant making them, except (1) when another statement "made in the course of the same plea or plea discussions" is in evidence and fairness requires that it should be considered in its context, or (2) in connection with a criminal proceeding for perjury or false statement that is given under oath, on the record, and in the presence of counsel. FRE 410.

- "Evidence that a person was or was not **insured** against liability is not admissible upon the issue whether the person acted **negligently or otherwise wrongfully**." FRE 411.

- Except as otherwise provided in FRE 412(b), "in any civil or criminal proceeding involving alleged sexual misconduct," the following is not admissible:

  - "Evidence offered to prove that any alleged victim engaged in other sexual behavior."

  - "Evidence offered to prove any alleged victim's sexual predisposition." FRE 412(a).

- Evidence given by **testimony of the judge** at the trial over which he or she is presiding is not admissible. FRE 605.

- Evidence given by **testimony of the juror** before the jury in the trial of the case in which the juror is sitting is not admissible. FRE 606(a).

- Evidence given by a juror concerning "any matter or statement occurring during the course of the **jury's deliberations** or to the effect of anything upon that or any other juror's mind or emotions as influencing the juror to assent to or dissent from the verdict or indictment or concerning the juror's mental processes in connection therewith," is not admissible, FRE 606(b), subject to the following exception:

  - A juror may give evidence as to "whether **extraneous prejudicial information** was improperly brought to the jury's attention or whether any **outside influence** was improperly brought to bear upon any juror." FRE 606(b).

- Evidence attacking or supporting the **credibility of a witness** (or a **hearsay declarant**—FRE 806) is not admissible, FRE 608, subject to the following exceptions:

- **Opinion or reputation** of the witness or hearsay declarant **for truthfulness**—but "evidence of truthful character is admissible only after the character of the witness [or hearsay declarant] for truthfulness has been attacked by opinion or reputation evidence or otherwise," FRE 608(a);

- Extrinsic evidence of **specific instances of conduct** of a witness or hearsay declarant may, if probative of veracity, be inquired into on cross examination of the witness, or on cross examination of a witness who has testified as to the character for truthfulness of another witness or hearsay declarant, FRE 608(b);

- Evidence of a witness's or hearsay declarant's **criminal convictions** to attack that person's credibility, is admissible in accordance with the rules specified in Rule 609.

- *The Procedural Rules*:

  - The party seeking to exclude relevant evidence must demonstrate how that evidence fits within the rule authorizing the exclusion. The proponent of the evidence must then demonstrate an applicable exception, by offer of proof if necessary, FRE 103(a)(2). The judge decides whether the evidence will be admitted. FRE 104(a).

  - The party seeking the admission of **specific instances of conduct** under Rule 404(b) must show (1) that a reasonable jury could conclude that the conduct occurred (which the judge decides under Rule 104(b)), and (2) that the conduct is probative of the purpose for which admission is sought (not merely propensity) (which the judge decides under 104(a)). FRE 404(b); *Huddleston v. United States*, 485 U.S. 681, 689–692 (1988). The evidence is excluded if the opponent shows that it is unfairly prejudicial under Rule 403 (which the judge decides under Rule 104(a)). If the evidence is proffered by the prosecution in a criminal case, advance notice to the accused must be given "of the general nature" of that evidence, if the accused so requests, unless advance notice is excused by the judge for "good cause." FRE 404(b).

- When evidence of similar crimes or acts in **sexual-assault or child-molestation** cases are offered by either the prosecution or a party, the party offering the evidence must give notice to either the defendant (in criminal cases involving evidence under FRE 413 & 414) or the party against whom the evidence is offered (in civil cases under FRE 415); and the party offering the evidence must "disclose" to either the defendant or the party against whom the evidence is offered "the evidence . . . including statements of witnesses or a summary of the substance of any testimony that is expected to be offered, at least fifteen days before the scheduled date of trial or at such later time as the court may allow for good cause. " FRE 413(b), FRE 414(b), & FRE 415(b).

- When "evidence of character or a trait of character of a person is admissible, proof may be made by testimony as to reputation or by testimony in the form of an opinion"; the cross-examiner is permitted to ask about "relevant specific instances of conduct." FRE 405(a).

- Evidence "offered to prove the sexual behavior or sexual predisposition of any alleged victim is admissible" only if:

     o "it is otherwise admissible" under the Federal Rules of Evidence, and

     o "its **probative value substantially outweighs** the danger of harm to any victim and of unfair prejudice to any party."

     o "Evidence of an alleged victim's reputation is admissible only if it has been placed in controversy by the alleged victim." FRE 412(b)(2).

6. *Privilege*:

   The truth-ascertainment goal of the trial must occasionally give way before the "weighty and legitimate competing" interests of privilege—society's determination that certain matters must be protected from public scrutiny. *Nixon*, 418 U.S. at 709.

- *The Substantive Rules*:

  - Evidence is not admissible if it is protected by a **privilege**, either as determined by "the principles of the common law as they may be interpreted by the courts of the United States in the light of reason and experience," or State law "in civil actions and proceedings, with respect to an element of a claim or defense as to which State law supplies the rule of decision." FRE 501.

- *The Procedural Rules*:

  - A party, person, or witness invoking privilege must establish the various predicate elements of that privilege. The proponent of the evidence must then demonstrate the applicability of any exceptions. The judge decides whether the evidence will be admitted. FRE 104(a).

7. *The Mechanics*.

The Rules of Evidence give the lawyers and the judge certain powers and responsibilities, which are designed to advance the goal that the contested proceeding be justly determined.

- *The Lawyers*:

  - In order to preserve an objection to a judge's ruling admitting or excluding evidence, the lawyer must either timely **object** or timely **move to strike** the evidence, and, unless the specific ground for the objection is apparent from the context, the lawyer must state the "**specific ground**" for his or her objection. FRE 103(a)(1).

  - In seeking the admission of evidence, the lawyer may have to show the judge "the substance" of that evidence *via* an **offer of proof**. FRE 103(a)(2). The judge may require that the lawyer make the offer of proof by **question and answer**. FRE 103(b).

  - If the lawyer wishes evidence to be considered for one purpose and not another, the lawyer must make that request and ask the judge so instruct the jury if a special **limiting instruction** is desired. FRE 105.

- *The Judge*:

    - In ruling on a point of evidence, the judge should, "to the extent practicable," prevent the jury from learning its substance until the evidence is admitted. FRE 103(c).

    - Hearings on the admissibility of a defendant's **confession** must be conducted out of the jury's presence. FRE 104(c).

    - When the **defendant is a witness**, the judge must hold a hearing out of the jury's presence on a preliminary matter concerning that defendant's testimony when requested to do so by the defendant. FRE 104(c).

    - If evidence is admitted for a **specific purpose**, the judge must so limit the evidence, and, if requested, so instruct the jury. FRE 105.

    - When a portion of a writing or statement is introduced, the judge, if requested to do so by an adverse party, must permit introduction of any other part of that statement or writing that fairness requires be **considered contemporaneously**. FRE 106.

    - When requested to do so and supplied with the necessary information, the judge shall take **judicial notice** of adjudicative facts that are not subject to reasonable dispute. FRE 201(a).

    - The judge must make sure that each witness takes an **oath or affirmation** that his or her testimony will be truthful. FRE 603.

    - The judge exercises "reasonable control over the mode and order" of **interrogating the witnesses** and the **presentation of evidence**. FRE 611(a).

- The **judge may call witnesses**, who may be cross-examined by all parties. FRE 614(a).

- The **judge may interrogate any witness**. FRE 614(b).

- The **judge may appoint an expert witness**, who shall perform such functions as the judge may direct and who may be called as a witness and cross-examined by any party. FRE 706.

- The **judge must sequester witnesses if requested** to do so; except that a party who is a natural person, a designated officer or employee of a party that is not a natural person, and any person "shown by a party to be essential to the presentation of the party's cause" need not be sequestered. FRE 615.

● *General Provisions*:

- A judge's erroneous evidentiary ruling may be reversed on appeal even though the lawyer has failed to properly preserve objection to that error if the error is "**plain**" and if it affects a litigant's "**substantial rights**." FRE 103(d).

- Any party may attack the **credibility** of any witness or hearsay declarant. FRE 607, 806.

- **Cross-examination** is generally limited to the **scope of direct examination** (and matters affecting the witness's **credibility**) unless the judge, in the exercise of reasonable discretion, permits inquiry by the cross-examiner into "additional matters as if on direct examination." FRE 611(b).

- **Leading questions** should generally not be used on direct examination, except when it is "necessary to develop the witness' testimony," or when the witness is "identified with an adverse party." FRE 611(c).

- **Leading questions** should generally be permitted on cross-examination. FRE 611(c).

- An adverse party is entitled to examine a **writing that a witness uses to refresh his or her memory while testifying,** and cross-examine the witness on that writing as well as introduce into evidence those portions of the writing that relate to the witness's testimony. FRE 612.

- If the judge, in the exercise of discretion, determines that the "interests of justice" so require, an adverse party is entitled to examine a writing that a witness has used **prior to testifying in order to refresh his or her memory for the purpose of testifying,** and cross-examine the witness on that writing as well as introduce into evidence those portions of the writing that relate to the witness's testimony. FRE 612.

- A **witness's prior statement** need not be either shown or disclosed to the witness before the witness is examined concerning that statement; upon request, however, the statement must be disclosed or shown to opposing counsel. FRE 613(a).

- Other than admissions by a party-opponent under Rule 801(d)(2), and unless the "interests of justice otherwise require," **extrinsic evidence of a witness's prior inconsistent statement** is not admissible unless the witness is given an opportunity to explain or deny the statement, and opposing party has an opportunity to examine the witness about the statement. FRE 613(b).

- A party that objects to the **judge calling or interrogating a witness** may object at the time or "at the next available opportunity when the jury is not present." FRE 614(c).

APPENDIX C

EVIDENCE AND ADVOCACY—USING THE RULES OF EVIDENCE TO WIN

1. Theme of the Case:

   - what is desired result of trial?
   - what are essential elements that must be proven?
   - what facts are consequential to each element? FRE 401, 402.
   - theme must be consistent with what the jury will believe.

2. How to Prove Facts:

   - **Witnesses**

     - Non-expert must have personal knowledge. FRE 602, 701.

       o   in-court witness

       o   out-of-court declarant

       ☞ *Strategy*: Out-of-court declarations are invulnerable to cross-examination.

     - Non-expert may give his or her opinion or inference as long as it "rationally based" on the witness's perception "and helpful to a clear understanding of the witness' testimony or the determination of a fact in issue." FRE 701.

       ☞ *Strategy*: Non-expert may give a FRE 701 opinion on the ultimate issue. FRE 704.

     - Expert witness must have "specialized knowledge" that "will assist the trier of fact to understand the evidence or to determine a fact in issue." FRE 702.

- In jurisdictions that follow *Frye v. United States*, 293 Fed. 1013 (D.C. Cir.1923), scientific evidence is not admissible unless the underlying principle is "sufficiently established to have gained general acceptance in the particular field to which it belongs." 293 Fed. at 1014.

- The United States Supreme Court has rejected the *Frye* test for the federal courts, holding that the doctrine was superseded by the adoption of the Federal Rules of Evidence. *Daubert v. Merrell Dow Pharmaceuticals, Inc.*, 509 U.S. 579, 113 S.Ct. 2786, 125 L.Ed.2d 469 (1993). *Daubert* recognized, however, that an expert opinion on a scientific issue must still pass muster under FRE 702:

    1) "The subject of an expert's testimony must be 'scientific . . . knowledge,' " which "implies a grounding in the methods and procedures of science," and must be based on "more than subjective belief or unsupported speculation." 509 U.S. at 589–590, 113 S.Ct. at 2795.

    2) The expert's "inference or assertion must be derived by the scientific method." 509 U.S. at 590, 113 S.Ct. at 2795.

    3) "[T]he requirement that an expert's testimony pertain to 'scientific knowledge' establishes a standard of evidentiary reliability." 509 U.S. at 590, 113 S.Ct. at 2795.

    4) "In a case involving scientific evidence, *evidentiary reliability* will be based upon *scientific validity*." 509 U.S. at 590 n.9, 113 S.Ct. at 2795 n.9. (Emphasis in original.)

    5) "FRE 702's 'helpfulness' standard requires a valid scientific connection to the pertinent inquiry." 509 U.S. at 591–592, 113 S.Ct. at 2796.

6) The trial judge decides under FRE 104(a) whether the proponent of the expert opinion has established a sufficient FRE 702 foundation. The trial judge should consider the following non-exclusive list of factors: (a) whether the underlying theory or technique can be and has been tested; (b) whether the theory or technique has been subject to peer review; (c) the "known or potential rate of error" for the theory or technique; (d) whether the theory or technique has been generally accepted in the particular field (the *Frye* test); (e) whether the probative value of the proposed testimony is substantially outweighed by the dangers of unfair prejudice (the test under FRE 403). 509 U.S. at 593–595, 113 S.Ct. at 2796–2798.

o Trial courts have discretion whether to admit or exclude *Daubert*-type evidence, and appellate review is under an "abuse of discretion" standard. ***General Electric Co. v. Joiner***, 118 S.Ct. 512, 515, 517, 139 L.Ed.2d 508 (1997).

o Prior to *Daubert*, jurisdictions that did not follow *Frye*, the admissibility of novel scientific evidence turned, variously, on an analysis of (1) whether the evidence would "assist" the fact-finder, FRE 702; (2) whether the evidence was based on valid data and methodology, FRE 703 (by implication) and 704 (by implication); (3) whether the evidence would either mislead the fact-finder or obscure the issue to be decided, FRE 403; or (4) whether the evidence met the threshold of relevance, FRE 401.[1]

■ Expert testimony may embrace "ultimate issue." FRE 704.

☞ *Strategy*: Expert witnesses make good "summation" witnesses through which to repeat evidence.

---

[1] *See, e.g.*, ***Christopherson v. Allied Signal Corp.***, 939 F.2d 1106, 1110-1116 (5th Cir. 1991) (*en banc*) (toxic tort); ***United States v. Downing***, 753 F.2d 1224, 1237 ff (3d Cir. 1985) (eyewitness identification).

- Tangible evidence

    - Must be what it purports to be. FRE 901.

        ☞ *Strategy*: Documents and other tangible items are invulnerable to cross-examination.

- Judicial notice — FRE 201.

    ☞ *Strategy*: Facts that are judicially noticed carry the court's imprimatur.

- Presumptions — FRE 301.

    ☞ *Strategy*: Temporarily shifts burden on opponent to offer evidence contrary to presumed fact; if opponent fails, fact is established.

3. Testimony

    - Direct-Examination (*non*-adverse witness)

        - Argue your case to jury through witness.

        - Every question and answer must advance theme.

        - When you enter a subject, you must close it.

        - Repetition

            o Looping

            o Go from "open" question to "closed" question.

            o Use transition "questions."

        - "Leading" is permitted on direct examination of non-adverse witness when that is "necessary to develop the witness' testimony." FRE 611(c).

- "Leading" is permitted on direct examination of non-adverse witness in connection with a hearsay statement by that witness that has been admitted against the examiner. FRE 806.

  - *Strategy*: Control witness, and stay as close to "leading" as you can without appearing to put words in witness's mouth.

    - Use choices ("Was he tall or short?")

    - Use words of facilitation ("Tell me whether or not ...")

- Direct-Examination (adverse witness)

  - "Leading" is permitted on direct examination of "a hostile witness, an adverse party, or a witness identified with an adverse party." FRE 611(c).

    - *Strategy*: Because you can lead as if on cross-examination, calling the adverse party may be a good way to establish part of your case and argue your theme to the jury. (*Caveat*: Some jurisdictions permit wide-open "cross" by adverse party's attorney; this permits your opponent to interrupt the presentation of your case. Under FRE 611(b), cross-examination is generally "limited to the subject matter of the direct examination" although the trial court "may, in the exercise of discretion, permit inquiry into additional matters as if on direct examination.")

- Cross-Examination

  - Argue your case to jury through witness.

  - Every question and answer must advance theme.

  - Purposes of Cross-examination:

    - Limit witness's testimony

    - Get help from witness

- Discredit witness

☞ *Strategy*: You must ask *some* questions (unless direct-examiner has omitted something critical to his or her case) — jury will not understand that there was nothing to cross-examine; it will believe that you were so devastated by the direct-examination that there is no rejoinder.

- **Impeachment**
    - Any witness may be impeached. FRE 607.

    - Prior inconsistent statements.

    ☞ *Strategy*: Although prior inconsistent statements must have been "given under oath subject to the penalty of perjury at a trial, hearing, or other proceeding, or in a deposition" to be admissible as *substantive* evidence, FRE 801(d)(1)(A), a prior inconsistent statement that does not meet these criteria may still be received for *impeachment* purposes. Both proponent and opponent are entitled to an instruction under FRE 105, telling the jury why the evidence was received and what the evidence may be used for.

    ☞ *Strategy*: A witness's prior statement need not be disclosed to the witness at the time of the examination (it must, however, be disclosed to opposing counsel, if he or she requests). FRE 613(a). If the statement is not admissible under FRE 801(d)(2) (statements—direct or vicarious—by the opposing party), extrinsic evidence of that statement "is not admissible unless the witness is afforded an opportunity to explain or deny the same and the opposite party is afforded an opportunity to interrogate the witness thereon, or the interests of justice other wise require." FRE 613(b).

    - Convictions. FRE 609.

- Out-of-court declarations, which, by their very nature, cannot be cross-examined, may, nevertheless, be impeached or rehabilitated "by any evidence which would be admissible for those purposes if declarant had testified as a witness." FRE 806.

- **Examination of Experts**

  - Establish extensive foundation for expert's opinion so jury will have reason to accept it.

    - ☞ *Strategy*: Do not "proffer" witness to the court as an "expert"—this will give opponent opportunity for examination-interrupting *voir dire*.

    - ☞ *Strategy*: Reject opponent's opportunity to "stipulate" to expert's credentials *unless* opponent is also willing to stipulate to the expert's opinion.

  - Do not permit expert to "sell" case to jury.

    - ☞ *Strategy*: As with every other witness, information should be plucked from expert.

      - Permits testimony to be broken-up into memorable parts, as with non-expert witnesses.

      - Permits repetition of favorable testimony, as with non-expert witnesses.

      - As with non-expert witnesses, stay as close to "leading" as is possible.

- Experts may rely on inadmissible facts or data as long as they are "of a type reasonably relied upon by experts in the particular field in forming opinions or inferences upon a subject." FRE 703.

- The facts and data that underlie the expert's opinion that are not admissible into evidence may, nevertheless, be disclosed to the jury so the jury can evaluate the expert's testimony. FRE 703 (by implication) and 705.

- Hypothetical questions no longer required. FRE 704.

  ☞ *Strategy*: Hypothetical questions can be extremely useful nonetheless.

    o Gives attorney chance to argue case to jury.

    o Gives opportunity for repetition of important material:

    1. Use hypothetical, *then*

    2. Ask direct question, as is permitted by FRE 704 (Do you have an opinion in this case as to whether . . .).

4. Tangible Evidence.

   - Must be what it purports to be. FRE 901(a).

     - How prove? FRE 901(b).

     - Self-authenticating documents. FRE 902

       ☞ *Strategy*: Foundations are simply laid:

       1. "Do you know what this is?"

       2. "What is it?"

- Two functions of tangible evidence:

    - Supplies substantive evidence needed to prove case.

    - Corroborates oral testimony of witness.

    - ☞ *Strategy*: Unless you must show exhibit to jury in the middle of the witness's testimony, do not move the exhibit's admission until after you have finished examining the witness. This will prevent your opponent from disrupting your examination with a *voir dire* on the exhibit. (NOTE: In most federal courts and some state courts exhibits will be marked and received into evidence prior to trial *via* a pretrial order.)

    - ☞ *Strategy*: Enlarge important exhibits. Make sure blown-up exhibit is legible—use press-type and highlighting to clarify and emphasize critical portions of documents (an illegible nurse's note will not be made more legible by making it bigger).

    - ☞ *Strategy*: Often not necessary to move corroborating exhibits into evidence. Receipt of exhibits that are not essential to case clutters the record, and interferes with jury's ability to focus on your theme.

- Charts and summaries of data or other material that "cannot conveniently be examined in court" are admissible to the same extent as the underlying materials. FRE 1006

    - ☞ *Strategy*: A well-designed chart or summary admissible under FRE 1006 can forcefully argue case.

- Demonstrative evidence.

    - To help jury understand witness's testimony.

    - Not necessarily prepared to be received into evidence.

        - ☞ *Strategy*: Can repeat critical testimony by having witness prepare diagram in front of jury *after* he or she has orally described event.

    - Lawyer can use charts and diagrams in opening statement and closing argument as an extension of his or her oral presentation.

INDEX

A Civil Action	163
Adams, Sherman	34
Alexander	2
American Journal	4
Aristotle	ix, 2
Belief in case	5, 21, 23
Berger, Margaret A.	107
Biased witness	135–147
Bleak House	3
Bright, Myron	113, 116, 117
Brookings Institution	8
Brown, Denise	61–63, 67
Brown, Nicole	4, 61–63, 75, 164–165, 167, 182, 183, 184
Buckner, Emory	121, 124
Burden of proof	33–35, 160, 163–164
Butzyn, Walter	161
Capra, Daniel L.	134
Carson, Edward	148
Charting a Future for the Civil Jury System	8
Churchill, William Spencer	5, 21

Clark, Ben	149, 150, 153–159
Clark, Marcia	21–22, 59–60, 67, 75–77, 83
Closing argument	159–164
Cochran, Johnnie	75–76, 79, 110–113, 128–130, 164–180
Cross-examination	89–92, 120–159
Darden, Christopher	21–22, 61–62, 67
D-Day	109
Davis v. Alaska, 415 U.S. 308 (1974)	135
Day care	7
Dean, John	92
DecisionQuest	190
Diagrams	80–82
Dialogue for Writers	64
Dickens, Charles	3
Direct-examination	59–106, 143–147
Douglas, Alfred	148
Egri, Lajos	10
Eisenhower, Dwight David	34, 109
Empathy	38–39, 89, 94, 165, 189
Equivocating witness	128–131
Ervin, Sam	92

Estes v. Texas, 381 U.S. 532 (1965)	3
Examination train	71
Examination funnel	72–73
Federal Rules of Civil Procedure	
Rule 11	3
Rule 32	132–133
Federal Rules of Evidence	190, Appendix A, Appendix B, Appendix C
Rule 105	134, 135
Rule 403	136, 137
Rule 411	136
Rule 602	182
Rule 607	29
Rule 611	64, 146
Rule 612	93
Rule 613	131–132, 134
Rule 615	39
Rule 701	91
Rule 703	115
Rule 704	114
Rule 801(d)	133
Rule 803(2)	116
Rule 803(4)	91
Rule 803(8)	115
Rule 901	82
Federal Rules of Evidence Manual	134
Ferguson, Colin	122–124
Fuhrman, Mark	29, 125–128
Garvey, Candace	4
Goldfine, Bernard	34
Goldman, Ronald	164–165, 182, 184

Gotti, John	32–33
Gravano, Sammy "The Bull"	32–33
Greenleaf, Stephen	5, 21
Grisham, John	64–66
Gyroscope	16
Hamilton, Lee	108–109
Harr, Jonathan	163
Hawthorne, Alec	5
Holmes, Oliver Wendell, Jr.	7
Homicide	106
How Jurors Respond to Complex Commercial Cases	6
Hughes, Langston	1–2
Hwang, Suein L.	10
Impact	5
Impeaching witnesses	131–135, 149
Introduction question	71, 72, 182
Ito, Lance	76
Jacobs, Stephen T.	106
Jury dynamics	160–161
Keker, John	108
Kelberg, Brian	110–111

Kenny, Peter J.	ix-x, 39
Klieman, Rikki	53
Koestler, Arthur	1–2
Laguzza, Ross P.	190–191
Lincoln, Abraham	5, 6, 16, 22–23, 106, 120, 152
Looping	72
Lundsford, Terry	6, 8
McElhaney, James W.	19, 25
Maas, Peter	32
Margaret, Kathryn	195
Martin, Michael M.	134
Mays, Willie	148
Melville, Herman	36–37
Nichols, Terry	22
Nixon, Richard M.	92
Nizer, Louis	7
North, Oliver	108–109
Occam's Razor	165
Ono, Yumiko	10
Opening statements	15–29, 30–32
Park, Allen	59–60, 67

Parloff, Roger — 125

Penthouse Int. Ltd. v. Dominion Federal S & L Assn., 665 F. Supp. 301 (S.D.N.Y. 1987), *aff'd in part and rev'd in part*, 855 F.2d 963 (2d Cir. 1988), *cert. denied*, 490 U.S. 1005 — 124

Persistence of Belief — 6–8, 160

Persuasion — ix, 13
   primacy — 13–14
   recency — 13, 14, 159
   repetition — 13, 14–15

Pilnak, Denise — 79, 164–180

Phillips, Ronald — 128–130

Rationalization and denial — 6–8, 14, 15

Reed, Anne Willis — 97–106

Reinhart, Boerner, Van Deuren Norris & Rieselbach — 97

Rock v. U.S. Postal Service — 39–58, 97–106, 153–159

Pope, Alexander — ix

Queensbury, Marquis of — 148

Rifkind, Simon H. — ix

Roosevelt, Theodore — 21

Rule in Queen Anne's Case — 131

Saltzburg, Stephen A. — ix-x, 39, 97, 129

Shakespeare, William — 39, 90

Shylock	39, 90
Simon, David	106
Simpson, O.J.	4, 21, 29, 59–63, 75–76, 79, 89, 108, 110–113, 125–131, 164–189
Slobodkin, Ralph	34
Stein, Mark	19–20, 23–25, 29
Stein, Sol	64, 74
Stern, Herbert J.	ix-x, 5, 9, 23, 39, 75, 77, 94, 120–121, 148
Stern, Isaac	1
Sullivan, Brendan	108
Summation	159–164
Surrogate witnesses	90–91
Ten Commandments of Cross-Examination	149–153
The Art of Cross-Examination	149–153
The Man to See	34
The Runaway Jury	64–66
Theme of case	8–13
Thomas, Evan	34
Tigar, Michael	22
Tobacco	7, 10, 14, 64–66
Transition question	71, 74, 184, 186

Triple Jeopardy	125
Truth in the courtroom	2–5, 6, 27, 33, 93 106, 120, 127, 131, 162
Trying Cases to Win	ix, 5, 120–121, 148
Uelman, Gerald	125–127, 129
Underboss	32
United States v. Glecier, 923 F.2d 496 (7th Cir. 1991)	108
University of Virginia Trial Advocacy Institute Introduction	1–2, 39, 153, 160
Vanatter, Philip	110–113, 125
Voir dire (of jurors)	16, 22, 190–195
Voir dire (of witnesses)	137–142
Voodoo Jurynomics	190–191
Watergate	92
Weinberg, Robert	160
Weinstein's Federal Evidence	107
When, if Ever, Does Evidentiary Error Constitute Reversible Error?	107
Wigmore, John Henry	62, 87
Wilde, Oscar	148
Williams, Edward Bennett	ix, 5, 34
Williams & Connelly	160
Wisewell, Mary	17

WXYZ-TV (Detroit, MI) 161

Younger, Irving 149–153, 159